Twentieth Century Architecture 15

Twentieth Century Architecture 15

edited by Elain Harwood and Alan Powers

Holy Houses

Places of worship in twentieth-century Britain

The Twentieth Century Society

2022

TWENTIETH CENTURY ARCHITECTURE is published by the Twentieth Century Society, 70 Cowcross Street, London EC1M 6EJ

NUMBER 15 | 2023 | ISBN 978-0-9556687-7-7

Designed and typeset in Sentinel and Equitan Sans by Nye Hughes
Printed in Belgium by Albe De Coker

The Twentieth Century Society gratefully acknowledges the generous support of the Golden Bottle Trust, Marc Fitch Fund and Thomas Ford & Partners

Individual authors have made their own acknowledgements in their articles. We would also like to thank Ayla Lepine and Matthew Saunders; and John East and Burns Guthrie & Partners for their photographs

Frontispiece: St Martin, Dixon Street, Wolverhampton, 1938–9 by Richard Twentyman (Elain Harwood)

CONTENTS

SIC DEVS DILEXIT MVNDVM

ALAN POWERS

1 Introduction – Holy Houses

Fig.1 St Mary the Virgin, Littlehampton, 1934–5 by W. H. Randoll Blacking (John East)

In 1998, *The Twentieth Century Church* appeared as volume number three in the series Twentieth Century Architecture. It followed an exhibition on the same theme at the RIBA Heinz Gallery in London, curated by Elain Harwood, Kenneth Powell and Alan Powers. Crowded into the gallery space were drawings and models showing the great variety of work in this field, much of it unknown. The journal repeated this pluralist and inclusive content, singling out individual architects such as Ninian Comper and F. X. Velarde, whose careers were later the subject of monograph studies. Longer surveys included an important contribution by Elain Harwood on the impact of the Liturgical Movement in the 1950s and 1960s, a theme that has subsequently been widely explored. The cover showed Robert Maguire and Keith Murray's significant contribution to the movement, St Paul's, Bow Common, London (1960).

A quarter century later, scholarship and general knowledge in this field has advanced considerably, notably through the Roman Catholic project for an inventory of church buildings, *Taking Stock*, carried out between 2005 and 2020 and including about 2,800 churches, Robert Proctor's incisive, well-documented and broad-minded study of the same denomination in the post-war period, and the C20 Society's online database.[1] The lack of either an equivalent inventory and a similar synoptic history of the Church of England's buildings after 1914 is troubling, and for both confessions the interwar decades remain a patchwork of knowledge, although the current work of Clare Price, a major contributor to this issue, is opening up new lines of enquiry for the 1920s and 1930s. These were the most prolific denominations in terms of building, but Nonconformists were also active, and although overall their numbers were beginning to decline, sects such as the Christian Scientists and Salvation Army founded in the late nineteenth century enjoyed their greatest period of growth, while the Quakers enjoyed a revival. Christian Science became fashionable among the social and political elite in the early twentieth century and enjoyed exceptional patronage in the interwar years. Among general studies, however, it is important to recognise how, since 1998, information on authorship and dates of church buildings of all kinds has been undramatically increasing through the revision of the Pevsner Architectural Guides and their expansion into Wales, Scotland and Ireland.

Within a period when stylistic choices seem in retrospect so diverse, it is possible through making comparisons between different faith groups and denominations to see some patterns. Nonconformists generally favoured simplicity without overt modernism, although Cecil Burns's Christian Science church in Tunbridge Wells is a notable exception and, had Methodism been included, a special place would be given to Edward Mills' church complex at Colliers Wood of 1937. Clare Price's detailed archival research on the connections between patronage and style, mediated by clergy and patrons acting individually or through organised structures of decision-making, goes a long way towards explaining the constraints imposed on Anglican architects. While a moderate form of modernism was a goal for some architects, such as D. F. Martin Smith at the John Keble Church, Mill Hill (more apparent internally than externally), we cannot assume that it was what many architects particularly hoped to achieve. Indeed, Duncan Gregory shows how a priest's desire for tradition led E. Bower Norris to produce one of his best buildings at St John Fisher, West Heath, Birmingham. That this happened in 1964 seems even more surprising, but only if we are subscribers to a 'spirit of the age' interpretation of history in which there are 'pioneers' and 'stragglers'. When examined in more detail, stylistic outcomes call such generalised theories into question.

When Peter Anson called his 1960 book about stylistic changes *Fashions in Church Furnishings, 1840–1940*, his assertion that such changes were often less than rational caused objections, but nonetheless carried a ring of truth.[2] The dynamic young vicar at St John, Ermine, Lincoln, chose his modern architect over a cup of tea, while the church authorities and congregation at Holy Trinity, Twydall, seem uniquely to have been led over several years towards a modern design by an architect not otherwise known for radicalism. It was rare for the architect to win out over a conservative clergy and congregation.

Much has been said about the overlaid design styles of churches in the nineteenth century, when architects and theorists promoted their concerns through lectures, books and periodicals such *The Ecclesiologist.* The nineteenth century cannot be understood without churches, but no similar assumption can be made for the century following. Yet there are similarities: the High Victorian Gothic Revival of William Butterfield and George Edmund Street had an urgency and individuality that has overshadowed what came before and after; similarly, the period most marked by the Liturgical Movement, between 1955 and 1965, has attracted a disproportionate share of attention. This represents a second concern – not a criticism for what it originally represented, but a fear that this has become the dominant theme in historiography, so that wars fought over fifty years ago are still being waged in academia to no very useful effect.

The movement's aims were ably expounded by Peter Hammond, Robert Maguire and other members of the New Churches Research Group (NCRG), through books and their journal, *Church Building Today* 1960–62 (later simply *Churchbuilding* in 1962–70 and revived as *Church Building* in 1984). They were zealous in condemnation of those who did not conform to their standards. Hammond admitted churches or re-orderings by traditional architects such as Comper or Stephen Dykes Bower that corresponded to liturgical ideas without a corresponding modernist style, but most strengthened their polemics by the coupling of centralised plan forms with the material realism of the New Brutalists, who themselves were admirers of Butterfield and Street.

This opening of an article from 1960 on 'Modern Architecture and Worship' by Nigel Melhuish, a member of the NCRG, gives a sample of the attitude of these zealots to earlier architecture, not just churches. 'The history of British architecture between the wars is a record of almost unrelieved mediocrity: it would be hard to name even ten buildings of that time which bear comparison with the work then being done abroad'.[3]

Fig.2 St Saviour, Eltham (Welch, Cachemaille-Day and Lander, 1931). The streamlined furnishings represent similar fashions in domestic *décor* and clothes, by Peter Anson, from *Fashions in Church Furnishings*, 1960 (1965 edition, p.324)

It was not only the designs of Gothic or Romanesque inspiration that were condemned, but, rather as Pugin and the Ecclesiologists reserved their sharpest criticism for those merchants of Gothic who might have been mistaken for members of their own tribe, the NCRG and their allies poured scorn on Basil Spence's Coventry Cathedral as 'a pavilion of religious art' or 'a ring-a-ding God-box'. Meanwhile Robert Potter, whose churches were commended by Hammond for incorporating a forward altar, moved from a style heavily influenced by Ninian Comper to embrace the open plans and inclusion of works of art having seen Spence's early designs for Coventry. Melhuish concluded his article by dismissing the possibility that choosing a modern style might solve the problem and called instead for 'the design not to come from a stylistic handbook, but from an understanding of the human activities the building had to serve'. As in contemporary thinking about liberating the theatre from a fixed stage or seating, the building might become little more than a shell.

But was this the only valid destination? In theatres, it was demonstrated that the traditional auditorium shape helped both actors and audience to communicate more intensely, while even the Victorian gingerbread decoration played a part in enhancing the experience.[4] The analogy with older churches has not been so closely argued, but at least it gives a suggestion that the 'unrelieved mediocrity' might have been achieved by people who knew something about what they were doing. Perhaps we no longer need to be so severe about decoration or even a little bit of gilding?

It has taken a long time for this dividing wall between the small number of canonic 'accepted' churches and the rest to be punctured with some observation spy-holes. The information available about church architecture in Britain of the twentieth century, almost regardless of style, is still severely limited. Certainly, active churches posting pictures of their buildings online has expanded the range beyond the pages of vintage building magazines and the useful but limited examples collected by the Incorporated Church Building Society in its three published volumes, but buildings need to be seen at their best through the lenses of skilled photographers.[5] To take one example, the parish church of St Mary at Littlehampton was rebuilt in 1934–35, as the third iteration on the original site, by the architect W. H. Randoll Blacking. This is hardly a name to conjure with, but the experience of this church interior – well-kept and free from clutter – with a Twentieth Century Society group in 2019 was a minor revelation. It confirmed the comment in the Buildings of England, reprinting an Ian Nairn text from the first edition of *Sussex*, 'Blacking clearly had a sound spatial sense and, like his master Comper, a sound sense of how to make religious spaces (they are not always the same thing), so that the result is far more a church than most 1930s religious buildings'.[6] How many others of this quality may there be to discover?

Extended literature about even the best known of mid-century church architects remains patchy. Juliet Dunmur's biography of Sir Edward Maufe, published in 2018, has not yet been joined by an equivalent study of his fellow cathedral designer, Sir Giles Gilbert Scott. Their equal in value and quality, as yet barely a recognised name, J. Harold Gibbons owes his rediscovery to Robert Drake, initially through Twentieth Century Society tours, followed by journal articles.[7] Thanks to the work of Dominic Wilkinson and Andrew Crompton, we have a book on F. X. Velarde in the series Twentieth Century Architects, and hope to add one in due course on N. F. Cachemaille-Day by Clare Price, to continue the trail blazed by Anthony Symondson in his book on S. E. Dykes Bower in the same series, and

Fig.3 Two spreads from Andy Foster, Nikolaus Pevsner and Alexandra Wedgwood, The Buildings of England, *Birmingham and the Black Country* (London: Yale University Press), images 118–25 (James O. Davies)

118. Sutton Coldfield, St Chad, by C.E. Bateman, 1925–7, interior (p. 441)
119. Birmingham, Alum Rock, Christ Church, by Holland W. Hobbiss, 1934–5, W tower (p. 272)
120. Sandwell, Oldbury, Warley, St Hilda, by E.F. Reynolds, 1938–40, interior (p. 567)
121. Sandwell, Oldbury, Warley, Our Lady and St Hubert (R.C.), by George Drysdale, 1934 (p. 567)

118 | 120
119 | 121

122. Birmingham, Longbridge, St John the Baptist, by George While, 1956–8 (p. 416)
123. Walsall, Darlaston, Bentley, Emmanuel, by Richard Twentyman, 1954–6, interior (p. 653)
124. Birmingham, Sheldon, Our Lady Help of Christians (R.C.), by Richard Gilbert Scott, 1966–7, interior (p. 282)
125. Wolverhampton, Whitmore Reans, St Andrew, W window, by John Piper and Patrick Reyntiens, 1967–8 (p. 752)

122 | 124
123 | 125

his earlier volume on Ninian Comper. We also published Gerry Adler's important monograph on Robert Maguire and Keith Murray, architects who led the move to liturgically-conscious church design and were equally important in secular as in sacred work. In these books, it becomes clear how important colour illustrations are to animating projects often recorded if at all only in black and white. This is not about taking sides in an old battle, because a united front is needed for a much bigger battle to come.

But this is only to cover a few of what are probably hundreds of names of architects doing work of quality both in its concept and construction within this period. As a demonstration, a two-page spread of pictures in the new revision of *The Buildings of England, Birmingham and the Black Country* shows four interwar churches, two exteriors and two interiors, all by 'local' architects: C. E. Bateman, Holland W. Hobbiss, E. F. Reynolds and George Drysdale.[8] Arguments about liturgical reform, anachronistic styles or comparison with 'progressive' architecture on a European track seem quite irrelevant – these are imaginative and quite diverse reworkings of well-digested historic sources, apparently continuing to give good service. That the Roman Catholic churches are generally listed, while Anglican coverage is patchy, is a testament to the value of *Taking Stock* and showing how other denominations need a similar study. This picture selection by the author of the revised volume, Andy Foster, followed immediately by another selection of four post-war churches, including Emmanuel, Bentley, by Richard Twentyman, is already enough to arouse curiosity, admiration and affection.

Hard times are no doubt coming, and all denominations will need to think how best to treat their legacy of buildings responsibly – we would hope with guidance from the designated authorities in the field. Most insidious are the changes that clergy and congregations implement against the grain and character of their buildings, afflicting fittings and spatial arrangements irreversibly, such is their desire for a complete makeover. Churches of all dates and styles can be seen as a burden and impediment to current trends of religious experience, a worry for architecture lovers as great as physical decay. The buildings of the major Christian denominations in religious use are subject to 'Ecclesiastical Exemption', regardless of their listed status, each operating its own systems of control. While appeals can be mounted by groups such as the Twentieth Century Society, the resulting Consistory Court hearings are expensive, and their verdicts often accept the loss of original features in pursuit of uncertain benefits.

The accelerated decline of church attendance and the burden of maintenance costs has put all places of worship increasingly at risk, and it is likely that those which are neither very old nor much celebrated will be among the first to fall from the tree. Demolition should be a last resort, especially in view of recent awareness in favour of refurbishment and re-use of all buildings on grounds of carbon emission saving. Conversion and adaptation have been successfully demonstrated in a number of cases, and it may be that the landmark value of places of worship in cities, towns and suburbs is better understood as a reason for saving at least the shell. Furthermore, well into the 1960s, most churches were of solid, traditional construction, and where innovation was required, architects like E. Bower Norris and Richard Twentyman still produced durable buildings, shown by Twentyman when faced at All Saints, Darlaston, with a bomb crater as his site.

Essential to the Twentieth Century Society's campaigns is the expansion of documentary knowledge of individual buildings and architects, more statutory protection and wider support for the retention of buildings and their fittings where appropriate. The purpose of a second journal on churches in the series is therefore to suggest some re-orientations in the existing historiography that could become instrumental in a life and death struggle.

Knowledge and understanding are the prerequisites. Time is short and there is still an enormous amount to discover and think about. Our thanks, in the meantime, to the contributors to this volume for sharing their explorations and insights, as well as to the generous funders who have made its publication possible.

NOTES

1 Robert Proctor, *Building the Modern Church: Roman Catholic Church Architecture in Britain 1955 to 1975* (Abingdon: Routledge, 2016)

2 Peter F. Anson, *Fashions in Church Furnishings, 1840–1940* (London: Faith Press, 1960)

3 Nigel Melhuish, 'Modern Architecture and Worship', *Frontier*, vol.3, Autumn 1960, p.168.

4 See Iain Mackintosh, *Architecture, Actor & Audience* (London: Routledge, 1993).

5 *New Churches Illustrated, fifty-two churches erected during the years 1926–1936* (London: Incorporated Church Building Society, 1936); *Fifty Modern Churches ... with a complete list of all consecrated Anglican churches erected in England since 1930* (London: Incorporated Church Building Society, 1947); *Sixty Post-War Churches; Churches, Church Centres; dual-Purpose Churches* (London: Incorporated Church Building Society, 1956). See also Michael Yelton and John Salmon, *Anglican Church-Building in London, 1915–1945* (Reading: Spire Books, 2007).

6 Elizabeth Williamson, Tim Hudson, Jeremy Musson and Ian Nairn, *Sussex: West* (London: Yale University Press, 2019), p.491.

7 Robert Drake, 'J. Harold Gibbons, an architecture of refinement', *Ecclesiology Today,* no.53, Winter 2016, pp.47–58 and 'J. Harold Gibbons – a closer look at some of his churches', *Ecclesiology Today,* no.54, Summer 2017, pp.39–58

8 Andy Foster, Nikolaus Pevsner and Alexandra Wedgwood, The Buildings of England: *Birmingham and the Black Country* (London: Yale University Press, 2022), illustrations 118–125.

CLARE PRICE

2 'To Build Economically without Sacrificing Reverence and Dignity'

New Church of England church buildings in the interwar period[1]

Fig.1 St Michael, Wythenshawe, Manchester, Nugent F. Cachemaille-Day, 1935–7 (Elain Harwood)

Since the polemical outpourings of the post-war liturgical reform movement, interwar church architecture in England has been consigned to a backwater for historians. Condemned for failing to anticipate that a few rare examples of experimental planning in other denominations across the Channel would become an irresistible revolution, designs have been criticised for both their eclecticism and their traditional styles. They were also categorised as cheap and unimaginatively planned, leading to the period being written off; many are unaware even of the volume of churches that were completed. Some 250 churches were built in the 1930s as the suburbs expanded and, since the preceding decade was similarly productive, the period should not be lightly dismissed.[2] Considering the financial problems of the period – depression, unemployment and the decline in philanthropy, that so many churches were built is remarkable.

The interwar period has been described as 'Janus-faced', an era on the threshold, not knowing whether to look backwards or forwards.[3] Its church architecture epitomises this characterisation, telling a history both of resistance to change and attempts to evolve new ideas. Inevitably there were false starts, with failed projects and a distinct lack of grand gestures; there are very few easily identifiable ground-breaking schemes. Instead, the foundations for future developments are spread across many churches where incremental changes, taken as a whole, indicate a significant transition in design approach. To understand why this was so, it is necessary to consider these buildings in their original context and examine the constraints under which they were conceived.

'INADEQUATE RESOURCES'

It is often forgotten that, between the wars, the church was a strong cultural and moral force, and a fundamental part of society. Post-war Marxist historians who have marginalised religion and condemned it as an irrelevance do not reflect the period accurately. The impact of secularisation on the bedrock of English life was still to be felt: Britain remained 'a highly religious nation' until the 1960s.[4] The Church of England was therefore under considerable pressure to build new churches in order to ensure that there was sufficient provision for the rapidly growing population in the suburbs. It was also a matter of obligation for the established church in England to provide facilities for every inhabitant regardless of their individual beliefs, not simply as a matter of aspiration, nor, although both elements are important, mainly as a social provision for a new community.

Existing parish churches had generally been built to serve the villages which were being swallowed up in the urban sprawl – buildings that were too small to accommodate the incoming population with little capacity for extension.

Frequently, the mission came before the physical structures, with priests and ministers settled in new neighbourhoods and providing a huge variety of community-building activities before permanent facilities were developed. Even those who did not attend for worship took part in such activities, so that churches made a significant contribution as social catalysts.

Translating the human presence of the church into bricks and mortar was a major problem and put a great strain on meagre diocesan resources. After the First World War construction prices rose, with the shortage of materials and especially men, and benefactor funding was increasingly hard to secure. Those inclined to give were more likely to donate sites, often in connection with sales of land for new housing estates, than to fund the construction of the buildings. The Church of England had relied on the state for assistance in times past, but now initiated fundraising schemes, such as the massive 'Forty-Five Churches Fund' launched by the Diocese of London in June 1930. An 'avalanche of building', Bishop Arthur Winnington-Ingram explained, had 'descended with such rapidity' that the diocese had entirely 'inadequate resources' to deal with it.[5] This was initially intended to provide funds for clergy stipends, building sites, parsonages, halls and churches. However, the plans were over-ambitious and costs underestimated, so that manpower and sites became the priority in order to get a foothold in a district. Dual-purpose buildings, combining a church and hall, often did duty until a 'permanent' church building could be erected, becoming parish halls once the proper churches were built; many survive in this use today.

Once this major initial coordinated effort was over, building the permanent church was left to the local congregations. They were expected to show their commitment to the church by providing a large portion of the building cost, even though many newly-relocated suburban dwellers had little disposable income. Redundant church sites in inner-city areas with declining populations were quite commonly sold to fill a funding gap, but this was generally unpopular and rarely offered until the local district had been seen to make its best efforts. Other sources of money included dwindling pre-war bequests and grants from funding bodies such as the Incorporated Church Building Society (ICBS).

More important for the outcome of the design than the funding raised was the choice of architect. Again, this was often led to the individual districts, with little help or guidance from the diocese or any other source. Some congregations defaulted to the local diocesan surveyor or architect, but a surprising number chose their architect after carefully researching the work carried out in their locality. Once an architect had been selected by the parochial church council, local involvement varied widely. This was an era of emancipation and the Church of England Assembly (Powers) Act of 1919 empowered ordinary members of the congregation serving on the parochial church council to have a direct input in the plans for a new church building, leading to some good working relationships between architects and their collective clients. Others were content to defer to the professional for the design of their church building. It was not unusual for there to be a mismatch between a local people who wished to have input and an architect who objected to their involvement as 'meddlesome interference'.[6] The changing dynamic between the congregation as client and the architect was an important determinant in the design of the final church building and depended a great deal on the attitude and stance of the architect within the professional debates of the time.

THE MIDDLE PATH

For architects, churches retained their prominence as respected commissions in the interwar period, their prestige undimmed in the minds of the majority of the profession and the public alike. As cathedral designers, for example, Sir Giles Gilbert Scott and Sir Edward Maufe were undeniably the 'starchitects' of their generation; even obtaining an ordinary parish church commission was still a mark of distinction. However, a commission could prove exceptionally challenging, with budgets ever decreasing, so that many architects struggled to realise their ambitions for such projects.

When compared to the exuberance of the Victorian Gothic Revival, the relative plainness of suburban interwar churches is undeniable. The Victorians were at the nadir of fashion and there was a deliberate policy to distance church design from the preceding century. As a result, the architects relied on proportion and the beauty of simplicity, reflected in the language they used at the time. This had the added advantage of keeping costs down, but the right way to achieve it was heavily disputed.

Much has been made of the conflict between traditional and modern styles during the interwar period and this certainly dominated the discussion in architectural journals of the time. Later narratives have assumed that church architects all fell into the traditional camp, whether vestigially Gothic, Byzantine or classical, with any construction in concrete almost entirely concealed. Many churches of the early 1920s continued earlier styles for the simple reason that they were designed before the First World War but only executed after it, with long building programmes owing to the changing funding climate. St Michael, Mill Hill, for example, was based on plans drawn up by W. D. Caröe in 1911 and constructed over many years in incremental stages beginning in 1921, never to be fully completed. Although their basic styling and influences were unchanged, pre-1914 plans nearly always had to be modified to take into account changing circumstances, usually by reducing the size of the building.

It was not uncommon for plans drawn up for local congregations before the First World War to be abandoned, and new architects commissioned, so that the eventual buildings were very different from those first intended for the site. Herbert Wills's proposed traditional basilica for St Alban, Golders Green, of 1914 was followed by a failed scheme from Ernest Trobridge in 1923, and only in 1932 was Sir Giles Scott's church finally built.

Fig.2 St Michael's Church, Mill Hill, W. D. Caröe, as designed in 1911 (Lambeth Palace Library)

By the 1930s the appearance and planning of new churches began to show signs of development. A new generation of 'school-trained men' with a 'necessarily wider outlook' brought the influence of the European Modern Movement – even if tailored to established ideas for form and materials – and they demonstrated a changed attitude to the role of community in church life.[7] Neither strongly traditional nor modern, the 'middle way' was attractive to many church architects and widely supported by an informed public, although its rationale has subsequently been forgotten or overlooked by historians.[8] This compromise position suited architects who were keen to evolve alternative concepts for a building type that transcended ordinary design solutions, described by Sir Giles Scott as 'a type of functionalism with which the functionalist is unfamiliar'.[9]

This shift towards a middle ground between traditional and modern architecture was recognised and reported in the architectural press.[10] In his annual roundup of new buildings in the *Architects' Journal* for 1933, Charles Reilly divided architects into three groups: 'Revolutionaries ... Evolutionists, and ... the As-You-Were Folks'.[11] Reilly classified all his church examples under the 'Evolutionists' heading. Rather than striking contemporaries as backward, these churches were contrasted favourably with many major civic projects, which for Reilly represented the traditional, unimaginative architectural contributions of the day.

Although there was a definite move to evolve and advance church architecture in the 1930s, there was also considerable resistance to the idea that change was necessary. Not surprisingly, there was a generational divide amongst church architects, with many older ones disapproving of what they considered to be 'merely eccentric' designs by architects who were 'showing off their own cleverness'.[12] Significantly, a handful of these highly respected senior figures, who in Sir Charles Nicholson's words found it 'difficult for [their] old eyes to appreciate the adventurous tendencies of a new generation', exercised both a direct and indirect influence in the selection of new church designs through their authorship of advisory publications and membership of key committees responsible for legal approvals and funding allocations.

Fig.3 St Alban, North Harrow, Arthur W. Kenyon, 1936–7 (Elain Harwood)

A move towards a new outlook was becoming unavoidable as traditional architecture involved expensive materials that could be ill-afforded. However, there were particular characteristics of church building that set it apart from other building types and caused particular difficulties, above all the need to convey permanence and a sense of the spiritual. These goals had to be achieved with limited resources at a time when the church was striving for community buildings that were attractive and approachable, to encourage attendance. New districts and architects alike needed guidance to help them achieve a church design that met the parish's requirements with an appropriate and 'worthy' building within budget.

'PROPERLY BUILT, CONVENIENTLY PLANNED AND DIGNIFIED IN DESIGN'

Unlike the Victorian decades, which were dominated by the Ecclesiological Society's dictatorship of every detail, there was no standard 'design guide' produced in the years after 1918, and an eclecticism was the result. For new suburbs without an established population, it would have been helpful for the Church of England or the dioceses to have assisted with a brief for their architects. Diocesan advisory committees were in their infancy, and the majority were tasked with overseeing repairs and war memorial installations, leaving little capacity for new churches. Those that did comment on new churches came into the process at a late stage and (as will be seen below) were often obstructive. With an inexperienced client, the lack of such guidance was keenly felt and bemoaned by many attempting to advise new districts on their projects. When assisting the Parochial Church Council of St Alban, North Harrow, with its competition brief, the architect Percy Lovell commented that he felt that the diocese could have helped 'a lot by giving more definite instructions'.[13] As a result of this vacuum, the ICBS' *Architectural Requirements and Suggestions* published to aid those approaching it for grants, became the recommended benchmark for church design.

The problem with using the *Architectural Requirements* as a de facto design guide was the traditional views of its authoring committee. Although the rules were regularly revised, they lacked any recognition of the changing circumstances of the local congregations or, indeed, of the evolving approaches of architectural colleagues. Ostensibly inviting reasonable standards of sound construction, the *Architectural Requirements* were narrowly framed to promote traditional

construction methods and assumed that plan forms too would follow precedent. Many churches guided in this way not surprisingly appeared traditional in style and form. The criticism voiced by the Southwark Diocesan Advisory Committee that 'better results could have been obtained by departing from the Gothic tradition which uninstructed local opinion insisted on' seems somewhat unjust; if they were expected to follow the available guidance, it was inevitable.[14]

Architects plainly followed the guidance too. The 1936 competition for St Alban, North Harrow, produced a series of designs that would have complied with these requirements, including the winning entry by Arthur Kenyon. Known for his work at Welwyn Garden City and for cinemas in streamlined modern styles, Kenyon was definitely not one of the 'As-you-were folks'.[15] He had not designed a church before, and his scheme assumed the building would not only have to comply with the published requirements but have to satisfy a conservative congregation. However, the local community at North Harrow wanted a forward-looking design and before launching the competition had approached Nugent Francis Cachemaille-Day. It clearly sought a building that was modern in conception and revised designs for St Alban's as built show that, once commissioned, Kenyon modified his design accordingly. Records show that the local church council contributed to the design process and exercised a measure of control, getting their way in wanting pews rather than chairs.

The committees who authored the *Architectural Requirements* allowed a measure of discretion in their application. Most often they were used by the older architects to promote their own viewpoint and to discourage innovation. Proposals by this old guard had an easier passage through the system than those of the younger generation such as D. F. Martin-Smith, Cachemaille-Day and Bernard Miller. The designs for All Saints, Hillingdon, built in 1931–2 by committee member Sir Charles Nicholson were passed without a single comment, for example. By contrast, the innovative plans for St Nicholas, Burnage, of the same date, were extensively criticised. Compliance with these regulations was expected by funding bodies such as the ICBS itself, and also the dioceses and Ecclesiastical Commissioners. The arbiters were the architects' committees of these bodies, whose members were firmly traditionalist.

The *Architectural Requirements* dictated that a church must be 'properly built, conveniently planned and dignified in design'.[16] The definition of what constituted 'properly built' was based on expectations of highly-specified traditional construction. Church buildings were rooted in the idea of longevity, and needed to establish their credentials in this regard whilst being economical to construct. The use of modern materials was becoming an economic necessity that church designers could not escape, but these materials also allowed a measure of freedom in what could be achieved. As the period progressed, the potential of materials such as reinforced concrete outside a purely structural use or as a cheaper way of mimicking older styles was realised, and the design freedom it brought recognised. St Michael, Wythenshawe (Cachemaille-Day, 1937) and John Keble (Martin-Smith, 1937) were built on waterlogged sites that demanded alternative constructional approaches, steering the architects towards concrete frames and diagrid roofs. Newer construction methods flouted the *Requirements* since they did not keep up with changing trends, for example retaining advice on wall thicknesses that only applied to traditional construction methods. St Christopher, Withington (Bernard Miller, 1935), St Michael, Wythenshawe and St John the Baptist, Tottenham (Seely & Paget, 1939) were all criticised for their thickness of screen walls inside concrete frames, even though the architects had all made it clear that the walls were not load-bearing. Other innovative uses of materials were discouraged: the experimental use of coloured concrete to adorn the tower of John Keble, Mill Hill, was condemned as 'rather puerile'.

Not only was traditional construction championed by the committees, there was also a clear tendency favouring conventionally planned schemes. The phrase 'convenient' planning was manipulated to favour the expected longitudinal nave and chancel arrangement and to snub any proposals that experimented with alternative layouts for the worship space. Attempts to re-think ancillary spaces such as vestries on different levels were questioned and there was a mysterious dislike for congregational toilet provision. Ernest Trobridge's elaborate and striking twin-naved scheme for St Alban, Golders Green, was rejected, not simply because of suspicions that it would not come within the budget, but mainly because W. D. Caröe and Herbert Passmore judged it to be 'incongruous and bizarre' and especially 'inharmonious' in its planning.[17] Interestingly, the archives of Trobridge's successor architect at Golders Green, Giles Gilbert Scott, contain similar experiments with twin naves and unconventional choir locations, so this clearly remained part of the parish brief. Scott's attempts to modify a more traditional cruciform

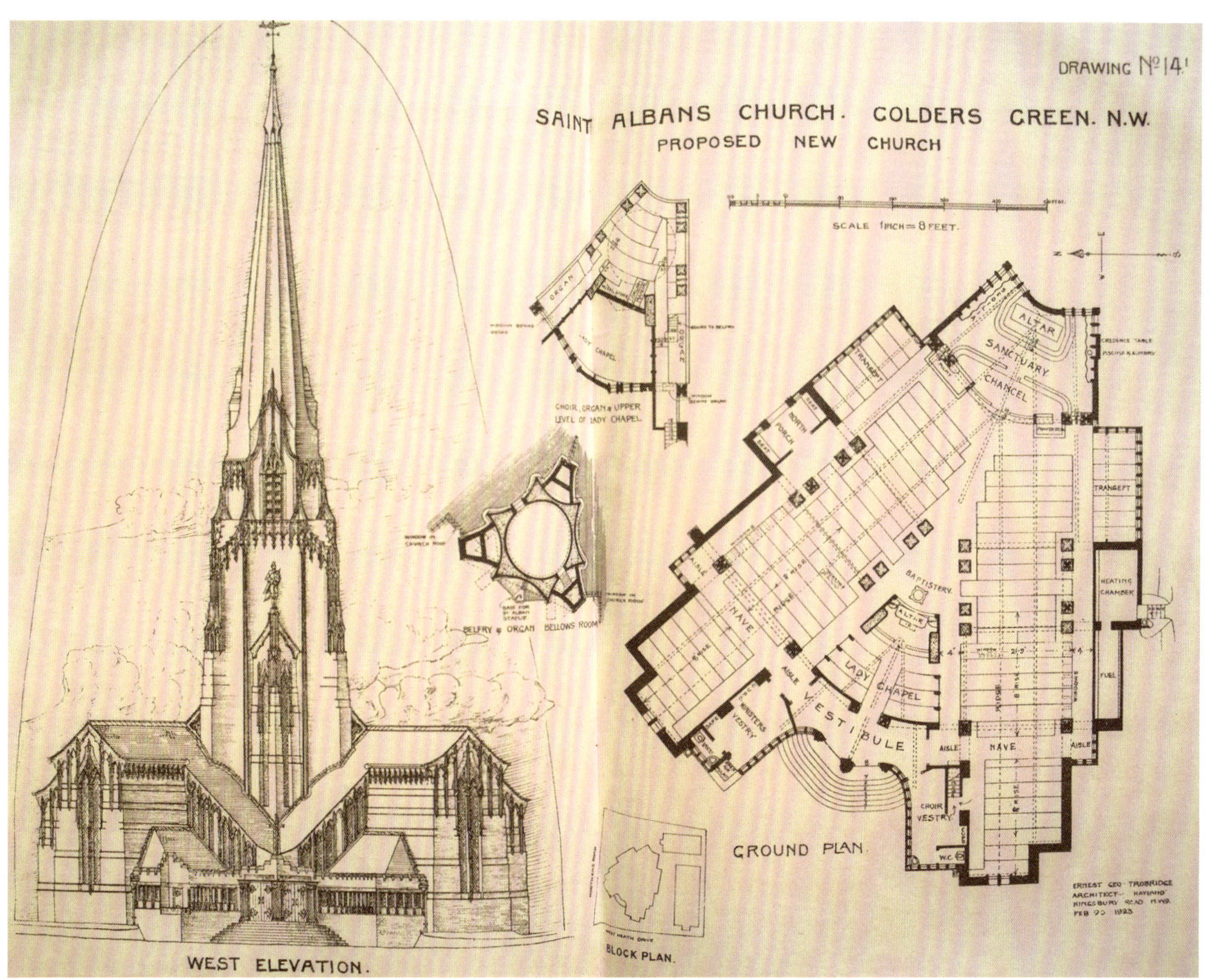

Fig.4 St Alban, Golders Green, proposed new church by E. G. Trobridge, 1923

plan to meet local requirements by placing the choir behind the altar in the eastern arm of the cross were also rejected. The conventionally planned church that was ultimately built conceals this fascinating design development, which was an early example of a trend to employ an unconventional plan within a traditional external appearance.

The John Keble church at Mill Hill was heavily criticised for the innovative placing of the choir in the middle of the nave. The architects on the ICBS committee squabbled over this one, and it was only the vociferous sponsorship of leading musical experts of the day such as Sydney Nicholson and Dr Geoffrey Shaw that saved the scheme from major alterations. The committee advanced the suggestions that a western gallery or seating the choir in the front two rows of the nave would

Fig.5 John Keble Church, Mill Hill, D. F. Martin-Smith, 1936 (John East)

serve the purpose just as well, misunderstanding the parish's key requirement that the church should reflect the idea of 'family worship'.[18]

Whether a design was 'worthy' was a value judgment made by panels of consulting architects, allowed by the phrase 'dignified in design', incorporated into the *Requirements* in 1938, presumably as the number of more modern designs proliferated. Both John Keble and St Nicholas, Burnage, were judged to be 'unworthy' designs and unlikely to inspire a spirit of 'reverence in worship'.[19] The star-shaped plan at St Michael, Wythenshawe, was considered not 'to have any great architectural value' and St Mary, Becontree, was dismissed as 'eccentric'. Despite the claim that there was 'no wish to limit architects in their architectural treatment', the opposite was clearly the case. This would have discouraged innovation, so that the 'fear of experiment' could also mean a fear of spending time and scarce resources on a scheme that would be rejected by these authorities.[20] The effect of this process was to supress innovative ideas and to put off parishes inclined to experiment, and had a very practical effect on what was built.

'TO DESIGN FOR COMPLETION AND ADORNMENT IN LATER YEARS'

The *Architectural Requirements* promoted the idea of 'building in instalments' – a strategy bound up with budgetary restrictions that also assumed that a certain method of design and construction was more important than the needs of the parish being served. However many years it might to complete, a church building was still expected to be elaborate, rich and costly. Committee member H. P. Burke-Downing declared that 'the aim must ever be kept before the architect that the building should testify to belief in the power of beauty to furnish an ennobling inspiration, and ... the worthiest offering to the Glory of God'.[21]

Even so, compromises had to be made in order to build a permanent church. Many districts suffered from having to worship in poor temporary buildings for many years: St Alban, North Harrow, and the John Keble church started life in tents; St Luke, Benchill, Manchester (1938 by Taylor & Young) began in a room in a dilapidated farmhouse, and many had ex-army huts or tin sheds which provided little insulation against either the winter cold or summer heat. The priority was therefore to achieve a well-built and completed structure, rather than an over-budget building that might never be completed.

In complete contradiction was the clause in the *Architectural Requirements* advising that building part of the church in a solid fashion was preferable to building the whole to a lower specification. Permanence of construction was paramount, and could be achieved through one of two routes: building part of a truly 'worthy' church with traditional construction to stand the test of posterity, with the intention of completing later, or devising a way to design an appropriate building that could be substantially built straight away within the parish budget. The problem with the first approach was that it failed to comprehend either the stringent economic reality of the time or that funding prospects would only get worse. It was well recognised that church buildings differed from others, but many of those involved still found it hard to accept that a new approach was necessary.

The failure of committee members to admit the changing circumstances is well seen in the six churches designed by Ernest Shearman between 1910 and 1933. These were St Matthew, Wimbledon (1910), St Silas, Kentish Town (1911), St Barnabas, Ealing (1914), St Gabriel, Acton (1929), St Barnabas, Temple Fortune (1932) and St Francis, Isleworth (1933). Gavin Stamp remarked that Shearman's churches displayed 'no stylistic development' and appeared to use the same kit of parts to produce near-identical churches because 'he could do nothing else'.[22] Shearman never responded to the fact that budgets became so restricted that the prospect of completion diminished with each church constructed; both St Barnabas, Temple Fortune, and St Gabriel were never finished to his design, and the latter still retains its temporary west wall. Other architects' elaborate and over-specified designs remained incomplete for the same reason. The first section of Caröe's church of St Michael, Mill Hill, was noted in 1920 as displaying 'an unusual amount of temporary construction'.[23] It was originally conceived before the First World War as a large, elaborate Gothic building intended to seat over 700 people and to be faced in Clipsham stone. Even a part-build of the chancel and half of the nave was still far out of the financial reach of the congregation in the 1920s. Although further sections were added, the original design was heavily comprised and the tower was never constructed.

Many churches suffered not only from losing their tower as their most elegant feature, but were thereby deprived of their geographical prominence in suburbs where wayfinding cues were frustrated by repetitious housing. St Michael, Mill Hill, never acquired its intended tower, nor did St Alphage, Burnt Oak (Nicholas & Dixon-Spain, 1927); St Mary, Cadishead (Robert Martin, 1927); St Crispin, Withington (Hubert Worthington, 1297); St Bede, Bolton (Frank R. Freeman, 1931) or St Michael, Tokyngton (Cyril Farey, 1932) to name but a few. Some of the architects on the committees agreed with the early Ecclesiologists that towers were a dispensable and redundant extravagance. Commenting on the church of Holy Angels, Claremont (Bradshaw Gass & Hope, 1926), W. D. Caröe doubted the scheme would come in on budget and that the option of not building the tower was one he actively favoured. Contrary to his predictions, however, the church was completed with funds in hand and the tower was built on a larger scale than originally intended.

Surprisingly, many of the architects on these committees who advocated part-build also placed their faith in the use of proportion as a substitute for decoration. Charles Nicholson considered that proportion was 'the real secret of architectural dignity'.[24] Clearly an incomplete church was one where the intended proportions were compromised. Comments were frequently based on how a certain feature would be appreciated once was the church was fully completed. It was noted that the arrangement of St Hilda, Audenshaw (Robert Martin, 1937) would 'look particularly well when the full length of the nave ceiling can be seen', but the church was never completed so could not be read as the architect intended.[25]

Not only did the *Architectural Requirements* favour part-build, the alternative of providing a structurally complete building on a less ambitious scale or using simpler construction was actively derided. Indeed, Stephen Dykes-Bower concluded that the architect had either to concentrate on using the money for 'the structure, or part of it and hope that its completion and proper furnishings may be added later' or he may instead build a 'modest building ... and derive what satisfaction he can' from the process, but in so doing would 'sacrifice his dreams'. By the time he wrote this in the late 1930s, he was obliged to conclude reluctantly that it would be 'foolish to ignore the fact that the chances of sustained generosity of this kind, in the circumstances of the times cannot be relied upon', admitting that the opportunities for completing a part-build church were diminishing very rapidly indeed.[26]

Building a structurally complete building, or one which felt complete but allowed for ancillary spaces to be added, was a challenge – especially if traditional construction, planning and design were assumed. Meeting the expectations of the district and the architects' committees that controlled funding and consents, often on imperfect sites, became the catalyst for innovation in the use of materials and design during the 1930s. Several architects realised that with a pragmatic approach, using modern materials and adopting an updated middle style, a satisfactory complete church could still be achieved.

Fig.6 St Gabriel, Acton, Ernest Shearman, 1929, showing the incomplete west end (Elain Harwood)

'THE ADVENTUROUS TENDENCIES OF A NEW GENERATION'

Rather than rejecting all precedent, those favouring a new approach were intent on working on an evolution of the Gothic – still widely believed to be the best basis for church design – leading to a series of churches that are perhaps best described as 'hybrids'. The combination of a modern exterior and conventionally planned interior in churches such as St Alban, North Harrow, and St Chad, Bolton (Richard Nickson, 1937) became an accepted form. They were subject to later disapproval in the post-war urge towards honest austerity.[27] An unusual internal plan intended to suit the worship needs of the local congregation, with a more conventional exterior, passed without recognition or comment in later years. One strategy was to place a

Fig.7 St Francis of Assisi, Gladstone Park, J. Harold Gibbons, 1933 (Elain Harwood)

Lady chapel behind the altar, meaning that the altar was closer to the congregation while giving length to the interior space, as in J. Harold Gibbons's churches of St Francis, Gladstone Park (1933), St Mary, Kenton (1936) and St Barnabas, Northolt Park (1939), all with Byzantine-style brick exteriors and steep roofs. Ideas for the architectural expression of family worship and plans to facilitate the gathering of the community were developing slowly, proving that this was no era of stagnation but of new concepts in the throes of development.

'AN ARCHITECT OF OUTSTANDING QUALITY'[28]

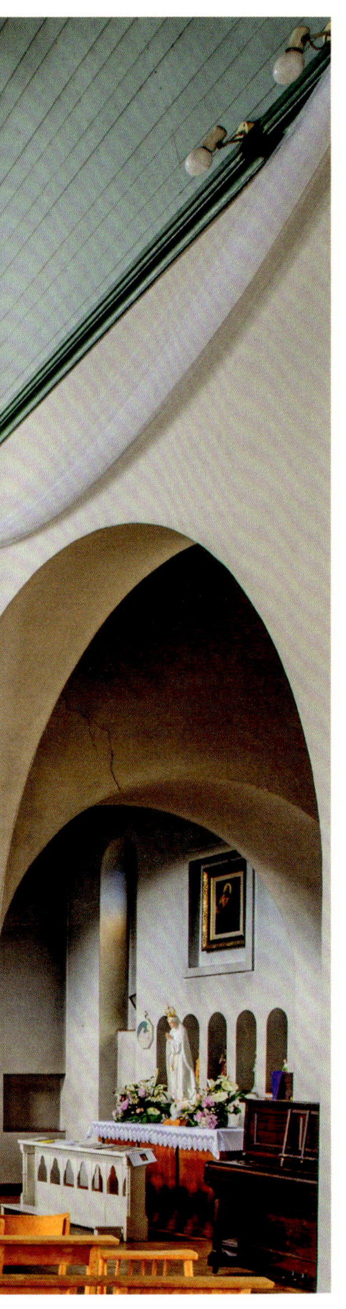

By far the most innovative architect at this time was N. F. Cachemaille-Day. He experimented with many of the key attributes of church planning that were to be recommended by the liturgical reform movement after the Second World War. While aware of the developments in church architecture on the Continent, he was also acutely conscious that many of the more outlandish examples published in the architectural press were not subject to the same requirements as those demanded by the Church of England, particularly in respect of the requirement for 'permanent' construction.[29] Instead, his approach was tailored to the local congregations, who wanted to express their worship through the form of their building; his success with these bespoke designs explains and validates the eclecticism of his churches.

Collaborating with a lively and interested local population, Cachemaille-Day's first church at Burnage in the Manchester suburbs was formative. It set the pattern for his extensive consultations with congregations, and showed his sensitivity towards budgets and the realisation that a complete church was worth more than the hope of one in an indefinite future. He often found novel solutions to the particular problems of a site, which at Burnage meant the noise from a tram route that led him to insert a raised Lady chapel as an acoustic buffer between the high altar and the road. His other churches were equally configured to express the particular requirements of their location and congregation.

Cachemaille-Day was a master at experimenting with shapes and materials. Concrete and steel frames achieved cost savings, while innovative solutions such as reinforced concrete foundations and roof structures dealt with difficult ground conditions, and at St Michael, Wythenshawe, the unusual star-shaped plan replaced a conventional longitudinal apsidal design to accommodate the angular shapes of the diagrid roof construction. At St Mary, Becontree, built with Welch and Lander in 1934, Gothic was reinvented as an appropriate style with simplified reticulated tracery set in modern plain rendered walls.

From the viewpoint of later developments in church architecture, Cachemaille-Day's most interesting designs arose when he worked with congregations that were trialling the 'Parish Communion'. While an early communion service (with few or no communicants), followed by Mattins and High Mass later in the morning, was the established norm, 'Parish Communion' encouraged congregational participation and the receiving of communion by all, at a time of day that would suit the majority – typically 9.00 am – often followed by a communal breakfast.[30] The origins of this movement are not clear, but seem to have begun before the First World War and spread gradually through the 1920s and 1930s. Cachemaille-Day specifically noted when the churches he designed were intended to express the idea of gathering as a family for communion. They did not all include the same elements. When reporting on St Mary, Becontree, he explained that the free-standing altar with altar rails on three sides was expressly 'to emphasise the feeling of family

communion'.[31] This focus on group participation ran parallel with the liturgical movement on the Continent, but the longitudinal nature of the Becontree plan (Gothic windows included) show how easily we can miss these more radical intentions, especially if later re-orderings have confused the picture. One of the defining principals of the liturgical movement was the concept of the celebrant facing the people, which required a freestanding central altar, but experiments of this kind were rare before the 1950s and the corporate feel of a family community in the worship space was instead expressed in different configurations of choir and congregational seating.[32] At St Paul, Ruislip Manor, Cachemaille-Day achieved this by putting the choir in the transepts next to and surrounding the altar, keeping its closeness to the altar without it getting between the congregation and the sacrament.

The churches of St Winfrid, Testwood (1938) and the Bishop Burroughs Memorial Church of the Epiphany at Gipton, Leeds (1936) represent the apogee of Cachemaille-Day's interwar work in liturgical planning. At Testwood the choir and congregation wrap around three sides of the altar, both at ground level and in galleries. The church hall was integral to the design with its flat roof intended as a terrace for breakfast. At Gipton, putting the choir behind the altar meant that the

Fig.8 St Nicholas, Burnage, Manchester, Nugent F. Cachemaille-Day, 1930–2, with Lady chapel behind the altar (Elain Harwood)

Fig.9 St Mary, Becontree, Nugent F. Cachemaille-Day, 1934, showing the brick tracery (John East)

Fig.10 Church of the Epiphany, Gipton, Nugent F. Cachemaille-Day, 1936 (John East)

church family could gather on every side, an idea originating from early designs for Wythenshawe. Putting the Lady chapel behind the sanctuary in both these churches, thus bringing the altar into a central position in the nave, was an idea repeated from Burnage.

The architects on advisory and approvals committees regularly disapproved of Cachemaille-Day's unusual approach. At St Nicholas, Burnage, the ICBS committee demanded a substantial number of alterations that, had they been carried out, would have added £900 to the bill – almost ten per cent of the total build cost. St Mary, Becontree, was condemned by the same committee as being 'of an eccentric character' and 'bizarre in the extreme' with a recommendation that the whole scheme needed 'reconsideration'. The windows in particular were considered

'unpleasant features', even 'abominations'. A robust response from the Archdeacon of Southend pointed out that it was not the role of the committee to turn down plans on 'the grounds of style and design' and accused them of being hostile to 'young architects of real ability'.[33] After this, the committees alighted on different reasons for complaint for almost every subsequent church by Cachemaille-Day, in addition to their habitual concerns about wall thicknesses. His church of St Paul, Dollis Hill, was criticised for 'irrationality'; the expense of a potentially striking decorative mosaic in the apse at St Paul, Ruislip Manor, was considered of 'doubtful' value and the use of concrete ribs at St Barnabas, Tuffley, 'disappointing in effect'. In a typical remark by the committees of the time, it was suggested that Tuffley would be better if 'a more traditional method of construction' were used.[34]

The committee members exercised unaccountable authority when they took on the role of assessing competitions, as when Edward Maufe rejected Cachemaille-Day's entry for that at the John Keble Church in Mill Hill. This featured a central location for the choir and a sanctuary surrounded on three sides by seating facing inwards. Since this clearly met the main competition requirements, it is difficult to understand Maufe's rejection – indeed he expressly avoided giving any clear reasons on this design, choosing instead as winner the design submitted by the brother of the church organist.[35]

Cachemaille-Day was always measured in his response to criticism, accepting suggestions with grace and attempting to modify his plans. He was careful not to compromise his design intent, however, and the needs and wishes of the local congregations were paramount in his proposals. The contemporary desire to champion community whilst expressing the new ideas of family communion was thus tailored to the individual circumstances of each district, with Cachemaille-Day experimenting with a different architectural solution on each occasion.

CONCLUSION

To produce a church within the tight budgets typical of the interwar years depended on the architect's ability to communicate with the client, be flexible over planning and willing to experiment with new forms and materials. Stringent economies forced many to compromise by denuding traditional forms of carving or mouldings, or worse, to run out of money with the project unfinished. The malign belief that part-build was a good solution left a legacy of buildings that are incomplete and unsatisfactory both as architecture and as functioning churches. The system of consents pitched two different generations of architects against one another: the new generation of school-trained architects against the 'old boy network'.[36] The committees of architects meddled in church projects, their over-arching influence of thought and attitude as to what was appropriate and acceptable in the design leaving its mark on the whole period. This had far wider repercussions than just the obtaining of funding; it influenced the entire ethos of church design of the day and helped to cement a superficial reading of ecclesiastical architecture of the period as backward-looking.

On the plus side, the same difficult conditions had an inspirational effect on other architects, leading to innovations that would pay for later, more revolutionary, changes in church building. For this to happen, the recognition that the needs and budgets of the congregations were changing was a vital starting point. These new suburban districts were fresh territories which required a revised understanding and a tailored approach to design. The aspiration to achieve a community drove a critical impetus behind church expansion, leading these new districts at last to get the types of space that they wanted for worship in place of an earlier generation's ossified preconceptions.

Church communities had two main requests, that the design should provide a space where all the people could see and hear, that also generated the feeling of being together as a family in church. Many permutations were suggested; more were proposed than were built. Combinations ranged from modern exteriors with conventional planning, to a traditional appearance outside and innovative uses of space inside. Given the cultural and social norms of the interwar period this was a totally understandable approach. The interior planning of these experimental churches is not unfamiliar to us today – it can be seen in many re-orderings of older churches to meet the needs of changing worship. In these, altars have been placed in the nave, chancels have become chapels behind and transept seating (now always chairs) rotated to surround the altar.

By separating the expectations of the outside of a church from the inside, the interwar church architects were standing on the threshold between the old and the new, trying to look backward and forward. Stepping back from later polemical writings that take these buildings out of this context, it is possible to identify these trends as a valid reflection of a specific time. Ultimately a re-evaluation is required that secures the interwar period in the timeline of twentieth-century ecclesiastical design, not as an eclectic or mixed-up muddle to be ignored or discounted, but as the 'missing links', necessary workings out that join the legacy of the Victorian ecclesiologists to the radicals of the post-war liturgical movement.

NOTES

1 N. F. Cachemaille-Day, 'Reinforced Concrete', *Church Times*, 7 October 1932, p.397.

2 Peter Hammond, *Liturgy and Architecture* (London: Barrie and Rockliff, 1960), p.68.

3 Alison Light, *Forever England: Femininity, Literature and Conservatism between the Wars* (London: Routledge, 1991), p.10.

4 Callum Brown, *The Death of Christian Britain* (Hoboken: Taylor and Francis, second edition 2009), p.30.

5 A. F. London, Bishop, 'Church Needs of Outer London', letter to *The Times*, 28 April 1930, p.19.

6 Charles Nicholson, 'The Design and Arrangement of Churches', in *Recent English Ecclesiastical Architecture* (London: Technical Journals Ltd, 1911), p.8.

7 Charles Reilly, *Representative British Architects of the Present Day* (London: Batsford, 1931), p.7.

8 Except those who have written on Giles Gilbert Scott such as Gavin Stamp and D. F. Lewis, both of whom recognised his identification with the 'middle line'. See Stamp, 'Giles Gilbert Scott: The problem of "modernism", *Architectural Design*, vol.49, *Britain in the Thirties*, 1979, pp.72–83.

9 Giles Gilbert Scott, assessor's report, Cathedral of the Holy Cross, Columbo, 6 March 1947, cited in David Frazer Lewis, 'Giles, Adrian & Richard Gilbert Scott', in Susannah Charlton, Elain Harwood and Clare Price, eds., *100 Churches 100 Years* (London: Batsford, 2019), p.163.

10 Charles Reilly, *Architects' Journal*, vol.79, 11 January 1934, p.65.

11 Charles Reilly, 'Built Now, the Year's Buildings', *Architects' Journal*, vol.77, 11 January 1933, p.47.

12 Charles Nicholson, 'Book Review: New Churches Illustrated', RIBA *Journal*, vol.44, no.7, 6 February 1937, p.358.

13 Percy Lovell, letter to G. Perry, secretary of the London Diocesan Fund, 6 August 1935, North Harrow St Alban Parsonage File, London Metropolitan Archives (uncatalogued).

14 Central Council of Diocesan Advisory Committees for the Care of Churches, *The Care of Churches: Their Upkeep and Protection*, eighth report, (London: Press and Publications Board of the Church Assembly, 1930), p.58.

15 Kenyon designed cinemas in Welwyn Garden City (1928), Rochester (1935) and Chatham (1936).

16 Incorporated Church Building Society, *Architectural Requirements* (London: ICBS, 1938).

17 Caröe & Passmore, Report to the Ecclesiastical Commissioners for England, 10 July 1923, file no.83079, Lambeth Palace Library.

18 Correspondence, John Keble, Mill Hill, ICBS file 12263, Lambeth Palace Library.

19 Committee of Honorary Consulting Architects, report 5 June 1935, John Keble, Mill Hill, ICBS file 12263, Lambeth Palace Library; Committee of Honorary Consulting Architects, report 1 July 1931, St Nicholas Burnage, ICBS file 12046, Lambeth Palace Library.

20 Bernard Miller, 'The Design of the Modern Church', *Architectural Record of Design and Construction*, vol.8, February 1938, pp.60–1.

21 H. P. Burke Downing, in Incorporated Church Building Society, *Churches for New Centres of Population* (London: ICBS, n.d. *c.*1930), pp.5–6.

22 Gavin Stamp, 'Review Essay', *Ecclesiology Today*, no.42, June 2010, pp.150–1.

23 ICBS report, 28 June 1920, Lambeth Palace Library.

24 Charles Nicholson, 'The Design and Arrangement of Churches', op. cit., p.7.

25 Robert Martin, 'Report to the Incorporated Church Building Society', 10 March 1938, p.2, ICBS file 12363, Lambeth Palace Library.

26 Stephen Dykes-Bower, 'Backgrounds and Practices', *Architects' Journal*, vol.83, 19 April 1937, p.744.

27 Hammond, op. cit., p.68.

28 Laurence King, 'obituary, N. F. Cachemaille-Day 1896–1976', *RIBA Journal*, vol.83, November 1976, p.484.

29 N. F. Cachemaille-Day, op. cit., p.397.

30 Gabriel Hebert, *The Parish Communion* (London: SPCK, 1937), p.3.

31 N. F. Cachemaille-Day, 'Report upon the proposed church of St Mary at Becontree', 7 May 1934, archive of Cachemaille-Day & Partners, 1928–1963, CaN/6, RIBA Drawings and Archives.

32 The first booklet published to explain this phenomenon was Basil Minchin, The Celebration of the Eucharist Facing the People (London: Darton, Longman & Todd Ltd, 1954).

33 Committee of Honorary Consulting Architects, report 4 July 1934 and correspondence, ICBS file for St Mary, Becontree, Lambeth Palace Library.

34 Committee of Honorary Consulting Architects, report 21 July 1938, St Paul, Dollis Hill, ICBS file 12473; Committee of Honorary Consulting Architects, report 6 July 1938, St Barnabas, Tuffley, ICBS file 12420, Lambeth Palace Library.

35 'Competition for the John Keble Church, Mill Hill', *Architect & Building News*, vol.140, 5 October 1934, pp.17–19. Any partiality was hotly denied, but Maufe would undoubtedly have recognised the hand of all competitors except that of the new designer Martin-Smith and would have been aware of the connections with the organist. Maufe was aware that the architects' committees did not favour Cachemaille-Day, being a member himself. Martin-Smith did not develop his designs much from this point, even after the war, which is interesting for the architect of what has been feted as the most liturgically aware design of the interwar period.

36 Gilbert Cope, 'The Sanctuary in the Parish Church', in William Lockett, ed., *The Modern Architectural Setting of the Liturgy* (London: SPCK, 1964), pp.32–41.

THIRD CHURCH OF CHRIST, SCIENTIST
HEAL THE SICK
CHRISTIAN SCIENCE READING ROOM
BERKELEY 1 DAY CLEANERS
UUJ 402
XUW 706

ALAN POWERS

3 Christian Science Churches

Fig.1 Third Church of Christ Scientist, Curzon Street, Westminster, Lanchester & Rickards, 1910–12

Mary Baker Eddy (1821–1910), the founder of Christian Science, stated in her writings that she saw no need for 'creeds and church organisations to sustain or explain a demonstrable platform that defines itself in healing the sick and casting out error'.[1] In the words of Paul Ivey, Christian Science was 'a church organized to reinstate primitive Christianity with its lost element of healing.'[2] When specialised buildings became necessary, she gave no specific instructions, but did not wish special attention to be drawn to them, giving more definite guidance for music which 'shall not be operatic, but of an appropriate religious character and of a recognised standard of musical excellence'.[3] This could be taken as an indication of a similar character in architecture, which resembles that of non-conformist places of worship, with their equivalent emphasis on the 'primitive'.

Christian Science was one of several unconventional religious organisations of the late nineteenth century whose relatively wealthy followers were able to commission buildings of substance from well-known architects. Sally Lessiter writes, 'A Christian Science Church has little to do with ritual or ceremony. There is no cross or special candles. A church has no altar, no communion table – as bread and wine is not given; there is no baptism, so no font. ... Never associated with saints or apostles, Christian Science churches are not named but numbered, First, Second, Third, etc. as each new one is formed in a town or city.'[4] The emphasis is on the spoken word, and the interiors assume the character of what Christopher Wren called an 'Auditory', tending towards uninterrupted rectangular or square plans, with an organ taking the place of an altar, and twin reading desks to either side of the platform, one for reading from the scriptures, the other from Eddy's treatise, *Science and Health*.[5]

The first church erected for Christian Science was in Oconto, Wisconsin, in 1886, a charming piece of 'American Gothic'. It was followed by the 'Mother Church' (First Church of Christ Scientist) in Boston, Massachusetts, in 1894, a Romanesque design by Franklin I. Welch overshadowed by its grand Italian Renaissance-style extension, begun in 1904 and completed two years later. The original designer for this phase, with a more eclectic scheme containing Ottoman and Byzantine elements, was a local architect Charles Brigham (1841–1925), who owing to ill health was superseded by the Chicago architect Solon Spencer Beman (1853–1914). Designer of several previous churches for the organisation, Beman put a more distinct classical imprint on the completion of Brigham's scheme, in line with the trend of the times, although the decoration included Tiffany glass in the dome.

In 1910, Bernard Maybeck's rightly-celebrated timber-built First Church in Berkeley, California set a standard for subtle planning and decorative richness unmatched by any successors. This was the result of his briefing from the congregation, seeing his problem as 'to design a church that would satisfy the joyous, holy feelings of an early Christian; perhaps an apostle.'[6] Berkeley was, then as now, a progressive community, although Maybeck's particular craft-based eclecticism would probably have been seen as old-fashioned rather than modern in most other parts of the USA by this date. Comparable in its centralised plan to Frank Lloyd Wright's contemporary and more austere Unity Temple (built for Unitarians) in Oak Park, Chicago, it has a riot of gilded decoration and carving, with interpolations of Gothic tracery that indicates a road not taken, not only for Christian Science, but for twentieth century architecture more generally.

Christian Science itself was eclectic in its formation, with some contribution from Hinduism, although Mrs Eddy seems to have absorbed this from the Transcendentalists whom she knew personally, including Ralph Waldo Emerson and Bronson Alcott.[7] The mingling of ancient religions was widespread in the late nineteenth century, contributing more, perhaps, than is usually acknowledged, to the Arts and Crafts ethos in Britain, as seen in W. R. Lethaby's *Architecture, Mysticism and Myth* (1890), and reflected in the rise of Theosophy, the foundation of another powerful woman, Helena Blavatsky. Within mainstream Christianity the Eastern Orthodox Church, represented in the Byzantine style, was attracting attention at the turn of the nineteenth century for its alternative creeds as well as its architectural style avoiding the western European binary of classical and Gothic.

Fig.2 First Church of Christ Scientist, Daisy Bank, Manchester, Edgar Wood, 1903–4 (Elain Harwood)

Fig.3 First Church of Christ Scientist, Sloane Terrace, first design by Robert Chisholm, 1908

The translation of such thinking into architecture is evident in the two architecturally unusual English Christian Science churches before the First World War. The First Church of Christ, Scientist at Daisy Bank, Rusholme, Manchester (also literally the first in England), was designed by Edgar Wood (1860–1935) in 1903–4. It was extended in 1905–7 and is now the Edgar Wood Centre. 'Always hounding a new ideal' and keen on drawing 'Arabic houses' on his holiday travels, Wood produced one of his most original designs, with a Y-shaped plan to gain more seating space, and decoration comparable in its controlled exuberance to Maybeck's Berkeley building although since shorn of several ornamental features.[8]

A different form of eclecticism is seen in the earliest London church, by Robert Fellowes Chisholm (1840–1915). The First Church of Christ, Scientist, in Sloane Terrace, opened in 1908, has been described as 'free Byzantine with Oriental touches'.[9]

Replacing a Wesleyan Methodist chapel on the site, the rejected first design is notably original, with its minaret-like turrets. As redesigned, the sheer surface of the stone frontage with shallow two-light windows is still exceptional for its time.

200th
ANNIVERSARY
BRAZIL

Fig.4 First Church of Christ Scientist, Sloane Terrace, Chelsea, Robert Chisholm, 1908 (Elain Harwood)

Fig.5 Second Church of Christ Scientist, Palace Gardens Terrace, Kensington, Thomas S. Tait of Sir John Burnet, Tait & Son, 1926

Chisholm's career was spent largely in Madras/Chennai, where he was the architect most closely associated with what became known as the Indo-Saracenic style, and he had returned to England and officially retired before gaining this commission, which departs from the norms of European styles becoming increasingly dominant in Britain after 1900.

There could hardly be a greater contrast between Sloane Terrace and its London contemporary, the Third Church of Christ Scientist in Curzon Street by H. V. Lanchester and Edwin Rickards, 1910–12, with a stagy baroque frontage closing the view from Half Moon Street – the only section of the building to survive. The *Architectural Review* commended the 'feeling of exceptional spaciousness' on a relatively small site. Although faced in Portland Stone with carvings by Harry Fehr, the construction was of concrete.[10] In Edinburgh, the First Church in Inverleith Terrace, 1910 was the work of Ramsay Traquair, stone-built with simple outlines and Romanesque round arches, now converted to offices.

In 1911, Sir John Burnet, an outstanding Scottish architect of his generation, designed a similarly Romanesque Second Church in London, on the site of an intended Swedenborgian church in Palace Gardens Terrace, but its completion was delayed until 1926, when his partners Thomas S. Tait and Douglas Raeside were jointly credited. The L-shaped site allowed for a spacious Sunday School and a square-plan church with continuous raked seating on three sides allowing 'all members of the congregation to be in view, not only of the speakers, but of each other'.[11] The ground-level spaces beneath the upper seating allowed for 'spacious vestibules' in which members could mingle before and after the service. These services were evidently popular, with seating for 1,000 and a loudspeaker system for a further 750 in the Sunday School. Hope Bagenal, becoming well known as an acoustic consultant, succeeded in avoiding any echo without the use of acoustic tiles.[12] The interior is notable for evident borrowings in the organ screen from Frank Lloyd Wright, a contribution from Tait whose interest in modernism was already becoming apparent, combined with mannerist classical details familiar from the firm's earlier work.

Fig.6 Eleventh Church of Christ Scientist, Nutford Place, Marylebone, Oswald P. Milne, 1926–7 (Elain Harwood)

The 1920s was the high point of growth for Christian Science and the decade when the largest number of churches in Britain were built. In his debunking book *Our New Religion*, 1929, the politician and historian Herbert Fisher (H. A. L. Fisher), described the atmosphere of a representative London church prior to a Wednesday afternoon meeting (the regular event apart from Sundays on what was commonly early closing day):

> *Motor cars and taxis discharge smartly dressed ladies before the steps which lead up to the august portals of the First, Second, Third, etc., Church of Christ Scientist, as the case may be, and these are mingled with converging streams of eager-looking pedestrians, mostly of the female sex. For a few minutes the members of the congregation chat with one another pleasantly in the spacious entrance-hall, and then by degrees drift into the church, a large lozenge-shaped room admirably constituted for sound, with, at one end, a graded hemicycle of seats, and at the other, in place of an altar, an organ, and before it a platform bearing two handsomely carved lecterns, one for the Bible, the other for Mrs Eddy's* Science and Health. *Everything in this spacious and well-furnished room indicates wealth. Not that there are images, pictures or crucifixes, or, save for two texts, any mural decorations; but a moment's inspection of the solid and finished workmanship of the building is sufficient to show that the absence of ornament is not the consequence of any lack of material means, but a reminder that Christian Science sprang from a Puritan root ...*[13]

This description would hold true of two other London churches, by former assistants of Edwin Lutyens who were briefly in partnership, Oswald Milne and Paul Phipps, the latter married to Nora Langhorne, sister of Lady [Nancy]Astor, MP and herself a Christian Science practitioner. Phipps designed the Seventh Church in Wrights Lane, Kensington, in 1919–24, with a rather austere Georgian exterior in which flat bands of stone substitute for frieze and cornice. Milne's Eleventh Church in Nutford Place, Marylebone, resembles Kensington Palace Gardens with its ramped corbeled brick main gable.

These designs are outshone by Herbert Baker's Ninth Church in Marsham Street, 1930 (now the Emmanuel Centre), where the Astor family went, and enough other MPs to justify installing a division bell in the building.

Baker benefited from receiving a very thorough brief from a Building Committee that included Waldorf and Nancy Astor and Lord Lothian, and also J. S. Braithwaite, who published an analysis of the requirements.[14] He successfully overcame the acoustic problems of a domed circular space for 1,000 people and an organ, ringed

Sylvia Young Theatre School
GR04 MGY

Fig.7 Ninth Church of Christ Scientist, Marsham Street, Westminster, Herbert Baker, 1926–30, with inscription by Laurence Turner (Elain Harwood)

with paired columns against the walls supporting arches over the windows. The plan is L-shaped, with the Sunday School and Auditorium leading off a lofty entrance foyer with a brick vault. Inside and out, the mood is more authentically Byzantine than that of the other churches. Indeed, this could be claimed as one of his best buildings, partly because while Baker enjoyed inserting decoration by artists, here he was restricted to inscriptions since 'the principles of the community were as antipathetic as those of Mahomedans to any representation of the works of the Divine Creator'.[15] While comparing Baker to Wren 'in being the amateur inspired by fine ideas but sometimes making howlers', C. H. Reilly acknowledged that 'his entrance hall, with its great apsidal ends, and his barrel-vaulted Sunday school are fine things, of which most people would not have seen the possibility'.[16]

These central London churches and their architects are relatively well-known, at least externally. Much less so is the work of William Charles Braxton Sinclair (1883–1962) who appeared on the scene with three major projects, in Southport, Putney and Bromley, all exhibited at the Royal Academy in 1927.[17] Sinclair had served in the Royal Engineers during the First World War, which may have taken him to Burma (Myanmar). His watercolours of that country and examples of decorative art are in the collection of the V&A.

His architectural style, however, reflects nothing of this experience, being a robust form of classicism in brick, blending seventeenth-century England and the Ecole des Beaux Arts in a manner popular ten years previously. There is a family likeness to them, all enjoying ample sites that allow for an all-round view, and displaying their square or octagonal double height auditorium spaces with chamfered angles and a pattern of pilasters and recessed brick panels, rising above the single-storey entrance hall.

Sinclair's Southport design was chosen from 36 competition entries because most of the others were long rectangles in plan and 'lost sight of the fact that the building was primarily a church', resembling instead 'public secular buildings and even places of amusement'.[18] This has been demolished, but the Bromley church was built according to the published drawings and survives unaltered, though recently closed. The Richmond church remains in use, with its fine portico of brick columns, differing considerably from the design published in 1927. This shows a U-shaped building with Sunday School and entrance wings projecting to create a courtyard, and a Dutch-style curved gable with central window lighting the auditorium that lies transversely behind it. A Sunday School was never built. The church was refurbished, with a new entrance to the Reading Room on Sheen Road, in 1996, by David Chipperfield.[19] Bromley is listed, but Richmond is not.

Sinclair's first Richmond design had a curly gable is suggestive of the First Church in the university quarter of Belfast by Clough Williams-Ellis, designed in 1922–3, but only completed fifteen years later with the local architect D. W. Boyd, the original scheme simplified to its advantage.[20] His signature is recognisable from the elongated proportions, smooth rendered surfaces, the copper-clad cupola, ironwork and the curved gable. To the eastern part of the corner site is a courtyard of subsidiary buildings with a garden, a pleasant grouping.

Christian Science was adopted with fervour by the artist Ben Nicholson when he was in California for health reasons during the First World War, and he made

Fig.8 First Church of Christ Scientist, Widmore Road, Bromley, W. Braxton Sinclair, 1928 (Elain Harwood)

Fig.9 First Church of Christ Scientist, Tunbridge Wells, Cecil Burns, 1931 (Burns Guthrie & Partners)

his first wife Winifred Nicholson, and subsequently Barbara Hepworth, equally enthusiastic. They saw a strong equivalence between the focus on purity and 'idea' and their artistic search for a spiritual form of abstract art.[21] There is no trace of a similar crossover into any of the Christian Science buildings of the 1930s, although one building stands out for an approach completely different to all its contemporaries. This is the First Church in Tunbridge Wells, closing the vista on a side road off the northern approach to the town, by the local architect Cecil Burns, 1932–33. The drum-shaped design reveals its concrete frame construction with brick infill, and in the manner of Auguste Perret, concrete is used for the glazing pattern of the windows, with a subtly-suggested cross motif. The projecting waterspouts drain the upper external balconies and obviate the need for downpipes. The plan was split to make a semi-circular auditorium fitted with a steep rake and curved benches, and ancillary accommodation to the rear. Some very modern light fittings made of horizontal squares of glass threaded on rods appear in the original photographs, and were presumably designed by the architect. Burns also designed the Kent and Sussex Hospital nearer the town centre, 1934, with spectacular spiral escape ramps in concrete at the end of each wing, since demolished. The Christian Science

Fig.10 First Church of Christ Scientist, Belfast, Clough Williams-Ellis, designed in 1922–3, completed in 1937 (Alan Powers)

Church was converted for secular use in 1960, with the window patterning altered and the auditorium floored over at an upper level. Its future is currently in question, since the building is difficult to adapt to other uses and probably too much altered to be listable.[22]

The 63 Christian Science congregations and their buildings, past and present, listed for the United Kingdom on Wikipedia, is an incomplete but telling list, including buildings not covered in detail here, very few of which are still in their original use – the Burnet and Tait Second Church and the Richmond church by Braxton Sinclair being notable exceptions.[23] The decline seems to have accelerated in the 1970s, but has continued ever since. In a number of cases, mostly without the protection of listing, alternatives have been found with other religious organisations, as is the case with the Belfast church and the church in Upper Parliament Street, Liverpool by W. H. Ansell, 1914, first built as the Temple of Humanity for the Positivist Church, and now used by a traditionalist Catholic congregation. This pattern reflects what has happened with the much larger number of American Christian Science churches. Some of the appropriate alternative uses, such as the Secombe Theatre in Sutton, Surrey, have also ceased, putting the future of still more buildings at risk.

Fig.11 First Church of Christ Scientist, Sheen Road, Richmond, W. Braxton Sinclair, 1939 (Elain Harwood)

The 1920s, when the majority of British Christian Science churches were built in response to the growth of the movement, is a period still out of focus to many architecture enthusiasts, neither fully traditional nor modern. This increases the jeopardy in which these buildings are placed and strengthens arguments for constructive reuse.

ACKNOWLEDGEMENTS

This article was originally drafted by David Brady, and the editors are very appreciative of his contribution. Further assistance was given by Chris Jones (Tunbridge Wells), Burns Guthrie Architects, Dr Timothy Brittain-Catlin, and Richard Fletcher (Edgar Wood Society).

NOTES

1 Mary Baker Eddy, *Science and Health*, (Boston: Christian Scientist Publishing Company, 1875), p.168.

2 Paul Ivey, 'American Christian Science Architecture and its Influence', https://www.marybakereddylibrary.org/research/american-christian-science-architecture-and-its-influence/, accessed 9 September 2022.

3 Mary Baker Eddy, *Manual of The Mother Church: The First Church of Christ, Scientist in Boston Massachusetts*, Article XVIII, (Boston: USA, 89th edition, The Christian Science Publishing Society, 1921, pp.59–60).

4 Sally Lessiter, 'Christian Science: worship, architecture and building use', in *The Chapels Society Journal*, vol.3, *All Chapels Great and Small*, 2018, p.56.

5 Christopher Wren, 'Letter of Recommendations to a Friend on the Commission for Building Fifty New Churches', Christopher Wren Jr., ed., *Parentalia* (London: Osborn and Dodsley, 1750), pp.318–21.

6 Frank Morton Todd, *Palace of Fine Arts and Lagoon* (San Francisco: Paul Elder and Company, 1915), quoted in Edward R. Bosley, *First Church of Christ, Scientist, Berkeley* (London: Phaidon Press Ltd, 1994), p.1.

7 Charles S. Braden, *Christian Science Today, Power, Policy, Practice* (Dallas: Southern Methodist University Press, 1958), pp.31–2.

8 John H. Archer, 'Edgar Wood' (Oxford: Dictionary of National Biography, 2004), the quote is from Wood's pupil, G. A. E. Schwabe. See also The Buildings of England, *Lancashire: Manchester and the South-East* (London and New Haven: Yale University Press, 2004), pp.469–71.

9 The Buildings of England, *London 3: North West* (London, Penguin Books, 1991), p.561. The Victoria County History, *Middlesex*, vol.XII, 2004, says that the 'Romanesque elements and tall tower of R. Chisholm's design faintly echo the original Mother church in Boston' (p.267).

10 'Third Church of Christ Scientist', *Architectural Review*, vol.32, August 1912, p.94.

11 'The Second Church of Christ Scientist', *Architectural Review*, vol.60, August 1926, p.65.

12 Hope Bagenal, 'Church Form and Christian Science', *Architects' Journal*, vol.65, 25 May 1927, pp.727–8

13 H. A. L. Fisher, *Our New Religion* (London: Ernest Benn, 1929), pp.151–2.

14 J. S. Braithwaite, 'Christian Science Churches', *Architects' Journal*, vol.74, 16 December 1931, pp.807–9.

15 Sir Herbert Baker, *Architecture and Personalities* (London: Country Life, 1944), p.154.

16 C. H. Reilly, 'Landmarks of the Year, A Retrospect of 1930', *Architects' Journal*, vol.73, 14 January 1931, p.62.

17 *Academy Architecture*, vol.59, 1927, pp.33–48.

18 Duncan A. Campbell, 'The Christian Science Church and Sunday School Competition, Southport', *Architects' Journal*, vol.61, 14 January 1925, p.123.

19 'Faith in the Community', *Architects' Journal*, vol.203, 14 March 1996, pp.33–42.

20 Richard Haslam, *Clough Williams-Ellis* (London: Academy Editions, 1996), p.59.

21 See Lee Beard, ed., *Ben Nicholson, Writing and Ideas* (London: Lund Humphries, 2019) pp.78–84.

22 The original scheme was published in *The Builder*, vol.145, 11 August 1933, pp.220, 222–3, and the alterations by Cecil Burns & Guthrie in *The Builder*, vol.199, 23 December 1960, pp.1168–9. See also letter from Brian G. W. Blackwood in *Architectural Review*, vol.115, January 1954, p.2.

23 https://en.wikipedia.org/wiki/List_of_former_Christian_Science_churches,_societies_and_buildings, accessed 9 October 2022

THE

WAR CRY

AND

OFFICIAL ORGAN OF THE SALVATION ARMY

WILLIAM BOOTH, Founder [Registered at the General Post Office as a Newspaper] BRAMWELL BOOTH, General

No. 2,035 INTERNATIONAL] LONDON, SATURDAY, JULY 24, 1915 [HEADQUARTERS PRICE ONE PENNY

OUR FOUNDER'S MEMORIAL, NOTTINGHAM

This beautiful building, erected by the citizens of Nottingham as a Memorial to her illustrious son, William Booth, was opened by the Duke of Portland on Monday, July 12th, on which occasion there was a striking demonstration of enthusiasm for and appreciation of the Work of The Salvation Army. General Booth received the building on The Army's behalf, and conducted the first public Meeting in it, with fifty-one seekers at the Penitent-Form.

—(*For fuller particulars see page 4*)

STEVEN SPENCER

4 'Even the poorest hall is the House of God':

Salvation Army halls in the twentieth century

Fig.1 William Booth Memorial Halls, Nottingham, 1915 by Oswald Archer, Salvation Army Architect's Department. Front cover of *The War Cry*, 14 July 1915 (Salvation Army International Heritage Centre)

When, in 1961, the *Architectural Review* summarised the requirements of a Salvation Army hall, the author emphasised the value of simplicity: 'it should be a simple meeting room, where the pattern of worship does not demand ... religious rites performed before the congregation, the service consisting of extemporary prayer and signing and teaching from the scriptures'.[1] A Salvation Army architect explained that 'gatherings are called "meetings" instead of "services" for liturgy plays no part in their worship ... Meetings are essentially of a "free and easy" nature and do not conform to a rigid programme. Music and song play a great part in these meetings. The right of anyone in the meeting to address the congregation is greatly exercised.'[2] As such, the layout and furnishings of a meeting hall have no liturgical significance; the Salvation Army does not perform communion and children are dedicated rather than baptised. The only object required in a hall is the Mercy Seat, also known as a Penitent Form, which is a plain wooden bench (or 'form') at the front of the hall, often integrated into the platform, where both existing Salvationists and those seeking salvation can kneel to publicly declare their conversion or to renew their commitment.[3] The Mercy Seat is 'functionally and visually the focal point of a Salvation Army hall' and has been called its 'sacred place'.[4] Halls also feature a platform at one end for preaching and leading the congregation in songs. The clergy, band and choir (known as songsters) are usually on the platform during a meeting and many halls were designed with direct access to it from an officers' room, band room and songster room.

In January 2021 the William Booth Memorial Halls in Nottingham became the first twentieth-century Salvation Army hall in England to be listed (at grade II). The halls had been built in 1915 as a memorial to the Salvation Army's founder, three years after his death, with funds raised by the people of his native city, including Sir Frank Bowden, principal shareholder of Raleigh Bicycles. The hall was designed by the Salvation Army's staff architect, Oswald Archer, in a neo-classical style. This marked a move away from the nineteenth-century 'citadels', whose fortress style had expressed the militaristic nomenclature and aesthetic adopted in 1878 when the revival society Booth had founded in the 1860s as the East London Christian Mission changed its name to the Salvation Army.[5] This 'Army' quickly adopted an array of militaristic trappings, including uniforms, ranks, brass bands and terminology – 'officers' for clergy, 'soldiers' for members and 'The General' to refer to William Booth. While 'corps' came to be used to refer to a congregation, a variety of terms were used to refer to the chapel buildings; originally known as 'barracks', by the late 1880s the name 'citadel' came to be applied to the larger halls, while smaller buildings were simply called 'halls' or 'corps halls'.

There are several difficulties attached to researching corps halls. There are no surviving administrative records from the architect's department at the Salvation Army's International Headquarters, and no statistics for the number of purpose-built halls constructed. I have identified 370 halls built between 1914 and 2019, although the total number was much greater. There is an indication of numbers from some years, for instance, the Salvation Army newspaper, the *War Cry*, reported that fifteen new halls had been built in 1976.[6] The three decades after 1910 were the most prolific years for new build halls. Numbers peaked in around 1932 when at least 42 new halls were built.[7] So, there would have been significantly more than a thousand new halls built since 1914, but no useful estimate is possible from the resources presently available. In 1934 Oswald Archer said that 'during his 30 years' experience ... he had supervised the erection of 300 to 400 halls', but that must be an underestimate.[8] Muratore and Willis, writing on Australian Salvation Army halls, admit that 'there has been very little scholarship on the built legacy of the Salvation Army in Australia, indeed worldwide'.[9] This article, sketching an outline and focussing on a few halls, aims to lay the groundwork for more detailed research.

The Pevsner architectural guides only rarely make reference to Salvation Army corps halls and often give more attention to the Salvation Army's social services buildings.[10] This attention follows a wider trend in architectural writing, which is understandable as some social centres were designed by high profile architectural practices. The most prominent include Ryder & Yates in Newcastle, who designed Hopedene Maternity Home in 1969 and a men's hostel in 1975 (as well as a social centre in Sunderland in 1982) and H. M. Lidbetter, who designed Booth House hostel for men in East London in 1967.[11] Lidbetter had worked with his father, Hubert (a specialist in Quaker meeting houses) on the Salvation Army's International Headquarters in the City of London in 1963 to replace one destroyed in the Blitz.[12] The Lidbetters' building was itself replaced in 1999 by a new headquarters designed by Sheppard Robson occupying only a fraction of the site.[13] The most high profile architect to work for the Salvation Army in the UK was undoubtedly Giles Gilbert Scott, consultant architect on the International Training College in Camberwell, south London, in 1929, though the in-house architects Gordon & Viner did most of the internal design.[14] Any work on halls by commercial architects seems to have always been 'under the supervision' of the Salvation Army staff architect and, perhaps because of this, their involvement seems to have been downplayed in the movement's literature. However, other sources show evidence of the widespread use of local architectural practices, such as John Hamilton & Sons of Glasgow who designed several halls in the Scottish lowlands between 1900 and 1910 in a Mackintosh inflected Art Nouveau style with characteristic lettering[15] and John Wilson Hays in County Durham who designed a series of halls across the north-east in the 1950s and 1960s.[16]

The Salvation Army's first staff architect, Major Edmund J. Sherwood, was appointed by William Booth in 1880 to extend centralised control over the design of all new corps halls.[17] He established a crenulated design in the 'style of a medieval fortress' which made these early halls stand out from the buildings of other Christian denominations.[18] Christopher Wakeling describes how the Sheffield citadel's 'battlemented turrets and parapets ... crown a busy elevation, supplemented by machicolations, arrow slits and cross-slip – as if the forces of darkest England were to be kept at bay by buckets of boiling oil and a volley of arrows'.[19] Although exemplary of the fortress style, Sheffield Citadel was actually designed by a commercial architect, William Gillbee Scott at the relatively late date of 1894.[20] Three of these early, crenulated citadels are listed at grade II in England and the elaborate (and atypical) citadel of 1896 built in Aberdeen by James Souttar in a Scots baronial style was the first Salvation Army hall to be listed, grade B, as early as 1977.[21]

The appointment of Oswald Archer as the new staff architect in 1906 saw the end of crenelated halls and the adoption of a freer Edwardian baroque.[22] However, some halls by Archer retain something of the citadel, with his Royston hall of 1911 described by the Buildings of England as having 'vestigial battlements' and Worthing of 1912 as being in 'an appropriately military stripped Baroque'.[23] Examples of this style can also be seen at Ware of 1907 and at York Street in Belfast of 1911.[24] In 1915 came his civilian design for Nottingham. David Blackwell, a later

Fig.2 Catford, 1925 by Oswald Archer, Salvation Army Architect's Department (Salvation Army International Heritage Centre)

Fig.3 Hemel Hempstead, 1954 by Lt-Colonel William Charles, Salvation Army Architect's Department. Showing the hall before the entrance and fenestration were altered in 2017 (Elain Harwood)

staff architect, wrote that under Archer 'the military type treatment gave way to a simplified classical style ... The elevation would be built of bricks with contrasting coloured brick plinth and moulded stone or terra-cotta dressings with exaggerated keystones'.[25] Archer would build in this style for the next two decades until his retirement in 1935, with characteristic halls at Tunbridge Wells (1921, demolished), Notting Hill (1924) and Catford (1925) – although the 'vestigial' fortress style can be found as late as 1927 at Bridgeton in Glasgow.[26]

Archer was the only staff architect until the late twentieth century to be an employee rather than an officer (although he was a Salvationist), since every staff architect from E. J. Sherwood onwards had trained as an architect after becoming an ordained minister. The graceful and uncharacteristic hall at Bradninch of

1936 was built to designs by Archer but completed by Brigadier James Vint, his successor as staff architect. Brigadier Vint designed halls for the new garden cities and suburbs, following Letchworth and Welwyn in 1936 with Wythenshawe in 1938.[27] Then came the Second World War and a hiatus in building for nearly ten years, during which time Lt-Colonel William Charles replaced Vint as chief architect.[28] Charles had trained as an architect at night school after becoming a Salvation Army officer.[29]

It was not until 1948 that the earliest post-war corps halls began to open, many of which were rebuilt around the surviving fabric of halls destroyed during the war, such as Portsmouth Citadel in 1949 (which incorporated foundation stones originally laid in 1898) and at Plymouth Exeter Street in 1951 which employed a modernised elevation.[30] At the small Brierley Hill Corps in the West Midlands, rented accommodation was replaced in April 1949 by a new hall in a prefabricated hut accommodating 250 people and costing £400.[31] The earliest post-war new build halls date from 1948 at Alexandria in Dunbartonshire and 1949 at Miles Platting in Manchester, Pontypool and a new hall for young people's meetings (usually known as the 'YP hall') at Gillingham, Kent.[32] These were built in the traditional style of pre-war halls, as was the simple red-brick hall built in 1953 at Coventry Stoke to replace a hall destroyed during the Blitz with a pointed gable and mullioned windows, which stands in sharp contrast to the first properly modern hall which opened at Hemel Hempstead in the following year.[33]

The old hall at Hemel Hempstead had to be vacated due to the building of the new town and compensation was received from the development corporation towards the cost of the new building.[34] It seems that conditions were also imposed on some aspects of the design of the new hall to keep it in character with the centre of the new town development (the hall sits on a corner of the new Market Square overlooking the River Gade), which may explain the radical departure from previous hall designs. The main hall seated 370 people and the building included a separate YP hall seating 175, classrooms and a kitchen, at a total cost of around £30,000. It was described by the *War Cry* in 1954 as 'the finest and latest architectural design in Salvation Army halls'.[35] In 2017 the hall was extensively refurbished, 'in keeping with restructuring the town centre', with significant alterations to the entrance and fenestration.[36]

Hemel Hempstead has earned a place in Salvation Army history as the 'first hall to be handled in a modern manner' and it became a 'model Army hall' with subsequent halls built in a similar style.[37] However the hall that received the most interest from the contemporary architectural press was that at Hendon of 1957.[38] This hall was one designed by a commercial architectural practice, C. Wycliffe Noble & Partners. Wycliffe Noble (1925–2017) was a Salvationist who would become the drummer with the Salvation Army's popular music group, The Joystrings, while continuing to practice as an architect, often travelling to concerts from business meetings with his drum kit in his red MG sports car.[39] The new hall at Hendon was accessed by a glazed entrance foyer with one slate wall and a louvred canopy outside (although this was filled in soon after the building opened). The meeting hall at the rear of the site seated 300 people and was a square of yellow Welsh brick with triangular clerestory windows and an acoustic domed roof. An elm Mercy Seat stood in its traditional place at the front of the platform. The building also housed rooms for the officers, band and songsters, as well as a small internal garden. The *Architects' Journal*, writing in 1962, recorded that 'Simplicity

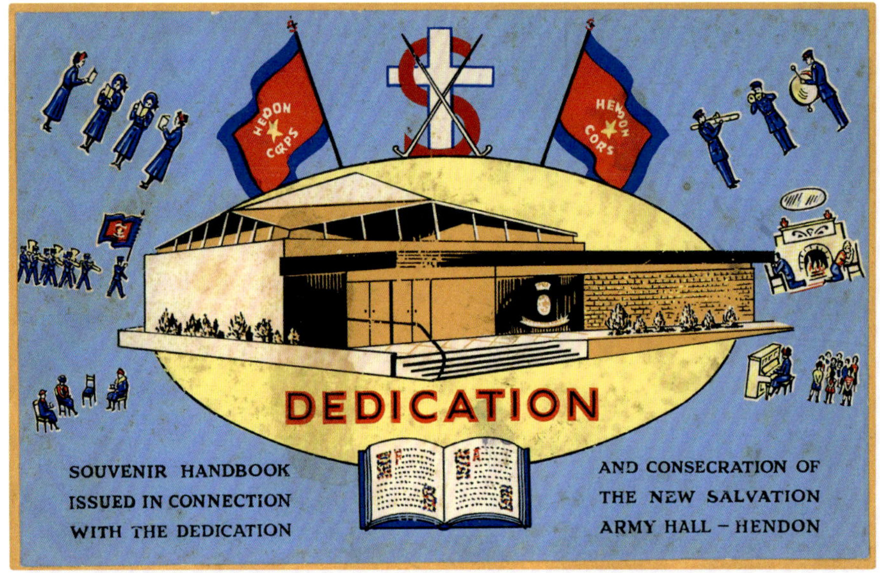

Fig.4 Hendon, 1957 by C. Wycliffe Noble & Partners. Souvenir Handbook for the opening of the new hall, June 1957. (Salvation Army International Heritage Centre)

has been the general aim, with clear definition of the various planes and lack of elaborate trim.'[40] The hall, which had cost £18,000, was extended in 1978 and then demolished in 2017, replaced by a new hall designed by Fbm Architects.[41]

Hemel Hempstead and Hendon represented a concession to wider architectural trends not previously evident in Salvation Army designs. However, while the description of Hendon as 'ultra-modern' in the *War Cry* indicated how different these halls were from their predecessors, it also indicated an ignorance of some of the more radical church designs adopted by other denominations in the 1950s, such as Handisyde and Stark's 1951 Festival of Britain Congregational church in Poplar and Edward Mills's Methodist church at Mitcham which opened the year after Hendon.

New halls continued to be built in the style of Hemel Hempstead and Hendon, particularly in older towns as part of substantial post-war redevelopment, as at Coventry in 1959. Here the hall, built as Basil Spence's Anglican cathedral was under construction, comprised a main hall and a junior hall in a suite of buildings dressed in grey, granite dash. A report on the opening in October 1959 describes those in attendance as 'overawed by the new surroundings'.[42] Oakley describes the structure as 'a concrete portal frame ... expressed externally on the outside of both the walls and the roof'.[43] This hall was demolished due to 'problems with a leaking roof and parts of the concrete structure' and replaced by a new hall in 2005.[44] A similar hall opened at Bath in 1964 but was clad in natural stone 'to reflect the architectural character of the locality'.[45]

Alongside these high-profile examples, the majority of halls designed at this time can best be described as unprepossessing, as exemplified by the small hall at Coalville, Leicestershire. Many of these, such as Stevenage of 1958, were based on a standard design developed by the Architect's Department for a small hall that could be cheaply constructed, continuing the nineteenth-century tradition of 'tin tabernacles'.[46] There are also any number of halls employing a more functional modern design, such as Jarrow of 1963 or Duke Street, Sheffield, built in 1964 amidst the slab blocks of Hyde Park as the second phase of the Park Hill development.[47]

Some halls, such as that at Romford of 1963, show a growing confidence in the use of a contemporary architectural style. The hall was designed by Ernest J. Lipscomb, a chartered surveyor at the Salvation Army's International Headquarters. Extending from a main suite of buildings is a dramatic circular YP hall where concrete piers alternate with glazing. The architect here referenced the Salvation Army crest, but the 33 piers also represent each year of Christ's life (a design also showing a clear debt to Spence's chapel of Christ the Servant at Coventry Cathedral). The extensive glazing extended to the senior hall in the main building, which had serrated walling 'designed to throw light mainly from behind the congregation' and, according to the Salvation Army press, 'You can see the Salvationists sitting, praying, clapping their hands and speaking of the joy they experience in living a Christian life ... The idea is to unite the internal with the external; it is an attempt to make the church and daily life one.' This increased glazing was to become a feature of modern halls into the 1970s, although the concrete piers at Romford can also be seen as a defensive structure referencing Christ's crown of thorns. The main building at Romford was replaced in 2008 with only the distinctive YP hall remaining.[48]

Although Major David Blackwell replaced Colonel Charles as chief architect in 1967, the 1970s saw a continuing use of extensive glazing to make halls 'more inviting and visually open to the public'.[49] This greater transparency was also reflected in the increased attention Salvation Army halls began to receive in the architectural press. The first to receive such coverage after Hendon was that in Albion Place, Oxford, in 1971 replacing an old citadel compulsorily purchased for demolition as part of the Westgate redevelopment plan by the Oxford Corporation, who also took an interest in the design of the new hall, which was by John Gilbert Fryman of Architects Design Partnership at a cost of £70,000.[50] A main hall on

Fig.5 Stevenage, 1958 by Lt-Colonel William Charles, Salvation Army Architect's Department. An example of the standard small hall design, with Tyrolean rendered panels (Elain Harwood)

Fig.6 Romford, 1967 by Ernest Lipscomb, Salvation Army Architect's Department. Showing the hall before the main hall (on the right) was rebuilt in 2008 (Salvation Army International Heritage Centre)

the first floor seated 400, with a secondary hall and 'facilities for ... a wide range of community activities for young and old' on the ground floor. Built on a corner site, the brick construction with reinforced concrete columns and floor slabs was given rounded external corners, producing 'a building consisting of a series of linked cylinders and rounded rectangles'.[51] A round tower was intended to house a lift to allow disabled access to the main hall. The architects wanted a design that was 'striking in character but free of excess. The simplicity of plan, elevation and section was a principal aim.'[52] The hall is now the UK headquarters of the German Hogrefe Publishing Group, with alterations to the entrance and the fenestration.

In January 1972, the *War Cry* wrote of Oxford that 'this distinctive building ... is in marked contrast to the traditional image of Salvation Army architecture'.[53] This ignored those halls built in a modern style since 1954, and also downplays how Oxford's tower and arrow-slit windows retained something of the bellicose spirit of E. J. Sherwood's fortress-like halls of the 1880s and 1890s. Even *Glass Age* remarked that 'something of a "citadel" style remains'.[54] It seems that ADP's new fortress style, with its mono-pitch roof and narrow, vertical windows, had an impact on other new halls in the 1970s. This is certainly true of that at Wood Green of 1975, which made much use of glazing and had long slit windows running the vertical length of the red-brick façade.[55] A similar design was employed at Clapton in east London, also of 1975, but here the mon-pitch roof of the meeting hall at the southern end of the building recalls Dewi-Prys Thomas's Quaker Meeting Hall at Heswall, Cheshire, of a decade earlier.[56] The design was in common use for much of the 1970s, and the new hall at Northampton East opened in October 1977 with two mono-pitch meeting halls giving the building an elegant, winged appearance.[57] Northampton East was one of many examples where an existing hall was replaced as part of a civic centre redevelopment, as at Hemel Hempstead, Oxford and Hertford, where in 1977 compensation went towards the £30,000 cost of a new hall.[58]

The 1980s saw the reappearance of a more vernacular tradition and a move away from some of the more definitive architectural statements made by halls of the 1970s. This was similar in spirit to Archer's tenure as staff architect, but with more modern forms. Wakeling also identifies the 1980s as a period when octagonal chapels 'gained momentum', citing the hall at Hereford of 1986 by ATP Group Partnership as an early example of this trend.[59] Hereford did indeed set the style of halls under the chief architects of the 1990s, Major Ray Oakley and David Greenwood. A new 'house style' was established with an octagonal meeting hall and separate 'ancillary rooms and flexibility for other uses' laid out in a linear fashion.[60]

Fig.7 Oxford, 1971 by John Gilbert Fryman, Architects Design Partnership. Showing mono pitch meeting hall above with secondary hall below (Henck Snoek/RIBA Collections)

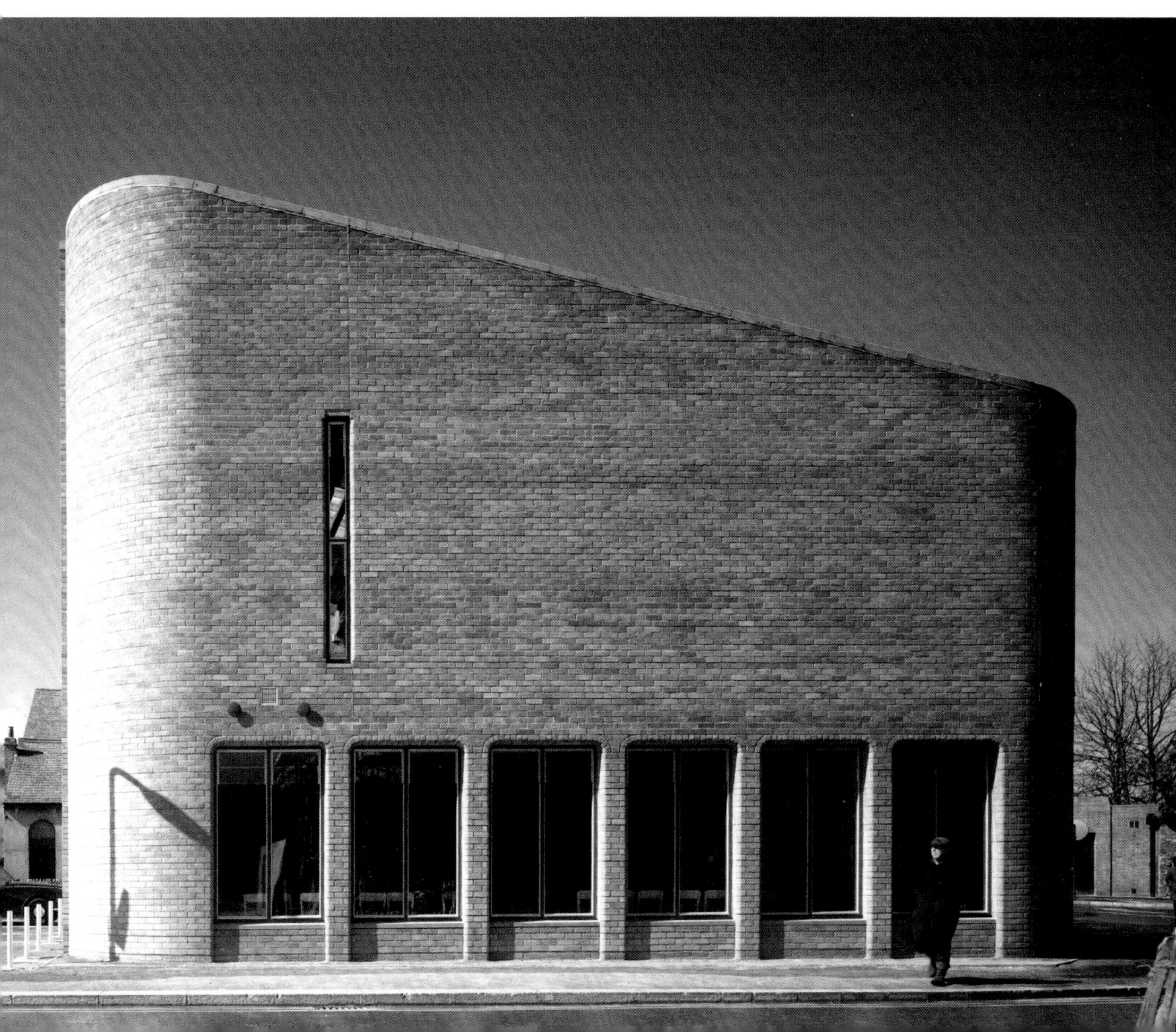

Prominent examples of the style were the Brighton Congress Hall of 1999, part of a design which 'incorporated references to the Regency environment' which replaced a demolished Victorian Congress Hall of 1883[61] and the 'workmanlike' new hall at suburban Nether Edge where work began in 1999 in advance of Sheffield Corps moving out of their 1894 Gillbee Scott citadel.[62] While a linear layout continued to dominate, octagonal halls were also built in different compositions, such as Belfast Sydenham in 1996, where Building Design Services placed the hall at the centre, lit by a clerestory, with the ancillary rooms massed around the edge, giving the complex a significant presence.[63] The octagonal hall continued to be popular into the 21st century, although commercial architectural practices often deployed stylistic variations following the closure of the Salvation Army Architect's Office in 2003.[64] The design for the new hall at Luton by the Ponsford King Partnership in 2003 was summed up in *Church Building* as 'simplicity is keynote to octagonal design'.[65] At the new Hadleigh Temple hall in 2003 BGA Architects updated the octagonal design with more glazing on the meeting hall and a weather-boarded cottage adjacent rather than single-storey ancillary rooms.[66]

When a new hall at Chelmsford was built in 2009 to replace one that had been in use since the 1970s, it eschewed the tradition of the octagon and embraced a radical design by Hudson Architects. It was the first hall since Oxford in 1972 to receive substantial attention in the architectural press, prompted in part by its winning the

Fig.8 Clapton, 1975 by Major David Blackwell, Salvation Army Architect's Department (Elain Harwood)

Fig.9 Brighton, 1999 by David Greenwood, Salvation Army Architect's Department (Salvation Army International Heritage Centre)

RIBA East of England Building of the Year and the national ACE/RIBA Award for Religious Architecture, both in 2009.[67] The building cost £2 million and included a 320-seat meeting hall and facilities for 'an extensive programme of support for local people ... [including an] indoor sports hall and outdoor play area'. Clad in Rheinzinc metal and red composite board incised with bible texts, 'interrupted by the iridescent face of a 42-foot tower', the hall presents a striking external appearance.[68] The structure of prefabricated timber panels is exposed in the meeting hall, giving it a 'barn-like feel'.[69] Wakeling calls Chelmsford 'a riposte to those groups who prefer to adapt retail hangars than to commission new places of their own in which to worship' and suggests that it could be a beacon to other denominations, writing that the hall 'invites comparison ... with the heady atmosphere of 1951, when new ways of building opened up fresh possibilities for Nonconformists'.[70] *Architecture Today* connected the zinc used in this contemporary hall to the traditional tin tabernacles, but its tower overlooking the dual-carriage Parkway harks back once again to E. J. Sherwood's fortress style, albeit now with reflective glazing and a silhouetted cross.[71]

Unusually for a Salvation Army hall, Chelmsford looks forward as well as back. While the Salvation Army in the nineteenth century was initially content to plough a separate and distinctive furrow in the architecture of its halls, by the early twentieth century it had largely established an architectural approach that adopted the designs of other denominations but which incorporated more elements from its bellicose antecedents than may at first be apparent. Some features still set these halls apart from other places of worship: the Salvation Army has no need of fonts or communion tables but does require plenty of space for band rooms and community activities. This, along with occasional economic necessity, has allowed a search for simplicity in its architecture which has gone hand-in-hand with the belief that this simplicity is itself a form of worship, that the design of the halls themselves put them close to God. As one Salvationist wrote in 1961, giving guidance on the maintenance of halls, 'never let us forget that [even] the poorest hall is the house of God'.[72]

Fig.10 [following pages] Chelmsford, 2009 by Hudson Architects (Elain Harwood)

JOHN 15:1. "I AM the true vine, and My Father is the gardener"
JOHN 10.11. "I AM the good shepherd. The good shepherd gives His life for the
JOHN 6:35. "I AM the bread of life. He who comes to me will never be hungry"
30
End

NOTES

1 'Hall of Worship for the Salvation Army, Hendon', *Architectural Review*, vol.130, July 1961, p.57.

2 Gerald Norwood's RIBA thesis on evangelical centres, 1954, quoted in Ray Oakley, *To the Glory of God: A history of the development of the Salvation Army in the British Isles as expressed, illustrated and symbolised through its buildings and some paintings* (Leamington Spa: privately published, 2011), pp.67–8.

3 Steven Spencer, 'Barrack, Citadel, Circus: Salvation Army halls, their development and use', Chapels Society Journal: No.3, *All Chapels Great and Small*, 2018, pp.70–1.

4 David R. Blackwell, 'Evolution of Corps Architecture in the United Kingdom', *The Salvation Army Year Book*, 1959, p.30.

5 Historic England list entry for William Booth Memorial Halls, King Edward Street, Nottingham (https://historicengland.org.uk/listing/the-list/list-entry/1454672, accessed 28 September 2021), Blackwell, op. cit., p.34.

6 *War Cry*, 11 December 1976, p.6.

7 These figures are based on sample years of the *War Cry* and *Salvationist*, the architectural press, the archives of the Salvation Army International Heritage Centre, online resources and webpages.

8 'Salvation Army and a Hall', *Bromley and West Kent Mercury*, 6 December 1935, p.11.

9 Renee Muratore and Julie Willis, 'Building Salvation: The architecture of the Salvation Army in Australia', *Fabrications: Journal of the Society of Architectural Historians, Australia and New Zealand*, vol.25:1, 2015, p.63.

10 Clare Hartwell, Matthew Hyde and Nikolaus Pevsner, The Buildings of England: *Lancashire: Manchester & the South-East* (London: Yale University Press, 2004), p.149 (Gilead House, Bolton, David Blackwell, 1984); John Gifford, Colin McWilliam and David Walker, The Buildings of Scotland, *Edinburgh* (London: Penguin, 1984), p.270 (Salvation Army Women's Hostel, John Hamilton, 1910).

11 Rutter Carroll, *Ryder and Yates* (London: RIBA, 2009), pp.107–115; Elain Harwood, 'Building of the Month: Salvation Army Men's Social Services Centre, Newcastle upon Tyne, Ryder and Yates', January 2010, https://c20society.org.uk/building-of-the-moth-salvation-army-mens-social-services-centre-newcastle-upon-tyne, accessed 28 September 2021; Survey of London, https://surveyoflondon.org/map/feature/450/detail, accessed 28 September 2021; Bridget Cherry, Charles O'Brien and Nikolaus Pevsner, The Buildings of England, *London 5: East* (London: Yale University Press, 2005), p.430.

12 Eleanor Gawne, 'Buildings of Endearing Simplicity: The Friends Meeting Houses of Hubert Lidbetter', Twentieth Century Architecture: no.3, *The Twentieth Century Church*, 1998, pp.85–92.

13 Oakley, op. cit., pp.164–73; 'Princess Royal opens new IHQ', *Salvationist*, 20 November 2004, pp.1, 3.

14 Oakley, ibid, pp.148–50. The most high-profile architect to work with the Salvation Army was Le Corbusier, who worked on two men's hostels in Paris: a converted barge and the Cité de Refuge. See Brian Brace Taylor, *Le Corbusier, the City of Refuge, Paris 1929/33* (Chicago: University of Chicago Press, 1987).

15 Ayr Citadel, New Road, 1905, was listed at category C in 1980 (http://portalhistoricenviornment.scot/designation/LB21702), Perth Citadel, South Street, 1905 listed at category C in 1977 (http://portal.historicenvironment.scot/designation/LB39640), Leith Citadel, Bangor Road, Edinburgh, 1910 listed at category C in 1995 (http://portal.historicenvironment.scot/designation/LB26756) and Govan Citadell, Golspie Street, Glasgow, 1903 listed at category B in 2004 (https://portal.historicenvironment.scot/designation/LB49789, all accessed 26 September 2021); Elizabeth Williamson, Anne Riches and Malcolm Higgs, The Buildings of Scotland: *Glasgow* (London: Penguin, 1990), p.590.

16 Including halls at Spennymoor 1954 (YP hall), Wingate *c.*1954, Ferryhill *c.*1957, Guisborough *c.*1957, Middlesbrough Cannon Street, *c.*1958, Alnwick *c.*1959, Birtley *c.*1964, Shotton Colliery 1965 ('New Hall in County Durham', *War Cry*, 27 February 1965, p.8), Easington Lane 1967 ('New Hall in the North-East', *War Cry*, 10 June 1967, p.7), West Hartlepool *c.*1967, Billingham *c.*1968, Hartlepool Citadel 1969 ('New Hall at Hartlepool', *War Cry*, 21 June 1969, p.10) and Middlesbrough Grangetown *c.*1969. For more details see the catalogue for the papers of John Wilson Hays held at Durham County Record Office (D/WH).

17 Spencer, op. cit., p.71.

18 Historic England list entry for Former Salvation Army Citadel, 24, 25 and 26 Lambton Street, Sunderland (https://historicengland.org.uk/listing/the-list/list-entry/1279897, accessed 26 September 2021); Christopher Wakeling, *Chapels of England: Buildings of Protestant nonconformity* (Swindon: Historic England, 2017), p.156.

19 Wakeling, ibid., p.194.

20 William Gillbee Scott (1857–1930) also designed citadels at Sunderland (1890), Middlesbrough (1890), Edmonton (1891), Page Green (1891), Penge (1891) and Belfast (1892).

21 York Citadel, Gillygate (1883) was listed in 1990 (https://historicengland.org.uk/listing/the-list/list-entry/1257749); Sunderland (1891) in 1994 (https://historicengland.org.uk/listing/the-list/list-entry/1279897) and Sheffield Citadel, Cross Burgess Street (1894) in 1995 (https://historicengland.org.uk/listing/the-list/list-entry/1279897), all at grade II; Spencer, op. cit, p.74; (http://portal.historicenvironment.scot/designation/LB19996), accessed 26 September 2021.

22 James Bettley, Nikolaus Pevsner and Bridget Cherry, The Buildings of England, *Hertfordshire* (London: Yale University Press, 2019), p.487.

23 Wakeling, op. cit., p.195 (Royston); Elizabeth Williamson, Tim Hudson, Jeremy Musson and Ian Nairn, The Buildings of England, *Sussex: West* (London: Yale University Press, 2019), p.731.

24 Bettley etc., op. cit., p.587.

25 Blackwell, op. cit., pp.33–4.

26 (https://canmore.org.uk/site/314197/glasgow-13-olympia-street-olympia-house), accessed 26 September 2021.

27 Letchworth stonelaying, *War Cry*, 5 October 1935, p.10; Welwyn Garden City, *War Cry*, 23 May 1936, p.10; Wythenshawe Corps History Book, 26 March 1938, C/WYN/1, Salvation Army International Heritage Centre (SAIHC), London. A new community centre added to the hall by

Ayshford Sansome won a Letchworth Garden City Heritage Foundation Award.

28 Blackwell, op. cit., p.35.

29 Oakley, op. cit., p.29.

30 'Portsmouth Citadel is Rebuilt', *War Cry*, 19 November 1949, p.5; 'Plymouth Looks to the Future', *War Cry*, 18 December 1948, p.3; for Plymouth see also Oakley, op. cit., p.66.

31 'New Salvation Army Hall', *Staffordshire County Express*, 7 May 1949 (copy held in Records of Brierley Hill Corps, C/BRY/1, SAIHC).

32 'New Hall at Alexandria', *War Cry*, 30 October 1948, p.2; Miles Platting, *War Cry*, 19 March 1949, p.2; Pontypool, *War Cry*, 26 March 1949, p.2; for Gillingham, see Oakley, op. cit., p.66.

33 *War Cry*, 27 March 1954, p.5; https://www.coventrytelegraph.net/news/coventry-news/congregation-angry-threat-church-3140462, 12 November 2004 (accessed 17 September 2021).

34 Hemel Hempstead Development Corporation, *Sixth Annual Report* (London: HMSO, 1953), p.279.

35 Oakley, op. cit., pp.66–7; 'The Challenge of the New Housing Estates', *War Cry*, 23 January 1954, p.8; 'A Model Army Hall', *War Cry*, 30 January 1954, p.4; letter from Wilfred Kitching, British Commissioner, to General Albert Orsborn, 'Hemel Hempstead New Halls', 22 September 1953, GEN/4/2/1, SAIHC.

36 'Reopening of Refurbished Hall', *Salvationist*, 20 May 2017, p.7.

37 Blackwell, op. cit., p.35; 'A Model Army Hall', *War Cry*, 20 January 1954, p.4.

38 Trevor Dannatt, *Modern Architecture in Britain: Selected examples of recent building* (London: Batsford, 1959), p.216; 'Hall of Worship for the Salvation Army, Hendon, *Architectural Review*, vol.130, July 1961, p.57; 'Salvation Army citadel, Brampton Grove, Hendon', *Architects' Journal*, vol.135, 6 June 1962, pp.1275–80.

39 Sylvia Dalziel, *The Joystrings* (London: Shield Books, 2013), p.23; 'More than a Drummer', *Salvationist*, 20 May 2017, p.20.

40 'Strategically Placed for Evangelical Thrust', *War Cry*, 22 June 1957, p.7; Souvenir Handbook issued in Connection with the Dedication and Consecration of the New Salvation Army Hall, Hendon, June 1957, C/HND/1, SAIHC; 'Salvation Army citadel, Brampton Grove, Hendon', *Architects' Journal*, vol.135, 7 June 1962, p.1276.

41 The Hendon Hundred: Corps Centenary Brochure, 1982, p.3, C/HND/1, SAIHC; 'Hendon', *Salvationist*, 22 April 2017, p.9; https://www.fbmarchitects.com/project/salvation-army-hendon-corps/, accessed 28 September 2021.

42 'Coventry City's New Buildings', *War Cry*, 17 October 1959, p.3.

43 Oakley, op. cit., pp.69–71.

44 https://www.coventrytelegraph.net/news/coventry-news/soaring-bill-for-new-citadel-3147293, 14 May 2004, accessed 17 September 2021.

45 Oakley, op. cit., p.71; 'Bath City Corps', *War Cry*, 4 April 1964, p.3.

46 Oakley, op. cit., p.67; for tin tabernacles, see Wakeling, op. cit., p.162.

47 'New Hall for Jarrow', *War Cry*, 27 April 1963, p.2; 'New Buildings', *War Cry*, 4 April 1964, p.3.

48 'Come Inside: You are Welcome', *War Cry*, 24 June 1967, p.10.

49 Oakley, op. cit., pp.73–5.

50 Oxford Corps Centenary Brochure, 1981, C/OXF/1, SAIHC; 'Simple Salvation: Salvation Army community service centre, Oxford', *Building*, vol.223, 11 August 1972, pp.37–9; "Praise for Oxford's New Hall', *War Cry*, 26 August 1972, p.8.

51 'Salvation Army, Oxford', *Glass Age*, vol.15, August 1972, p.34.

52 'Salvation Army Centre, Oxford', *Interior Design*, December 1972, p.847; *Building*, vol.223, 11 August 1972, pp.35–9.

53 'New Halls at Oxford', *War Cry*, 8 January 1972, p.2.

54 'Salvation Army, Oxford', *Glass Age*, vol.15, August 1972, p.34.

55 Oakley, op. cit., p.72.

56 *War Cry*, 15 March 1975, p.10; for Heswall, see Wakeling, op. cit., pp.245–6.

57 *War Cry*, 29 October 1977, p.9.

58 https://hertforshirechurches.wordpress.com/2016/07/08/salvation-army-former-baker-street-hertford/, accessed 28 September 2021; Hertford Corps History Book, 5 February 1977, C/HRT/1, SAIHC.

59 Wakeling, op. cit., p.254.

60 Spencer, op. cit., p.78.

61 Nicholas Antram and Nikolaus Pevsner, The Buildings of England, *Sussex: East* (London: Yale University Press, 2013), p.173; Oakley, op. cit., p.76; Patrick Spears, 'Salvation Army redevelopment, Park Crescent Terrace, Brighton', *Church Building*, no.72, November/December 2001, pp.10–15.

62 Ruth Harman and John Minnis, Pevsner Architectural Guides, *Sheffield* (London, Yale University Press, 2004

63 'Salvation Army premises in Sydenham, Belfast', *Church Building*, no.40, July/August 1996, p.19.

64 The last chief architect was Patrick Spears who, along with several former colleagues, continued to work on Salvation Army halls via the consultant firm of Swanke Hayden Connell Architects (Oakley, op. cit., pp.34–5).

65 'The Salvation Army, Luton', *Church Building*, no.84, November/December 2003, pp.34–9.

66 https://www/bga-architects.com/hadleigh-temple, accessed 25 August 2021.

67 Since the mid-1990s new halls had come to be featured with some regularity in *Church Building* magazine, but the interest in Chelmsford went much wider: 'Something to Believe In', *Building Design*, no.1874, 26 June 2009, pp.12–15; 'Hudson Architects' Salvation Army Chelmsford Corps', *Architecture Today*, no.199, June 2009, pp.28–34; 'Salvation Army Citadel Corps', *Church Building*, no.119, September/October 2009, pp.52–5; Inida Wright', https://www.architectsjournal.co.uk/archive/hudson-architects-provide-salvation-in-chelmsford, accessed 20 July 2022.

68 Wakeling, op. cit., p265.

69 John Lyall, 'Hudson Architects' Salvation Army Chelmsford Corps', *Architecture Today*, no.199, June 2009, p.30.

70 Wakeling, op. cit., p.265.

71 *Architecture Today*, no.199, June 2009, p.20.

72 Memorandum on the Maintenance of Properties issued by the Salvation Army National Headquarters Property Department, 1 January 1961, C/CIC/1, SAIHC.

The Religious Society of Friends
Quaker Meeting for Worship Every Sunday at 10.30am
All are Welcome
THE LAND IN FRONT OF THESE PREMISES HAS NOT BEEN DEDICATED AS A PUBLIC RIGHT OF WAY OR HIGHWAY
QUAKER MEETING

JOHANNA ROETHE

5 'In keeping with our way of worship': Quaker meeting houses of the twentieth century

Fig.1 Heswall Meeting House, 1961–3 by Dewi-Prys Thomas and Gerald Beech (Alun Bull, Historic England Archive, DP168482)

Quaker meeting houses are unique among places of worship. The largely silent form of worship favoured by the Quakers only required spaces which permitted introspection, and in the absence of a design programme or any liturgical requirements there were few constraints which shaped their planform or style. Furthermore, there were no incentives to embellish them in any way, since one of the founding tenets of the Religious Society of Friends was that meeting houses were no more holy or special than other structures. Together with the Quaker values of simplicity and equality, this resulted in buildings which appear plain and functional to outsiders, without familiar furnishings like an altar, font or pulpit, and without decorations like paintings or stained glass. Meeting houses have historically been a diverse group, a homogenous style only briefly emerging in the decades either side of 1800.[1] Every meeting (and indeed individual Friends) might have their own ideas about what a meeting house should look like and discussions might be lengthy before a consensus could be found. This discourse around the most suitable architectural language for a meeting house continued in the twentieth century, with novel styles and construction methods supplying a new vocabulary to express the Quaker ethos.

Like other denominations, Quakerism experienced a building boom in the twentieth century and particularly in the decades after 1945. Of the 253 purpose-built meeting houses still in use in England, Wales, Scotland and the Channel Islands (the area covered by the Britain Yearly Meeting), the largest group dates from the twentieth century (94), compared with 70 from the nineteenth, 56 from the eighteenth and 28 from the seventeenth.[2] Nearly a third (83) were built between 1918 and 1999. Many more were restored or extended during the period, and many new or re-established meetings chose to convert buildings, not least due to financial and environmental reasons. This was a return to the approach taken by the earliest Quaker meetings who used converted houses or farm buildings for their worship. This article, however, will focus on purpose-built meeting houses and explore how meetings and architects responded to the task of their design.

The increased and accelerated building and re-building activity appears to have been partly related to an increase in membership over the first half of the century. British Quakers have always been a relatively small group with an overall trajectory of decline from a peak of about 55,000 members in 1680.[3] This downward trend continues, but the first half of the century saw a slow but steady increase from 17,346 members in 1900 to a peak of 21,643 in 1958, a 25 per cent increase.[4] The largest increases occurred just before the First World War, between 1906 and 1910 and, after flat-lining in the interwar period, at the beginning of the Second World

War, in 1939–41. The latter increase was undoubtedly related, at least in part, to the war-time attraction of the Quakers' pacifist stance. This upward trend was reversed in the second half of the century, with a decline in membership of 24 per cent to 16,486 in 2000 with a brief slowing in the 1980s. While the reasons for erecting a new meeting house could be manifold, it seems likely that the post-war boom and the continued building activity into the 1980s, albeit on a smaller scale, were connected to this mid-century peak in membership numbers and the hope for a continuation in growth.

INTERWAR MEETING HOUSES

The design of the early twentieth-century meeting houses continued late Victorian and Edwardian developments; they varied in style, planform and, sometimes, function. Many had additional rooms to accommodate mission halls and adult schools, although some meetings chose to erect separate buildings for them. Quakers were heavily involved in the Arts and Crafts and garden city movements: the architect Barry Parker was a Friend and several Quaker industrialists and philanthropists, like Cadbury and Rowntree, built garden suburbs. At Bournville, this included a meeting house of 1905 designed by William Alexander Harvey, although at the Rowntrees' New Earswick near York Quakers initially used the multi-purpose Folk Hall. Other new meeting houses included the Golders Green Meeting House at Hampstead Garden Suburb of 1913 by Fred Rowntree and that at Letchworth

Fig.2 Harrow Meeting House, 1935 by Hubert Lidbetter (Elain Harwood)

Fig.3 The meeting house at Weston-super-Mare, built in two phases in 1953 and 1956 (Steven Baker, Historic England Archive, DP236015)

of *c.*1907 by Robert Bennett & Benjamin Wilson Bidwell. These strong links to the garden city movement and a preference for the Arts and Crafts style continued into the interwar period and beyond, with an emphasis on good quality, contextual design and domestic scale. Examples include H. Clapham Lander's building at Welwyn Garden City of 1925–6 in the Arts & Crafts style, while Hubert Castle's meeting house of 1939 at Wythenshawe, Manchester, adopted the mansard roof of the slightly earlier housing in the area by Barry Parker.

Neo-Georgian meeting houses first appeared in the 1920s, generally on a domestic scale, such as Ernest Hickman's building at Northfield, Birmingham, of 1929. The first large-scale building in the style was Friends House of 1924–7 in Euston Road, London, the administrative headquarters of the Religious Society of Friends. Designed to complement the Georgian houses of the wider area and the Euston Arch, Hubert Lidbetter's competition-winning design took the form of an imposing four-storey building of brick and Portland stone with three Doric porticos *in antis*.

Friends House launched the career of the Quaker architect Hubert Lidbetter (1885–1966) as the most prolific twentieth-century architect of meeting houses, although it is somewhat of an anomaly in his oeuvre. No other meeting house was anywhere near as expensive, its final cost being £191,262. Most of Lidbetter's subsequent meeting houses were small, either in an Arts and Crafts style like Harrow of 1935, or a blend of neo-Georgian and vernacular features like Brentwood of 1957. While he was not keen on overtly modern architecture, his large urban meeting houses at Birmingham (1933) and Liverpool (1941) were less historicist than most of his buildings, although this was partly due to financial constraints.[5]

Fig.4 Croydon Meeting House (right) of 1956 by Lidbetter, beside the Adult School Hall of 1908 by W. Curtis Green, photographed by Paul D. Barkshire in 1992 (Historic England Archive, DD003706)

Practical considerations also influenced his design for Watford (1953), originally a strikingly modern meeting house of single-storey cubic volumes with flat roofs, with the meeting room behind an ancillary range with a recessed central entrance. In fact, part of its radical appearance was due to the fact that Lidbetter had planned the future addition of wings and a second storey.[6] It is possible that he intended the completed building to be closer to his earlier meeting house of 1939 at Sutton Coldfield, which had a very similar planform and main elevation combined with a hipped roof over the meeting room and some decorative features such as a moulded concrete door surround.

POST-WAR MEETING HOUSES

Of the 83 meeting houses dating from after 1918, over half were built in the 1950s (eighteen) and 1960s (26). The causes of this increased building activity were manifold. Bombed meeting houses had to be replaced, for example at Weston-super-Mare (1953 and 1956), at Hammersmith (1954–5) and Croydon (1956), both by Lidbetter, and at Canterbury (1956 by J.L. Denman). Some new meetings like Brentwood and Stevenage wanted their own, purpose-built premises. Due to shifts in population, established meetings found they had either outgrown their building, as happened at Oxford, or wanted something more compact, as at Coventry where the old meeting house of 1897 was considered too large. Meetings in urban centres came increasingly under pressure to give way to development. In

Fig.5 An undated photograph of the interior of Canterbury Meeting House, 1956 by J.L. Denman (RIBA Collections)

Bournemouth, an exchange was agreed with Marks & Spencer, who acquired the site of the Edwardian meeting house and in return funded the construction of a new building by Dexter & Staniland in the suburb of Boscombe, opened in 1962. Other historic meeting houses were preserved by new owners and converted to other uses. In Bristol, the eighteenth-century meeting house was sold in 1956 to the City Council, who converted it to a registry office, and a new meeting house was built on the burial ground of a former Quaker workhouse.[7] After the boom of the 1950s and 1960s, building activity slowly tapered off. Of the purpose-built meeting houses currently in Quaker ownership, only ten were built in the 1970s, eleven in the 1980s, and three in the 1990s.

Stylistically, the 1950s marked the transition to more modern styles of architecture, although this was a slow process. Friends generally opted for traditional forms and materials, particularly at historic locations like Oxford, where Thomas Rayson prepared a Cotswold vernacular design built in 1954–5, and Canterbury, a meeting house of 1956 in a blend of domestic neo-Georgian and Arts and Crafts styles by J.L. Denman. Hitchin, designed by the Quaker architect Paul V. E. Mauger (1896–1982) and built in 1958–9, was the first prominent modern meeting house. The old meeting house was sold to the rural district council for use as offices and its successor built on the old burial ground nearby. In order to minimise the impact on burials it was decided to raise a first-floor meeting room on pilotis. *The Friend* reported divided opinions, ranging from 'thank goodness you are building a place of

Fig.6 Hitchin Meeting House, 1958–9 by Paul V. E. Mauger (Elain Harwood)

worship in a contemporary idiom' to 'a hen-house on stilts'.[8] The building elicited comments beyond Quaker circles: *The Guardian* described it 'as up to date as a supermarket', implying a somewhat uneasy tension between the modern style of commercial buildings and its use for a place of worship.[9]

These reactions demonstrate that questions of architectural style and decoration in meeting house design were problematic for many Quakers. Aware that their buildings would be seen as representative of their values, they were hesitant about too much outward show. This was not new to the twentieth century; similar discussions had taken place in the 1840s, for example, over the use of classical columns.[10] In his 1961 book on the history and development of meeting houses, Hubert Lidbetter, then in his 70s, warned against 'the restless eccentricities which so frequently mar the modern places of worship and detract from their true function'.[11] Although not universally accepted, his opinion carried some weight, for between 1935 and 1957 he was surveyor to London's Six Weeks Meeting (now the London Quakers Property Trust), the only official architect's post in Quaker circles. Lidbetter's argument about fitness for purpose as a place of worship was echoed in 1980 by the Quaker historian and architect David M. Butler who wrote about site swaps such as that at Bournemouth: 'occasionally through transactions in town centre sites we have more money than we need and perhaps an architect not of our choice as part of the bargain. How difficult it is then to resist tropical hardwood, veneers, polished marble facings, special-effect lighting! All these and more are to be found in a few post-war meeting houses, complications which do not help them to fulfil their purpose.'[12]

Others objected to overt architectural flourishes due to additional costs or fears about future maintenance. For example, in 1967 Lidbetter's son Martin, who took over his practice, had to change his design for a new meeting house at Sutton after the meeting expressed its anxiety about the proposed hyperbolic roof, the chief concern being the 'effect of this form of roof structure on the worshipping group'.[13] He substituted a pyramidal roof with some regret, fearing 'that the result will now inevitably be a second best'.[14] An elliptical paraboloid roof in laminated timber at Nottingham's meeting house, of 1960–1 by Bartlett & Gray, experienced weather-proofing problems and was replaced by a plainer design in 2006–7.

Yet functionalism suited the Quaker ethos and many meetings embraced the new materials and forms on offer. For example, Nottingham Meeting House was hailed by Friends for successfully combining modern design with the 'simplicity of approach and layout which seems in keeping with our way of worship'.[15] Innovative plan forms began to appear. Some meetings even commissioned what may be described as 'statement buildings' by Quaker standards, such as the Brutalist meeting house at Blackheath of 1971–2 by Trevor Dannatt and the post-modernist one at Sheffield of 1989–91 by Michael Sykes of the Sykes Able Partnership.[16] Another unusual building is that at Heswall, Wirrall. Influenced by the sandstone outcrop on the site, in 1958 the architects Dewi-Prys Thomas and Gerald Beech designed a building with a prow-like meeting room on the first floor, whose vertical strip windows give it further upward emphasis. According to Thomas, the approach

Fig.7 Sheffield Meeting House, 1989–91 by Michael Sykes of the Sykes Able Partnership (Elain Harwood)

Fig.8 Wanstead Meeting House, 1966–68 by Norman Frith, in a photograph of 1969 by Peter Baistow, with the burial ground in the foreground (Architectural Press Archive / RIBA Collections)

to the building (erected in 1961–3) was intended to reflect a spiritual journey: 'The 'yard' from the world outside is gained by a slight ramp which is sympathetic to the rise of the rock itself on the profile of the ground here. On passing through the cleft between the main block and Resident Friend's accommodation we feel that we are passing into a private part of the world, like the atrium of the Early Christian Church'.[17] Although early Friends had eschewed any resemblance to church buildings, post-war Quakers and their architects used such ecclesiastical comparisons more frequently. Another example is Mauger's description in 1968 of the newly opened Wanstead Meeting House, likening a layout with discrete functional spaces to the arrangement of 'the monasteries of the Western Church for worship, living and working'.[18]

However, most post-war meeting houses aimed to be unostentatious, blending into their surroundings. Neo-vernacular designs re-appeared in the late 1970s and continued into the 1990s, less as a reaction to modernism and more as a logical continuation of early twentieth-century trends in Quaker architecture. At East Garston, Berkshire, a new meeting house with laminated cruck frames and weatherboarded walls opened in 1979, designed by the Quaker John Bangma. Others followed a more domestic red-brick idiom, including Richard Fraser's 1988 meeting house at New Earswick and Edwin Trotter's building at Scarborough of 1990, while Keswick of 1995 by the Manning Elliot Partnership reflects the vernacular traditions of the Lake District, with white painted rough-cast render, a Cumbrian slate roof, and sash windows with stone architraves.

SEATING AND CENTRAL PLANS

A new feature in post-war meeting houses was the emergence of central and polygonal plans. They were almost unknown in earlier Quaker buildings, the only known pre-twentieth-century example being the octagonal meeting house built in 1680 at Burlington, New Jersey.[19] The central plan became possible because the main constraint on the internal seating arrangements disappeared in 1924, when the London Yearly Meeting (the central body which in 1995 was renamed the Britain Yearly Meeting) agreed to discontinue the practice of having 'recorded ministers'. These were Quakers with an acknowledged gift of spoken ministry, who with the elders would have sat on benches on a raised platform (also known as the 'stand'), with the rest of the meeting on benches facing them, a layout which best fitted an oblong plan. Use of the stand had been waning for some time before 1924, and in the early twentieth century it and the rows of benches for the congregation were increasingly replaced by chairs. The chairs initially replicated the historic layout of benches, as at Leonard Brown's Peterborough meeting house (1936), but in the post-war period came to be arranged in a circle, which is the most common arrangement today.[20] The furnishings of post-war meeting houses were frequently of high quality and designed for the building. Surviving contemporary sets of chairs from the early and mid-twentieth century are increasingly rare but can be found for example at Chelmsford (1957–8), Bournemouth and Heswall. Many meeting houses, including older ones, have high-quality furnishings made by the Brynmawr Furniture Company (fl.1929–39) of South Wales, one of several local initiatives with Quaker involvement which aimed to ease unemployment.[21] Examples of the company's work can be found at Harrow and a full set of oak chairs, table and benches at Malvern (1937–8), a building by John Ramsay Armstrong, architect to the Bournville Village Trust.

A central plan became the logical architectural expression of the new seating arrangement. Square meeting rooms were the most popular and an early example is that at Welwyn of 1925–6. Polygonal meeting rooms started to appear from the late 1950s, such as the octagonal example at Stevenage of 1959 by William Barnes with laminated timber trusses. Norman Frith's building at Romford (1961) has a hexagonal meeting room with one fully glazed wall with staggered glazing bars. The same architect also played with the shape at Wanstead (1966–68), where the hexagonal meeting room is flanked by three further hexagons containing ancillary

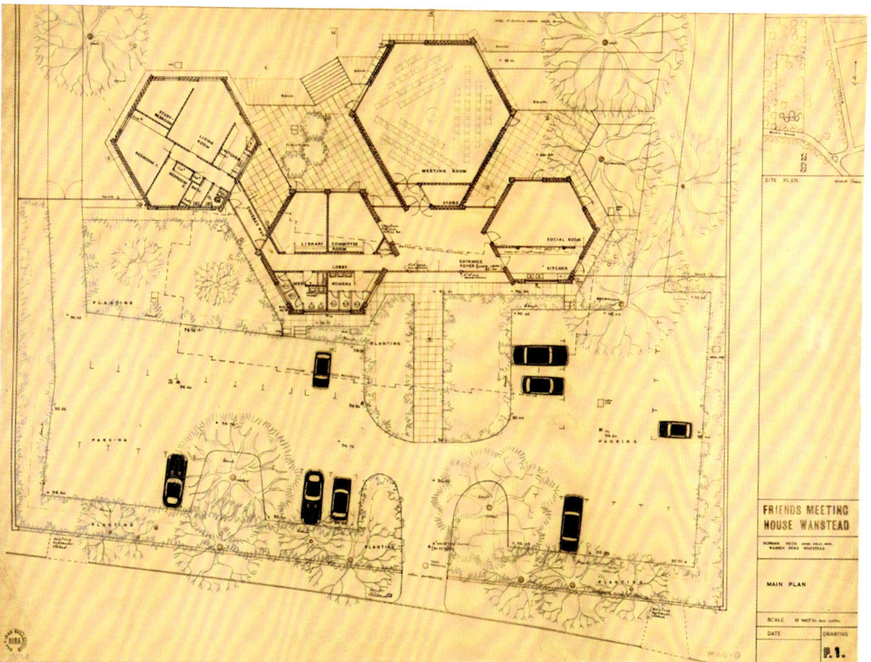

Fig.9 Undated plan of Wanstead Meeting House by Norman Frith (RIBA Collections)

spaces and accommodation for a resident Friend. Frith, a member of the Wanstead meeting, developed this plan in order to keep other activities away from the main meeting room.[22] At Cheltenham, which opened in 1985, Arnold J. Brownrigg of C. Frank Timothy Associates continued this theme of imposing geometrical symmetry on the entire plan, not just the meeting room, by designing a building of three staggered squares.

Fig.10 Blackheath Meeting House, 1971–2 by Trevor Dannatt (Elain Harwood)

At Maidstone (1976), Frith designed a hexagonal meeting room under a folded roof at the head of an oblong block of ancillary spaces, an arrangement repeated by Barber, Bundy & Partners at Reigate (1983–4). Keswick Meeting House of 1995 combined both forms by means of a canted apse, reviving another uncommon meeting room plan which can be found, for example, at the neo-Gothic meeting house at Exeter (1876) and at the 1950s building at Weston-super-Mare. The rare oval meeting room at Redditch (1974), Worcestershire, projects above the lower ancillary spaces to the rear of the building; its architect was Selby James Clewer, chief architect of the Bournville Village Trust. Another option for the plan of a meeting room was a square with chamfered corners. That at Blackheath explored this tension between an octagonal space and a square, its chamfered corners emphasised internally by hidden natural lighting. Externally, this is further accentuated by turning the building through 45 degrees, so that a chamfer faces the main approach. Frequently likened to a chapter house, the main meeting room was described by the *Architectural Review* as a 'calm but climactic' space.[23] The traditionalist Lidbetter did not agree with the increasing use of central plans: 'circles and octagons are all very well in their way and though by no means unQuakerly, they hardly seem to fit in with the Quaker mode of worship'.[24]

The absence of fixed seating resulted in a highly flexible meeting room, with few furnishings specific to Quakers. This suited most meetings who wished to play a stronger role in their wider communities by renting out their building to other uses; for example, Redditch Meeting House was used from the start additionally as a council-run day nursery. But the balance between a building which is primarily a meeting house and one that is completely multi-functional has sometimes been difficult to strike. David Butler posed this as a rhetorical question: 'Is [the modern meeting house] to be a social centre which includes a room more or less convenient for meetings, or a well-fitted meeting room where other users may make the best of it?'[25]

In addition to the main meeting room, most buildings included ancillary facilities such as a kitchen, toilets, a smaller meeting room, a room for children during the silent meeting for worship, and a flat for a warden or caretaker. Other related accommodation on the same site could include housing, especially of the types which the meeting felt were lacking locally. The social responsibility which had prompted Quaker interest in garden cities and model workers' housing reappeared in the post-war new towns with schemes at Ifield near Crawley and at Redditch to remedy shortages of accommodation for single persons and single parents. 'Camfield' – the new building by Graham Christopher, Ernest Chew and A.J. Morley opened at Ifield in 1971 – is attached to a meeting house of 1675–6 and a fifteenth-century hall house. Later, the focus appears to have turned to sheltered housing. When a new meeting house was built on the Quakers' historic site at Reigate, the scheme included twenty flats for the elderly. Similar flats were built in conjunction with the meeting house of 1987 at Carlton Hill, Leeds (designed by Michael Sykes), and at Scarborough for the Joseph Rowntree Housing Trust.

CONCLUSION

Quaker clients and the designers of modern meeting houses grappled with the same issues of style and decoration that had occupied their predecessors for over two hundred years. In many cases, the Friends' attitude to architecture was 'what happens inside is more important'.[26] As an architect and Quaker, David Butler thought that: 'It appears characteristic of Friends throughout the whole course of their history either to take virtually no notice of the physical surroundings of worship or deliberately to reject notice of them.'[27] And yet, when engaged in the task of selecting a design or an architect for a new meeting house, Friends were keen that their building was not only functional but also dignified, appropriate for its primary use and respectful of its surroundings. A number of twentieth-century meeting houses won Civic Trust Awards (e.g. Hitchin, Heswall and Blackheath) and RIBA regional awards (e.g. Nottingham).

While modern buildings form a substantial group among Quaker meeting houses, they are also the least well-known, as attention has too often focused on the more picturesque earlier buildings associated with the founders of Quakerism. Frequently under-appreciated, they are vulnerable to alterations and even closure due to shrinking congregations. In 2020, the total number of members was 12,125, a lower figure than in 1900, although this is bolstered by an additional 6,902 regular 'attenders'.[28] In a climate of rationalisation, twentieth-century meeting houses can be a valuable asset as they can be more flexible in plan than older buildings, and can generally accommodate additional or alternative uses. But they may also be considered a liability if there are problems with the original construction, or even an easy development opportunity without any heritage constraints. A recent joint initiative by Historic England and the Religious Society of Friends has sought to approach this strategically by commissioning reports on all meeting houses owned by the Society in Great Britain and the Channel Islands. These reports offer an overview of the buildings' heritage significance, their current use and management, and their vulnerability to change, providing an invaluable tool for their future management.[29] As a result of that project, the listing grades of six meeting houses were upgraded and eleven more were newly added to the National Heritage List for England, including the twentieth-century buildings at Malvern, Croydon and Blackheath. However, many more meeting houses deserve recognition as an important part of recent Quaker history and a modern expression of the Friends' values.

ACKNOWLEDGEMENT

Much of the research for this article was undertaken while working in 2014–16 on the Quaker Meeting Houses Heritage Project, which was commissioned by the Religious Society of Friends and Historic England from the Architectural History Practice.

NOTES

1 See Johanna Roethe, "Of singular elegance and dignified simplicity': Quaker Meeting Houses and their architects' in Megan Aldrich and Alexandrina Buchanan (eds.), Studies in Victorian Architecture and Design, vol.7, *Thomas Rickman and the Victorians*, 2019, pp.113–131.

2 For information on individual meeting houses, see David Butler, *Quaker Meeting Houses of Britain*, (London, Friends Historical Society, 1999), 2 volumes; and the reports by the Architectural History Practice on the website of The Quaker Meeting Houses Heritage Project (2014–16), http://heritage.quaker.org.uk/, accessed 29 May 2019.

3 A.D. Gilbert, *Religion and Society in Industrial England: Church, chapel and social change 1740–1914*, (London, Longman, 1976), p.40.

4 The membership figures for the twentieth century come from the annual tabular statement, which is published with the proceedings of the London (now Britain) Yearly Meeting (various titles), Friends House Library. The early-twentieth-century tabular statements do not include statistics about the number of attenders, who are not full members but can attend meetings for worship. Thus, the figures cited here exclude them.

5 Eleanor Gawne, 'Buildings of endearing simplicity: the Friends Meeting Houses of Hubert Lidbetter', Twentieth Century Architecture, no.3, *The Twentieth Century Church*, 1998, p.91.

6 An upward extension was built in 1970 and a new frontage in 2004 but neither were to Lidbetter's design and they have obscured the original building. Neil Burton, 'Friends Meeting House, Watford', 2015, http://heritage.quaker.org.uk/files/Watford%20LM.pdf, accessed 29 May 2019.

7 The eighteenth-century meeting house in Quakers Friars, Bristol, is now a restaurant.

8 Basil Donne-Smith, 'Hitchin's new meeting house' *The Friend*, vol.116, 24 October 1958, p.1356.

9 'Hitchin Quakers' up-to-date meeting house', *The Guardian*, no.35242, 21 October 1959, p.6.

10 See Roethe 2019, op. cit., p.191.

11 Hubert Lidbetter, *The Friends Meeting House. An historical survey...*, (York, William Sessions Ltd/The Ebor Press, 1961), first edition, p.44.

12 David M. Butler, 'The Making of Meeting Houses', *Friends' Quarterly*, vol.22, July 1980, p.323.

13 Letter from Margaret Arnold (Clerk to Sutton Preparative Meeting) to H. Martin Lidbetter, 17 May 1967, Sutton Preparative Meeting Minutes, volume 7 (1963–8), MGR11C/Sutton, Friends House Library.

14 Letter from H. Martin Lidbetter to Margaret Arnold, 25 May 1967, Sutton Preparative Meeting Minutes, volume 7 (1963–8), MGR11C/Sutton, Friends House Library.

15 Ian Hyde, 'A new venture for Nottingham', *The Friend*, vol.119, no.24, 16 June 1961, p.807.

16 Trevor Dannatt did not agree with the label 'Brutalist' for his Blackheath Meeting House. Interview with Catherine Croft and Tess Pinto in 2019, audio recording at https://c20society.org.uk/news/listing-success-for-trevor-dannatts-blackheath-friends-meeting-house/, accessed 30 May 2019.

17 1958 report by Dewi-Prys Thomas as quoted by Emma Neil, 'Quaker Meeting House, Heswall', 2015, http://heritage.quaker.org.uk/files/Heswall%20LM.pdf, accessed 29 May 2019.

18 Paul Mauger, '[Wanstead Meeting House]', *The Friend*, vol.126, 25 October 1968, p.1326.

19 Susan Garfinkel, 'Letting in "the World": (Re)interpretative tensions in the Quaker meeting house', *Perspectives in Vernacular Architecture*, vol.5, 1995, p.82.

20 Photographs of 1936 in the collection of Peterborough Local Meeting. There has been so far no systematic investigation of the modern seating arrangements of meeting houses.

21 Gethin Evans, 'Cymru: concern, conscience and caution: Quaker cameos in Welsh history', *The Journal of the Friends Historical Society*, vol.69, 2018, p.10.

22 E.B., 'New Meeting House for Archery Lodge Site', *The Friend*, vol.124, 21 October 1966, p.1238.

23 The original text says 'climatic' but it is clear from the context that the author meant 'climactic'. 'Meeting House, Blackheath, London', *Architectural Review*, vol.153, April 1973, p.267.

24 Undated lecture by Lidbetter, Lidbetter papers, Friends House Library, quoted in Gawne, op.cit., p.88.

25 Butler 1980, op.cit., p.322.

26 Frank Stillwell, 'Official opening Sheffield', *The Friend*, vol.149, 22 February 1991, p.248.

27 Butler 1980, op.cit., p.316.

28 Britain Yearly Meeting of the Religious Society of Friends (Quakers), *Patterns of membership, including the 2020 tabular statement*, 2021, p.2, www.quaker.org.uk/documents/tabular-statement2021, accessed 11 August 2021.

29 See the overview report and the individual reports on http://heritage.quaker.org.uk/.

DUNCAN GREGORY

6 'The Unproclaiming and Noble Frame',
or 'Modern, without being Modernist': The Churches of Ernest Bower Norris

Fig.1 Sacred Heart, North Walsham, 1934–5 (Elain Harwood)

The 1950s and 1960s were exciting times for the designers of Roman Catholic churches in England. Two seismic shifts had blown away centuries of tradition and led to a period of innovative and experimental building. The dual impacts of the Modern Movement and the Second Vatican Council (1962–5) brought new materials which encouraged a break with traditional building styles and new liturgical thinking that revolutionised the way the buildings were used. Priests began to face their congregations and share Mass in their own language as altars were brought forward and their rails removed. The architectural expression of the relationship between clergy and congregation was revolutionised.

Developments at the vanguard of this architectural revolution have been well documented. But there is another story, that of the quiet majority of architects who modified their work in an iterative rather than a revolutionary way, and whose work has been overshadowed. Ernest Bower Norris (1889–1969) was one of those.

Between 1920 and 1969 Norris built over sixty Catholic churches, as well as schools and secular commissions, from practices in Manchester, Stafford and briefly London. His work was published in the contemporary architectural press, but has since faded into obscurity. In 1965 he was honoured by having a primary school in his adopted hometown of Stafford named after him. By the 1990s the school's headmaster had no idea who Norris was, and the school has since been renamed.

Norris built in the Byzantine-Romanesque style, popular with Catholic architects in the early and mid-twentieth century. It claimed an authenticity of Christian practice predating the great schisms between eastern and western churches, and between Catholics and Protestants. It claimed in bricks and mortar a legitimacy which had been denied British Catholics over centuries of state and social persecution. Conveniently, it had the advantage of being cheaper than Gothic, and the decorative mosaic interiors could be finished later as funds became available.

Norris had travelled widely and was well aware of developments in Europe and, among other modernist works, had visited Auguste Perret's St Joseph the Worker at Le Havre (1951–4). He preferred, however, to use reinforced concrete for economy of structure while presenting a more traditional appearance externally. This choice led to success in his own time but has since condemned him to obscurity. His talent is recognised in the listing of six early works, but two of his finest, St Edward the Confessor, Macclesfield, Cheshire (1939) and St John Fisher, West Heath, Birmingham (1964) remain unprotected, while St John Vianney, Blackpool (1958) was turned down for listing in 1999.

Norris was born in Didsbury, Manchester in 1889, the sixth of seven children. His father, a staunch Methodist, was a registrar of births and deaths. He was

Fig.2 St John the Baptist, Rochdale, perspective by Henry Hill, c.1914 (Diocese of Salford / HHAA)

educated at Manchester Grammar School and served articles with James Harold France while studying architecture at the School of Art. There he met Henry Hill, a fellow student one year older and a member of an established Catholic family; Norris converted to Catholicism around this time. After graduating in 1909 Norris spent some time travelling in Italy while Hill joined his father, Oswald Charles Hill, an architect practising at No.9 Albert Square, Manchester. Oswald Hill had important links to the Catholic hierarchy through his cousin, the vicar general of the Diocese of Salford.[1] He had designed a school for Canon Henry Chipp at Rochdale in 1902, and later the firm accepted the commission to build a church.[2] On his father's death in 1911, Henry Hill took over the practice, aged just 23, with Norris his chief assistant from 1910 to 1914.[3] Norris also worked for Sir Edwin Lutyens, perhaps in 1914–15, but the two men later fell out over the building of Campion Hall in Oxford.[4] In 1915 Norris enlisted in the Royal Navy and seems to have been stationed in the London area manning anti-aircraft guns protecting against Zeppelin attacks.[5] Henry Hill joined the Royal Flying Corps and received the Military Cross for bravery in 1916, but was lost in action in October 1917.

Demobbed in February 1919, Norris quickly submitted his nomination to become an associate of the RIBA. He described himself as chief assistant to Henry T. Sandy of Stafford, who had taken over Hill's Manchester practice.[6] The following year Norris was made a partner in Sandy's firm, and they traded as Sandy & Norris from Stafford, but used the style Hill, Sandy & Norris for work from the Manchester office. Henry Sandy died unexpectedly in January 1922 at the age of 53, leaving the 33-year-old Norris as the sole partner.[7]

The spectacular church of St John the Baptist, Rochdale (listed grade II*), is officially attributed to Norris in conjunction with Henry Hill. A perspective in the Salford Diocesan Archives, dated from before the war, was signed by Henry Hill and shows the design almost as built. But while it was customary for the senior partner to sign all the drawings, the handwriting on the sheet appears to be Norris's. The client, Canon Chipp, asked for a Byzantine church, and the dominating feature is a reinforced concrete dome 68' in diameter and only five inches thick, lit from a ring of 36 small windows. Between the pre-war perspective and the final project built in 1923–5, the detail at ground level was simplified and the campanile omitted because of reasons of cost, but the main form of the upper part remained the same. The interior has extensive decoration by Eric Newton (1893–1965), grandson of Louis Oppenheimer (1830–1900) who founded a firm in Manchester manufacturing mosaics in 1865, many for the Roman Catholic church. Newton, who took his mother's maiden name in 1918, worked for the company until the mid-1930s while developing a career as an art critic.

THE BASILICA PLAN

The English Martyrs, Sparkhill, Birmingham, built in 1923, aligns in date with the great domed structure in Rochdale, sharing its Byzantine-Romanesque style, with a flanking campanile, but it follows the alternative and more commonly found basilica plan form of a nave and aisles. Internally, a nave of seven bays has arcades of Siena marble columns terminating in an apsidal sanctuary. The timber king post roof is left exposed, recreating the effect of the fourth century AD, when Christianity had just been legalised as the state religion of the Roman Empire and the basilica hall of justice was adopted as a model.[8]

According to the *Architectural Review*, Sparkhill's design 'was evolved from a study of the Byzantine Churches of Rome at the express wish of the client ... All unnecessary features were eliminated in order to get an effect of extreme simplicity.'[9] The specific source was the seventh-century San Giorgio in Velabro, which may hold the key to one of the quirks of Sparkhill, whose Siena marble columns are unusually short and were later criticised for their 'stunted height'.[10] Early designs show taller columns, more in line with conventional expectations, but somewhere in the building process they were shortened.[11] The explanation for this may be that until the mid-1920s San Giorgio had a raised floor that concealed its column bases. These were only exposed after the completion of Sparkhill in a restoration programme that stripped away later additions. It appears that while Norris was adjusting the Sparkhill designs to shorten the columns, work was being planned in Rome to lengthen them. Some decorative marbles and mosaics were added at Sparkhill, but for a similar church with a completed scheme one should

Fig.3 St John the Baptist, Rochdale, built 1923–5 (John East)

Fig.4 English Martyrs, Sparkhill, Birmingham, 1923 (Elain Harwood)

look to the Sacred Heart and St Catherine, Droitwich, built in 1921 by another regional architect, Frank Peacock, whose mosaic interior by Gabriel Pippet (1880–1962) was mostly completed by 1932, making it a rare English example of a completed Byzantine-Romanesque decorative scheme.

After Sparkhill, Norris designed St Anne's, Blackburn (1926) and St George, Hanley (1927–8, Now St George and St Martin) in a similar basilica style. Although the building was one of Norris's cheapest, the western elevation at Hanley is particularly fine, with smooth purple brickwork offset with red framing to the doors and windows, and carved stone 'kneelers' where to buttresses terminate at the height of the aisle roofs. It was built for, and mostly funded by, a coal-mining community during an economic recession and the project was complicated by mine workings running under the site. However, at its opening the church was described by the Archbishop of Birmingham as 'a glorious church amid depressing surroundings'.[12]

In 1924, Norris adapted his basilica style to produce a dramatically different church, St Joseph's, Leyton, east London, with a massive, monumental west tower, rectangular on plan and tapered towards the top. Norris explained the requirements:

> *The design of this Church was largely dictated by the need for a large mass and striking elevation due to its situation amongst the unbroken monotony of terrace houses, yet serving as suitable War Memorial to the Fallen.*[13]

Such striking west towers became a popular motif in the years after 1900. Norris's father had retired to the Isle of Man, where in 1909–10 Giles Gilbert Scott had built Our Lady Star of the Sea and St Maughold, Ramsay, one of the first of his many designs in this manner. In 1923 Norris designed an unbuilt church in Port Erin, clearly influenced by Scott's local precedent, whose 'sturdy proportions' aimed for a form which would be 'architecturally satisfying' while able to 'withstand the continuous gales experienced on an exposed site'. It is a form typical of German Romanesque designs, often extending into paired towers at the top, and in simplified form popular with progressive German designers after 1920, notably Dominikus Böhm. It masks the roof of the nave and aisles behind, a solution used much earlier by Nicholas Hawksmoor at St Mary Woolnoth and Christ Church Spitalfields. St Joseph's is softened by classical stone string courses and shallowed pilasters projecting at the corners, a little more emphatic than Scott's work on the Isle of Man. Norris proceeded to build another seven churches in this style including Sacred Heart, Tipton, Birmingham (1940).

THE INFLUENCE OF FRANCIS REYNOLDS

A design similar to that proposed for Port Erin was adopted fifteen years later at St Edward the Confessor, Macclesfield (1939), where sheer undecorated brick walls flank a more elaborate carved stone centrepiece rising to full height. This commission was privately funded, allowing for high-quality interior fittings. This design is attributed to Francis Maurice (Frank) Reynolds (1910–67), who joined

Fig.5 Norris's unbuilt design for Port Erin, 1923 (HHAA s868)

Fig.6 Sacred Heart, Tipton, 1940 (author)

Fig.7 St Edward the Confessor, Macclesfield, 1939 (author)

the partnership in the early 1930s. He was a cousin of Henry Hill, their mothers being sisters, and before the age of 21 he had studied at the Manchester School of Architecture and spent time in Italy and France.[14] He then joined Sandy & Norris in Stafford for 'office experience' and by 1932 was in the Manchester office producing drawings for an unbuilt chapel at the Salesian College, Shrigley. The first church on which he was significantly involved was St Winefride, Lymm, near Warrington (1933), a humble building heavily influenced by Norris's earlier work at Sacred Heart, Wadhurst, East Sussex.[15] Henry Hill's mother lived nearby and appears to have worshipped at Lymm, bequeathing £50 to the rector of St Winefride's for 'an annual mass for deceased members of the Hill family'.[16]

The relationship between Norris and Reynolds is somewhat unclear. Reynolds worked in the office at Albert Square, Manchester, where drawings were labelled as by Hill, Sandy & Norris. However, when published, the churches were often attributed to Norris & Reynolds. Buildings from the Stafford office continued to be attributed to Sandy & Norris. In 1946 they parted, with Norris retaining the Stafford office and Reynolds operating from Albert Square in partnership with William Scott as Reynolds & Scott.

St Cecilia, Tuebrook, Liverpool (1931, grade II), shows an evolution from Norris's earlier designs. 'Conceived on sturdy lines, owing to the fact that the building is situated in the centre of villas of the usual suburban type', as the *Architects' Journal* explained, the west front has paired octagonal bell turrets which make it an unusually sculptural church for Norris.[17] Most of the design elements were re-used from other projects, the turrets from an early design for St Anne's, Blackburn, and the projecting wings with roofs at right angles to the direction of the nave were trialled in an unbuilt project in Southampton. A preliminary drawing for Tuebrook shows these as sloping shoulders like those at Leyton and in an early design for Hanley. The west window in this design is influenced by Rochdale and Leyton, although in the built version it is reduced from five to three lancets. Internally, the barrel-vaulted ceiling is reminiscent of Leyton and a convent chapel at Southam, but the arcade is broken by transept-like tall arches, lightening the interior effect.

The following year Norris designed a new building for the Convent of St Joseph, Stafford (1932), which includes a first-floor chapel as well as dormitories, refectories and a gymnasium. It is said to have been inspired by convents in the south of France and Spain, although it may show the influence of Norris's more exotic travels, particularly a trip to Buenos Aires in 1929.[18] Portuguese baroque influences appear at SS Peter and Paul, New Brighton, Wirral (1935, grade II). This unusual church was shaped by a strong-minded parish priest, Fr Mullins, whose zeal with the collection plate was only matched by his energy on the international stock and currency markets, dealing in high-risk German loans, a Brazilian trading company

Fig.8 St Dunstan, Moston, Manchester, 1937 (Elain Harwood)

and the Russian rouble in order to fund the project.[19] He had studied in Lisbon and wanted a church like the Estrela Basilica there.

Among the fine churches ascribed to Norris & Reynolds in the 1930s were St Dunstan, Moston, Manchester (1937, grade II), based on Norris's unbuilt design of 1925 for a church in Wanstead, London. A design published in 1928 shows an Italian Renaissance style Greek Cross, with an octagonal dome topped by a lantern.[20] The Wanstead design was modified for an unbuilt Norris and Reynolds scheme of 1933 for the John Bosco Memorial Chapel at the Salesian College, Shrigley, Macclesfield. The nave was elongated to form a Latin cross with Romanesque styling and sawn-off gables as at New Brighton. Several variants survive in the archive of the Manchester practice, two of which were drawn by Reynolds in 1932.[21] This design, together with constructional details from New Brighton, seems to have influenced not only the Moston church but also St Willibrord, Clayton, built in 1938. This was attributed by Pevsner to Reynolds, and while it should be ascribed to Hill, Sandy & Norris – as confirmed by *The Builder* and a drawing in the Stafford practice archive – some of the detailing, particularly the low-arched side chapels, seem out of character for Norris and suggest that Reynolds played a larger role in the design.[22] Pevsner suggested that it was inspired by Walter Tapper's Our Lady with St Thomas of Canterbury, Gorton, (1927), but the concrete structure is a repeat of that at New Brighton.[23] The concrete contractor for both projects was Holst, and the handling of the barrel roofs and the transepts is very similar. Internally, the stripped classicism of the arches and pilasters are also variations of New Brighton.

St Dunstan's is in the firm's basilican tradition but with the addition of transepts and an octagonal crossing tower. The structure is faced in brown brick with dressings of stone and red brick. It has the characteristic long high west window, and lancets along the nave. The interior has Oppenheimer mosaics and was praised at the time for achieving a spacious effect on a restricted site.[24]

St Willibrord's is a very fine Byzantine church of reinforced concrete faced in brick. Due to the orientation of the site, the north street elevation is the most prominent, with three monumental transept-style projections, each with a single lancet window in an inset surround. The central bay has a low, octagonal tower topped by a flat dome. Internally, the nave ceiling is formed into saucer domes and the side chapels are entered through three diminishing circular arches, an Odeonesque touch.

Norris reused the triple-transept plan at St Thomas of Canterbury, Tean, Birmingham (1938) and much later at St John Vianney, Blackpool (1958). At Tean, it was a cost-saving device, because by bringing the roof tiles down between the transepts he significantly reduced the number of bricks required.[25] This feature reappeared at Reynolds & Scott's Blessed Sacrament, Preston (1955).

ART DECO AND MODERN INFLUENCES

The mid-1930s saw the emergence of a consistent set of forms which was used extensively by Norris, and later by Reynolds & Scott. The first example is Our Lady of Perpetual Succour, Bulwell. It has a tall nave in the basilican style but without the side aisles seen in the 1920s. Most of these churches had towers, with a more modern feel than the campaniles of the 1920s. They clearly echo early Christian basilicas such as the tenth-century San Francesco, Ravenna, but are reinterpreted for the mid-twentieth century.

Variations of this style continued to be built from the 1930s into the early 1960s.

Fig.9 St John, Heswall, Wirral, 1939 (author)

One of the best early examples is Our Lady and St Brigid in Northfield, Birmingham (1936). Using minimal decoration, Norris relied on height and proportion to create a simple, elegant building with a satisfying interior. St Alphonsus, Brooks Bar, Manchester (1936, no tower), and St Charles Borromeo, Rishton, Blackburn (1937–8) are similar but with lancet windows and pointed-arch arcades. One device often incorporated in these churches is the addition of a shallow projection behind the square-ended chancel that framed the high altar or reredos in a small arch. In the surviving drawings it first occurs in a 1933 design for Holy Trinity, Garston, which coincided with the arrival of Frank Reynolds.[26] One of its most effective deployments is at Our Lady and St John, Heswall, Wirral (1939) by Norris & Reynolds, where again simple proportions are used to striking effect. Andrew Derrick notes the similarity between the chancel arch here and that at Velarde's more progressive English Martyrs at nearby Wallasey (1953).[27]

Art Deco inflexions in the underlying Romanesque model can be detected in some of the churches discussed, but it is particularly pronounced in certain examples from the mid-1930s. The earliest was an unbuilt design for Holy Trinity, Garston, from 1933. This was followed by Sacred Heart, North Walsham, Norfolk (1934–5, grade II) and St John Fisher and St Thomas More, Wythenshawe, Manchester (1935) – described by Peter Anson as 'far and away the best church Mr Norris has yet given us' but demolished in 2012.[28] The last in this group was Holy Name, Great Barr, Birmingham, completed in 1938.

North Walsham marked a new construction technique. Until this point Norris had used concrete to recreate traditional forms, but here he chose longitudinal concrete beams to support the roof, removing the need for arcades and thus improving the sightlines. He still chose to express the nave and aisles, through a change in the ceiling height that also emphasises the form of the beams. As described in *The Tablet*:

Fig.10 St John Vianney, Blackpool, 1958 (Elain Harwood)

> *The architect has resolved that North Walsham's Catholic church shall have nave and aisles, but he gives them without using any detached piers. The roof of his nave is carried on two beams of reinforced concrete which span the whole length of each aisle, with no need of supporting pillars. Thus there is no point in the nave or aisles from which the Sanctuary cannot be clearly seen.*

The reviewer declared the result to be 'modern, without being Modernist'.[29]

LATER WORK

After Reynolds's departure from the practice, there is less variety in building style. Churches tend to be adaptations of the tall, aisleless basilicas like Bulwell, exemplifying a movement towards the 'noble simplicity' later advocated by the Second Vatican Council. Norris's first post-war church was St Patrick, Stafford, completed in 1951. It is a modernised form of Romanesque, praised for its 'almost monastic simplicity' and yet achieving a satisfying elegance by the use of graceful proportions and subtle detailing.[30]

A more unusual post-war church is St John Vianney, Blackpool (1958). In compensation for its position at the bottom of a hill, Norris designed an imposing west tower to elevate the church and give it a commanding scale.[31] It is similar to the tower at Leyton, but with its prominent hipped roof it echoes earlier precedents, such as the Porta Serrata in Ravenna of 1583. The inspiration might equally have come from closer to home. Reynolds & Scott designed churches in a similar style in the 1950s, as did Arthur Farebrother, another Manchester-based architect. Because of the corner plot, both west and south elevations are prominent at Blackpool. The location on a corner plot at Blackpool means that both west and south elevations are prominent. For the south, Norris uses a design of three projections similar to St Willibrord's; the north elevation is similar but because it is mostly hidden the details are less clearly expressed. Like St Willibrord's, the nave is formed of three reinforced concrete saucer domes, supported on Romanesque arches, but unusually the Blackpool church has an ambulatory behind the high altar, also cast in reinforced concrete. The intention was to decorate the sanctuary with marble and mosaics, but this remains unexecuted.[32] Norris also built Our Lady of the Assumption, Blackpool, in 1961, a late-career church that shows him at his best. Standard motifs are deployed in a new combination on a well-proportioned building to provide a pleasing and functional church, somewhat conservative but effective.

In all of these churches, Norris used a standard set of elements, described by Robert Proctor as an 'architectural kit'. He constantly rearranged them to produce

Fig.11 Our Lady of the Assumption, Blackpool, 1961 (Elain Harwood)

Fig.12 St John Fisher, West Heath, Birmingham, 1964 (Elain Harwood)

a group of buildings which, while displaying individuality, share a strong family resemblance.[33] This could be criticised as showing a lack of imagination, but Norris demonstrated considerable ingenuity in the reinvention of his patterns. As known quantities, they allowed him to predict costs and schedules accurately, freeing him from the 'burden of perpetual discovery' associated with modernism. This predictability helped him to retain the support of the influential diocesan offices, ensuring further commissions.[34]

While still building simple brick basilicas, Norris also experimented with more contemporary styling, beginning at Sacred Heart, Bilton, Rugby, built in 1958–61. His design of 1959 for a church at Woodthorpe, Nottingham, was rejected in favour of an even more ambitious design by Gerard Goalen. Ironically, Goalen's spire replaced Norris's vaults at New Brighton in advertisements for Holst concrete.

One intriguing design from this period is for a cathedral in Tanga, Tanzania, dated 1960. Although contemporaneous with Frederick Gibberd's Liverpool Cathedral, Norris's cruciform design is firmly rooted in the traditions of the practice. The long nave would have accommodated 900 worshippers, with a further 144 in the transepts; there are no chapels at the heads of the aisles, but three are located in the ambulatory behind the altar.

The end of Norris's career saw a return to the Greek Cross plan originally seen at Rochdale. His initial design for Ratcliffe College Chapel, published in 1957, showed a traditional basilican building with three side projections in the style of St Willibrord's, but later that year he made a new design featuring a central drum reminiscent of St John, Rochdale, possibly also influenced by Jean-Baptiste Hourlier's Notre-Dame-de-Victoire, Lorient, Brittany.[35]

At St John Fisher, West Heath, Birmingham, which opened in 1964 when Norris was 75 years old, we can see how the Greek cross plan was still in his mind. Here, however, he was obliged to use timber rather than concrete for economy, and the result is a near-flat octagonal cap like that at St Willibrord.[36] The spacious and well-proportioned interior gives clear lines of sight towards the high altar. Rounded arches separate the central nave from the transepts and sanctuary, and smaller arches lead through into chapels and ancillary spaces – making a complex perspective of related shapes. The fittings are of high quality, including pews of African walnut and an enamelled aluminium ciborium. Most of the seating is the central octagon under the fifty-foot diameter dome. The sanctuary and narthex occupy the east and west arms. There is *dalle de verre* by Jonah Jones (1919–2004), abstract in the clerestory windows and figurative for four lancet windows in the short faces of the octagon. Jones wrote that 'the context of Mr Bower Norris's architecture has always suited my work. Its scale and detail are the unproclaiming and noble frame for the various works that adorn it'.[37] Sadly his sculpture of St John Fisher above the west door is now lost.

For Our Lady of Windermere and St Herbert, also from 1964, Norris needed to provide for varying numbers of tourist congregants visiting the Lake District. His solution was a pentagonal central core, extended by two naves to provide extra seasonal capacity, which he described as resembling a pair of shorts, where one leg could be closed off in winter – though this neat analogy unfortunately places the baptistery in the gusset.[38] In this unusual design, the pentagon has a clerestory of abstract *dalle de verre*, while the reredos and high altar are against the liturgical east side and a sanctuary fills about half the space. The walls to each side of the sanctuary are arcaded, leading to chapels and access to the vestries. The two remaining sides of the pentagon, facing the sanctuary, open into the naves. The baptistery and narthex sit between them, with a doorway from the narthex

Fig.13 St John Fisher, West Heath, interior (author)

into each nave. The baptistery is in the main body of the church rather than the narthex.

Cyril Horsley, successor to the practice, confirms that Norris played an active part in the design of the Windermere church, showing that even in his seventies he was playing with new ideas. Externally the building works well, but the interior arrangement is less successful. Pews can be placed in the main body of the pentagon, but in 2019 seating was only in the naves, distancing the congregation from the sanctuary and dividing it.[39] An earlier iteration of the plan is based on an octagon rather than a pentagon, with 124 seats in the main block close to the sanctuary. Externally the main block seems taller and is topped by a tower that seems to show the influence of St Joseph, Le Havre, in a similar manner to Reynold's collaboration with Gibberd at the De La Salle training college chapel, Hopwood Hall, Rochdale (1965).

Our Lady and St Pius X, Habberley, Birmingham, Norris's final church, opened posthumously in 1970. In contrast to his other late works, it shows no outward concessions to liturgical, architectural or societal changes of the previous decade. It appears that the priest, possibly a Fr Proudfoot, was a 'dyed in the wool traditionalist' and Norris, ever pragmatic, supplied what the client requested.[40]

CONCLUSION

Norris was a frequent and ambitious traveller, visiting Quebec in 1923, Buenos Aires in 1929, Bombay in 1930 and New York in 1937. In 1969 he stopped off in Durban en-route to Australia, where after dining in the hotel restaurant he called reception to complain that the oysters he had been served were bad. The following morning, 25 April, he was found dead in his room, having suffered a heart attack.[41]

Norris left a legacy of fine buildings, even though the congregations who worship in them are often unaware of the designer. While they are conservative when compared to those of many contemporaries, this was a conservatism not through ignorance, but by choice. Its rationale seems fairly clear, for Norris enjoyed the financial success that his practice brought. His motto was that 'the best is only just good enough': he kept a cellar of half bottles of champagne to enjoy with meals and always travelled first class. This success was dependent on the on-going patronage of diocesan authorities. Architects were appointed by parish priests, whose taste was described in 1907 by Giles Gilbert Scott as 'appalling'.[42] But bishops often recommended architects to parishes, and designs had to be approved by diocesan offices. Most had favourite architects who would build many churches in those areas, and whose reputation for dependability was key for future commissions. This was a commissioning model that did not encourage innovation.

Robert Proctor notes that the churches were built mostly in suburbs, for a target audience unconcerned by ideas of authenticity, craftsmanship and stylistic avant garde. Their taste can be belittled as 'middlebrow', but in its service Norris drew on influences from around the world and across the centuries. Proctor also argues that as much thoughtfulness and creativity goes into the production of a 'good-typical' church as into a modernist one, and this is conspicuous in many of Norris's churches.[43] His legacy has suffered from unfortunate timing. The liturgical and architectural changes which happened at the end of his career rendered many of his buildings old fashioned before they were even paid for. In fact he has left a group of elegant, functional churches which have stood the test of time and most of which continue to serve the purpose for which they were built.

ACKNOWLEDGEMENTS

The author would like to thank Cyril Horsley and David Freeth of Horsley Huber Architects Ltd, the successor practice to Sandy & Norris in Stafford; Andrew Derrick, Elain Harwood, Brenda Ward and the many priests, nuns, parishioners and archivists who gave generously of their time to make this study possible.

NOTES

1 Andrew Derrick, 'Twentieth-Century Roman Catholic Church Architecture: A characterisation study' http://www.hrballiance.org.uk/wp-content/uploads/2018/12/RC-C20-Characterisation-Final-July-2014.pdf, p.30, accessed 5 June 2022.

2 'St John's School, Rochdale, classroom', STF1092, practice archive of Horsley Huber Architects.

3 Ernest Bower Norris, Nomination Papers (Associate 02822), 1919, RIBA Drawings and Archives.

4 David Frazer Lewis, 'Lutyens's Designs for Campion Hall, Oxford', Twentieth Century Architecture, no.11, *Oxford and Cambridge*, 2013, pp.54–5.

5 Lieutenant Commander M. D. Spencer, email to the author, October 2019.

6 RIBA Nomination Papers, op. cit.

7 'Obituary, Mr H. T. Sandy', *The Builder*, vol.122, 27 January 1922, p.169.

8 John A. Hilton, The Artifice of Eternity: The Byzantine-Romanesque Revival in Catholic Lancashire (Ormskirk: North West Catholic History Society, 2008), p.5.

9 'The Church of English Martyrs, Birmingham', *Architectural Review*, vol.54, December 1923, p.208.

10 *English Martyrs Sparkhill: Golden Jubilee of Consecration 1946–1996*, unpag., P47/T6, Birmingham Diocesan Archives.

11 STF11887, Horsley Huber Architects archive.

12 'Roman Catholics' New Church', *Staffordshire Sentinel*, cutting labelled (incorrectly) October 1925, P261, Birmingham Diocesan Archives.

13 *Catholic Church Construction (illustrated)*, undated cutting, Horsley Huber Architects archive.

14 Francis Maurice Reynolds, Nomination Papers (Fellow 4238), 1947, RIBA Drawings and Archives; Robert Proctor, 'Designing the Suburban Church: The mid-twentieth-century Roman Catholic churches of Reynolds & Scott', *Journal of Historical Geography*, vol.56, 2017, pp.113–33.

15 Francis Maurice Reynolds, Nomination Papers, op. cit.; Reynolds-Scott_601–472_0280, Manchester Metropolitan University Special Collections; *Brick Builder*, no.24, December 1931, pp.1 (cover), 16, describes the Wadhurst church as 'a homely little structure in excellent taste'.

16 Will of Mary Josephine Hill, <ancestry.com>.

17 'St Cecilia's Church, Liverpool', *Architects' Journal*, vol.74, 16 September 1931, pp.363–6.

18 'Some Notable Ecclesiastical Brickwork: Designed by Mr E. Bower Norris', *Brick Builder*, no.31, September 1933, pp.13–16.

19 'ss Peter & Paul Church: Recollections by J. Higgins'; Letter from Bishop Moriarty to Bishop Singleton, October 1932; Jennie Hargreaves, 'My Beloved Church', recollections, p.17, Shropshire Diocesan Archives.

20 'An Artist in Brickwork: Some work of Mr E. Bower Norris, *Brick Builder*, vol.3, October 1928, pp.10–16.

21 Reynolds-Scott_601–462_0280–1, Manchester Metropolitan University Special Collections.

22 'Manchester – Catholic Church in North Road' (tender), *The Builder*, vol.153, 6 August 1937, p.264.

23 Nikolaus Pevsner, The Buildings of England: *Lancashire South* (Harmondsworth: Penguin, 1969), p.337; revised Clare Hartwell and Matthew Hyde, *Lancashire: Manchester and the South-East* (London: Yale, 2004), p.363.

24 'St Dunstan, Moston, Manchester: E. Bower Norris and F. M. Reynolds,' *Architectural Record of Design and Construction*, vol.8, February 1938, p.74.

25 'New Church of St Thomas of Canterbury', *Catholic Building Review*, southern edition, 1954, pp.87–8.

26 S810, Horsley Huber Architects archive.

27 Andrew Derrick, op. cit., p.45.

28 Peter Anson, The Churches of Ernest Bower Norris, FRIBA', *Art Notes*, vol.1, nos.5–6, May-August 1938, p.70.

29 'A Good, Cheap Church', *The Tablet*, vol.163, 26 May 1934, pp.654–5.

30 'St Patrick's R. C. Church, Stafford', *Catholic Building Review*, southern edition, 1954, pp.87–8.

31 'New Church of St John Vianney, Blackpool', *Catholic Building Review*, northern edition, 1959, p.168.

32 'New St John Vianney Church, Marton', *Blackpool Gazette & Herald and Fylde News*, no.7469, 21 August 1959, p.17.

33 Robert Proctor, *Building the Modern Church, Roman Catholic church architecture in Britain* (Farnham: Ashgate, 2014), p.21

34 Proctor, 'Designing the Suburban Middlebrow', op. cit., pp.113–135.

35 'Ratcliffe College Chapel', *Catholic Building Review*, southern edition, 1957, pp.109–11; Proctor, *Building the Modern Church*, op. cit., pp.22,43.

36 Proctor, *Building the Modern Church*, op. cit., p.22.

37 Jonah Jones, 'Windows and Statues', in *Church of St John Fisher, souvenir brochure*, 31 March 1964, P55, Birmingham Diocesan Archives.

38 Cyril Horsley, Horsley Huber Architects, to the author, 30 November 2019.

39 'Windermere – Our Lady of Windermere and St Herbert', Taking Stock, https://taking-stock.org.uk/building/windermere-our-lady-of-windermere-and-st-herbert/, accessed 5 June 2022.

40 Cyril Horsley, 30 November 2019. The church has been demolished and replaced by housing.

41 Horsley, ibid.

42 Derrick, op. cit., p.42.

43 Proctor, 'Designing the Suburban Middlebrow', op. cit., pp.113–14.

CHRIS KENNEDY AND AIDAN RIDYARD

7 Richard Twentyman: Church Architect of Distinction

Fig.1 All Saints, Darlaston, with portal decoration by Don Potter (John East)

(Alfred) Richard Twentyman (1903–79), known to friends and colleagues as Dick, was a successful West Midlands architect whose church designs show his evolving responses to the modernist movement in England in the period before and after the Second World War. Practicing in Wolverhampton in the West Midlands, he was geographically, socially and culturally distant from London and has consequently somewhat disappeared from view; in compensation his regional status allowed him to enjoy a relatively relaxed life with time to indulge his personal interests, including fast cars and motor hill-climbing.

This article focusses on two out of his thirteen churches, to demonstrate the importance of social, religious and professional influences in their design and show his development as an architect. There is no central archive of his professional papers and drawings, which are distributed over several record offices and local church archives. All his churches are still standing, however, and only one is inaccessible to the public.

Twentyman and his younger brother John Anthony (Tony) (1906–88) were originally destined to follow their father into the engineering firm, Henry Rogers, Sons, & Co. Both brothers were educated at Wellington College and read engineering at university, Richard at Pembroke College, Cambridge and Tony (by odd coincidence) at Pembroke College, Oxford. Tony left early to join the firm, then became a professional sculptor whose artistic contacts proved useful to his brother. After Cambridge, Richard went on to qualify at the Architectural Association in London in 1931 before joining the Wolverhampton practice of H. E. Lavender & Co., which became (E. C.) Lavender & Twentyman in 1932–3. During Twentyman's career the firm was renamed Lavender, Twentyman & Percy in 1942, and Twentyman, Percy & Partners in 1960.

Both brothers inherited creative talents from their parents. Their mother, Grace Evill (1867–1954), was a cartoonist and a friend of the New Zealand-born artist Frances Hodgkins. Their father, Harold Edward Twentyman (1869–1946), worked initially as an industrial draughtsman and designer for Rogers & Co. and later became its managing director and chairman. He was also a skilful woodturner, becoming a master of the Worshipful Company of Turners, where a competition is still named after him today. Anthony encouraged Richard to take up watercolour and oil painting. He had earlier approached John Piper to paint their family home at Bilbrook Manor, where the unmarried brothers lived all their lives until their mother's death, when they moved to Claverley in Shropshire. The commission led indirectly to Piper's stained-glass window at Twentyman's St Andrew's Church in Whitmore Reans in 1965, the only occasion he introduced any stained glass into his churches.

Fig.2 St Martin of Tours, Parkfields, Wolverhampton, from the west (John East)

Although Twentyman might commission a single sculptural piece placed either externally or internally as a counterpoint to his simple church designs, he resisted further embellishment. Several works were commissioned from an Eric Gill pupil, Donald (Don) Potter, a member of the Scouts whose skills as a sculptor were recognised early on by Richard Baden-Powell, the founder of the Scout Movement. Anthony Twentyman was also a Scout, and met Potter when both were Scout leaders in the 1920s. This led to Potter's first commission from Richard Twentyman for his church of St Martin, Wolverhampton, in 1939, shortly before he became a much-respected art and craft teacher at Bryanston School. The architect and sculptor worked well together and further commissions followed.

TWENTYMAN'S CHURCHES

Apart from one Methodist church and two crematorium chapels, Richard Twentyman's eleven new churches, mainly in the Wolverhampton area, were for the Church of England. His career divides into three phases, beginning with St Gabriel, Walsall, and St Martin, Parkfields, Wolverhampton, both completed in 1939. They were somewhat disparagingly categorised by the writer Derek Mills as being in the 'power station' style, their brickwork sharing similar north-European sources.[1] Although forward-looking, these represented a pronounced glance back at tradition. After the war, his work developed into the more recognisably modernist forms, until his last two churches, built in 1965, St Andrew, Whitmore Reans, and St Andrew, Runcorn – which show him adapting to the contemporary evolution of the liturgy as well as keeping pace with architectural developments.

St Martin, Wolverhampton (1939) is taken here to represent his early work, and All Saints, Darlaston (1952) that of the post-war years. The quality of both is recognised in their grade II listing. Built to meet the demographic demands of expanding suburbs, they not only show how his design ideas changed, but at the same time some of his consistent features over time.

ST MARTIN, PARKFIELDS, WOLVERHAMPTON

Twentyman won an architectural competition for St Martin's in 1938, judged by Sir Charles Nicholson. A letter of recommendation later that year from the Lichfield Diocesan Trust was fulsome in its praise: '[Lavender and Twentyman] are easily the leading firm of Architects ... and have a very wide experience ... at the moment they are Architects to the new Rough Hills Church and Vicarage [i.e. St Martin's] ... I do not think you can do better.'[2]

Wolverhampton was expanding in the early twentieth century, merging with the towns of the Black Country to form the wider conurbation after the Great War. The population reached 133,190 in 1931 and 147,000 by 1942, with employment in mechanical engineering, commerce and finance, but dense urbanisation meant generally poor-quality housing and derelict land.[3] The provision of council housing was seen as one solution to these problems. St Martin's was first planned for the Cockshutts and Rough Hills area of collieries where few people lived, but by 1931 over 5000 council houses had been built in Wolverhampton, including the Rough Hills and Parkfields estates.[4] Built with a bequest from the Marson family of Tettenhall, St Martin's was a response to this housing expansion, and to the need to offer religious and social services to the workers and families on the estates.

A former slag heap with mine workings underneath, the site required a deep, reinforced-concrete foundation raft to bridge on to more stable clay at an additional cost of £1,500, some ten per cent of the construction budget. St Martin is stylistically similar to its contemporary 'sister' church of St Gabriel, Walsall. Brick-built and rectangular, both were described by Nikolaus Pevsner, in his final volume in the Buildings of England series, as 'impressively blocky'.[5] St Martin's was designed for a congregation of 515 people, including seating in the choir and chapel, and cost around £15,450 including fittings.[6] The broad face of the tower faces the road across a generous entrance court, formed by a pantile-covered brick cloister of three bays – to the south connecting with the vicarage, that comes forward to frame the space. These arches echo the broad, deep-set, round-headed, red-painted west

Fig.3 St Martin of Tours, cutaway (Aidan Ridyard)

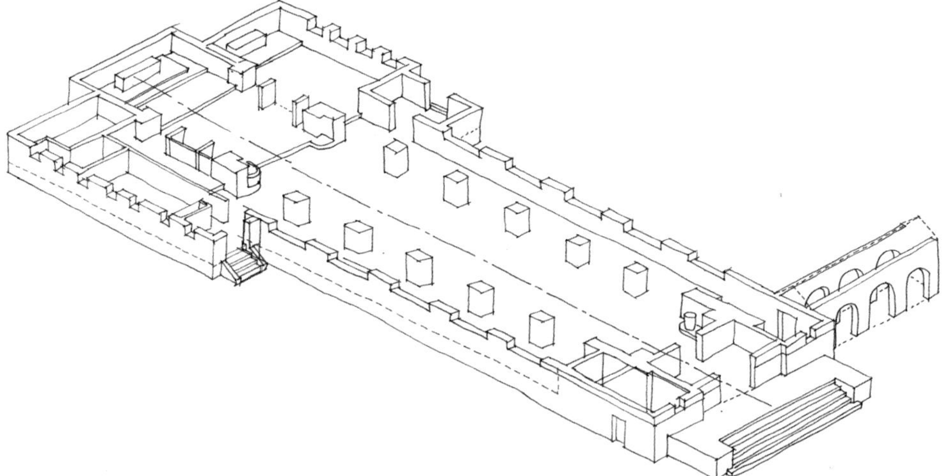

Fig.4 St Martin of Tours, nave looking east (John East)

door at the base of the massive rectangular tower whose neo-Romanesque feeling is probably owed to work by Dominikus Böhm.[7] It also quite closely resembles another St Martin's: the Garrison Church at New Delhi of 1931 by Edwin Lutyens's former assistant A. G. Shoosmith, especially in the stepped pyramid effect created by the low projections of the aisles to either side. Wide stone steps lead up to the main entrance. The plain wall between the doorway and the four tall round-arched bell louvres is set off by Donald Potter's three-ton solitary vertical stone figure of St Martin with his broken sword to striking effect.

Externally, the fortress-like design is continued on the north and south façades. There are six double, clear-glazed, narrow round-arched lights in steel frames on each side of the nave at clerestory level, a double set of rounded lights in the chancel taller than the nave windows, vestries to the north and a chapel to the south. A set of paired triple lights in the sanctuary provides the light that Twentyman regarded as an important 'material' in his churches, using deep reveals to conceal the source while flooding the space with light. As Le Corbusier wrote, 'architecture is the masterly, correct and magnificent play of masses brought together in light'.[8] None of the many arches inside or out has imposts, each forming a pure uninterrupted curve. The aisles have four-light brick mullioned windows. The east wall has a raised brick cross, a detail which would become a recurrent Twentyman feature.

The interior has a traditional layout with separation of the chancel from the nave with a step leading to oak choir stalls, and a plain round arch with rails and steps to the altar separating the chancel from the sanctuary. Colours, now quite vibrant, were originally muted.[9] The sanctuary ceiling was light pink on pale grey wood squares; the chancel and nave ceiling was grey with painted grey-blue beams on a north-south axis; nave walls were putty-coloured. One of the architectural features signalling a break from tradition and used also at St Gabriel, is the replacement of traditional aisles by passageways punctuated by six low rounded arches either side of the nave, an idea which evolves over time in later Twentyman churches. The narrow vestigial aisles create more space for a wider nave so that all can see the altar. Each arch originally had a suspended lamp orb above it, attached on the end of a projecting timber beam. The lamps have been replaced by clusters of three hanging lamps on each beam, although the originals remain in storage.

ST MARTIN, TWENTYMAN AND CHURCH ART

Apart from Potter's figure of St Martin, his first sculpture after leaving Eric Gill, he carved a tall, round, tub font at the south-west end in Clipsham stone with sculpted figures of celebratory saints and an elm cover surmounted by a remarkable figure of a cross-legged baby being held in a raised hand.[10] On the square-panelled, rounded oak pulpit, Potter carved an Agnus Dei, setting a patten for future architect-sculptor collaborations.

The issue of church decoration and furnishing has always been the subject of much debate and disagreement.[11] Peter Anson summarised the situation between 1920 and 1940:

> *Fashions were seldom stable or uniform. On the one hand there were imitation Gothic or Baroque altars, pulpits ... etc.; on the other streamlined furniture which would have looked equally at home in, say, ... the new Shakespeare Memorial Theatre at Stratford-on-Avon, or in any typical cinema.*[12]

Judging from his use of decoration and furnishing at St Martin and in his later churches, Twentyman would have been more in sympathy with Anson's second, more modernist categorisation, but still adopting a restrained approach. In the only writing by him that has been identified, Twentyman states his position:

> *Sculpture either inside or outside the building can help to humanize it, but sentimentality or slickness must at all costs be avoided ... very dramatic effects are out of place ... design should be simple; excessive austerity can be avoided by the use of pleasant materials, such as wood, and by the intelligent use of colour.*[13]

In common with many of his contemporaries, Twentyman believed in the notion of a *Gesamtkunstwerk*, and accordingly would often design his own wooden chairs, pews, pulpits, altars and altar rails so that his churches could present an internally consistent decorative style.

INFLUENCES

Pevsner's evaluation of St Martin exemplifies his concern for discrepancies of architectural progress through time as a mark of overall significance, commenting that '1939 is just a little late for all this; if it were 1933, it would be remarkable – at least in England'.[14] This supposed time-lag could be attributed to the provincial location both of the practice and the work, but there was little else of this date anywhere in the country to satisfy his criteria. St Martin was reviewed by the *Architect and Building News*, and R. J. McNally included both it and St Gabriel in his selection of *Fifty Modern Churches*, along with examples such as Cachemaille-Day's St Barnabas Tuffley, a similarly monumental building of 1939 with narrow elongated windows.[15] Edward Maufe's slim volume of European church architecture of 1948 traced earlier 1920s' developments in German and Swiss

Fig.5 St Martin of Tours, Lady chapel (John East)

expressionism and Nordic monumentalism which influenced British architects; Hugo Schlösser's Sankt Georgskirche (1929–30) in Stuttgart is a case in point.[16] In a letter written in 1979, Lawrence Israel acknowledged the debt owed by British architects of the time to north European architecture:

> *The 30s was a transitional period and architects were influenced by the Scandinavians and Dutch. The buildings which had a considerable impact were Dudok's Hilversum Town Hall in Holland, and in Stockholm Gunnar Asplund's Crematorium, Ragnar Östberg's Town Hall and Ivar Tengbom's Concert Hall.*[17]

James Thomas argues convincingly that the unusual design of Albi Cathedral (1282–1512), especially the use of narrow passages cut through internal buttress walls, resulting in a sheer surface to the exterior, influenced much nineteenth and twentieth-century church design. Maufe used the idea for Guildford Cathedral, the drawings for which were published in 1932, a project that might have influenced Twentyman in the design of St Martin's which, like Guildford, had 'pure cubic forms, unbroken straight lines, and a lack of decorative detail'.[18] Both allow for a clear view from the west to the east wall, and both architects arranged for shafts of light to fall obliquely onto the sanctuary from high windows. Twentyman's influences also included such well-known examples as Karl Moser's Church of St Anthony, Basle (1927) with its well-lit, spacious interior; Rudolf Schwarz's Corpus Christi, Aachen (1930), a minimalist box lit from high windows, and Fritz Höger's 1933 church on Hohenzollernplatz, Berlin with its internally buttressed nave bays pierced by passage aisles and tall windows. He would also have been aware of secular neo-classical buildings in Britain, such as Giles Gilbert Scott's Cambridge University Library (1931–40) and, more locally, Lyons and Israel's Wolverhampton Civic Hall of 1934.

Twentyman and his clients would have followed the arguments about church design prompted by changes in the liturgy in both Anglican and Roman Catholic denominations, set in motion by Pope Pius X in 1910, emphasising community involvement in services and greater interaction between celebrant and congregation.[19] At one extreme, writers such as Peter Hammond prioritised the activities taking place and the functions arising from them, referring to 'a craving for visual effect' in the more theatrical intentions of the previous generation of architects.[20] Maufe and others aimed for a more transcendental approach, since, as he wrote, 'the religious mind seeks the infinite ... there should be a certain mystery – there should be spaces in which the imagination can play'.[21] Hammond took an opposite view, criticising Maufe's views and writing in *Towards a Church Architecture* that 'we should be heading towards rather plain brick boxes with no tricks'.[22]

St Martin and Twentyman's later church designs provide a balanced response to these arguments. His ecclesiastical clients showed a preference for modern approaches without revolutionary design, while Twentyman was concerned with the functionality of liturgical spaces and also with the psychological and aesthetic effects of the space on congregations, as can be seen in his developing mastery of concealed lighting. There was no serious incompatibility in these aims.

ALL SAINTS DARLASTON

Fifteen years, including the Second World War, separate St Martin from All Saints, Darlaston. Both churches share common features, but All Saints signals an evolution from the neo-Romanesque to a more radical approach that Twentyman developed through the 1950s, to the extent that there has been speculation that at St Martin Twentyman was implementing the ideas of his architect partner Ernest Lavender, and that All Saints might therefore be his first wholly original church building.[23] Although, as a relatively new partner in the practice, Twentyman might have worked closely with Lavender on St Martin, he is given sole authorship in the list of churches compiled by his retired practice partner, John Hares.[24] Moreover, in the fifteen intervening years, even provincial England had developed a light, everyday form of modernism, with simpler structures supported on slender pillars, flat-roofed aisles and large areas of glazing, creating more space and light.

Twentyman was sympathetic to such developments, commenting that 'now we have a live, contemporary style, it would ... be unreasonable to use any past one'.[25] One of his postings during his war career in the Royal Engineers was in Palestine, where he may have seen and been influenced by the 'White City' of Tel Aviv, built from the 1930s onwards following Bauhaus ideals. In Britain, there was less concern that religious and secular buildings should be distinguished from one another, at least externally, supported by the comment from Hammond that 'there is no reason why the technology and materials of churches should be in any way different from normal building, in fact they have to be the same (the ideation of the

Fig.6 [following pages] All Saints, from the south-east (John East)

FRIENDS ENGINEERING
& FABRICATION

commonplace and so on)'.[26] This view was somewhat more ambiguously expressed by the Bishop of Salford that 'some of our modern churches might be mistaken for factories or swimming pools'.[27]

BACKGROUND TO CONSTRUCTION

All Saints, Darlaston, a Gothic Revival church by G. E. Street from 1871–2 containing stained glass by Burne-Jones, was destroyed by bombing on 31 July 1942. A replacement was required, and furthermore one that responded to the population expansion in the West Midlands. In the area of Darlaston served by All Saints, municipal housing went back to 1920 and 3,500 new council homes had been built by 1965, many to house those working in local firms, some involved in light engineering, others like GKN and Rubery Owen with an international reputation for heavy engineering. During the war, such firms were fully employed providing essential armaments including tanks, aircraft parts and shells.[28] The Atlas Works, owned by GKN, was spread over twenty acres and employed 3,000 people by the end of the war, while F. H. Lloyds had the largest foundry in Europe.

The Diocesan Bishop of Lichfield responsible for the Darlaston church, as well as the bishops of Birmingham and Coventry, realised that the growing population and housing expansion required a parallel community development in church and hall provision if the Anglican Church was to fulfil its social purpose, and if new residents were not to become totally secularised. Stretton Reeve, Bishop of Lichfield from 1953 to 1974, having raised £1 million in the late 1950s and early 1960s, launched a further seven-year 'Bishops Campaign' to raise another £1 million for funding new church construction in 1966; donors included local companies as well as the church commissioners, the diocese and parishioners. He justified these campaigns since there were now 'huge new housing estates ... [where] young married people with children were to be found in their thousands, and it was the prime duty of the Church to be where the people were'.[29] As early as August 1942, the church council had formed a restoration committee and made plans for the rebuilding of the church. It raised £10,000 towards the new church from local businesses and parishioners as well as the diocese, and received £28,320 from the War Damage Commission.

THE DESIGN OF ALL SAINTS

Twentyman's church, designed to seat over 300 people, was built directly over a crater fifty feet deep and forty feet across left by the bombing. Concrete piles were sunk twelve feet below floor level and, over the crater itself, they were sunk a further eight to twelve feet.[30] The reinforced concrete brick-faced structure has a curved barrel copper roof over the nave, providing maximum height for the size of the church. Externally on the south elevation, six small square-headed lancet windows mark the rhythm of the six internal nave bays. Above the lancets, the façade begins to dissolve into a grid of steel-framed windows between deep stone mullions, creating a much lighter aspect than St Martin. The south elevation is dominated by a row of eighteen tall windows each with six rectangular lights reaching to eaves level. The expanse of windows stretches from the south-west porch externally down the south elevation of the nave terminated by the projecting side of the bell tower. To the east of the tower the width of the vault narrows. Below the windows, the Lady Chapel projects southwards and eastwards beyond the east wall of the sanctuary with six small two-light windows on the upper wall and an apsidal east end. Here, Twentyman's usual Flemish garden wall bond quickens into a normal Flemish bond to cope with the curvature, as at the circular tool house at his Bushbury Crematorium opened in 1954. It has a domed copper roof topped by a mast and five-pointed star, another recurrent motif.

The north elevation has six bays, with a tall window in the first western bay only, and five two-light windows high on the walls of the remainder. The north wall of the sanctuary has five tall windows matching those on the south side. There is a large Latin cross in relief at the external east end of the church, a common Twentyman feature, and a circular window high up on the west end. The slender tower is constructed of two concrete planes faced in brickwork. It has a large opening high on its west and east sides in which two church bells are hung on show above each other. The tower differs from St Martin's keep-like structure, and functions more as a modernist landmark visually connected to its surrounding residential and commercial community.

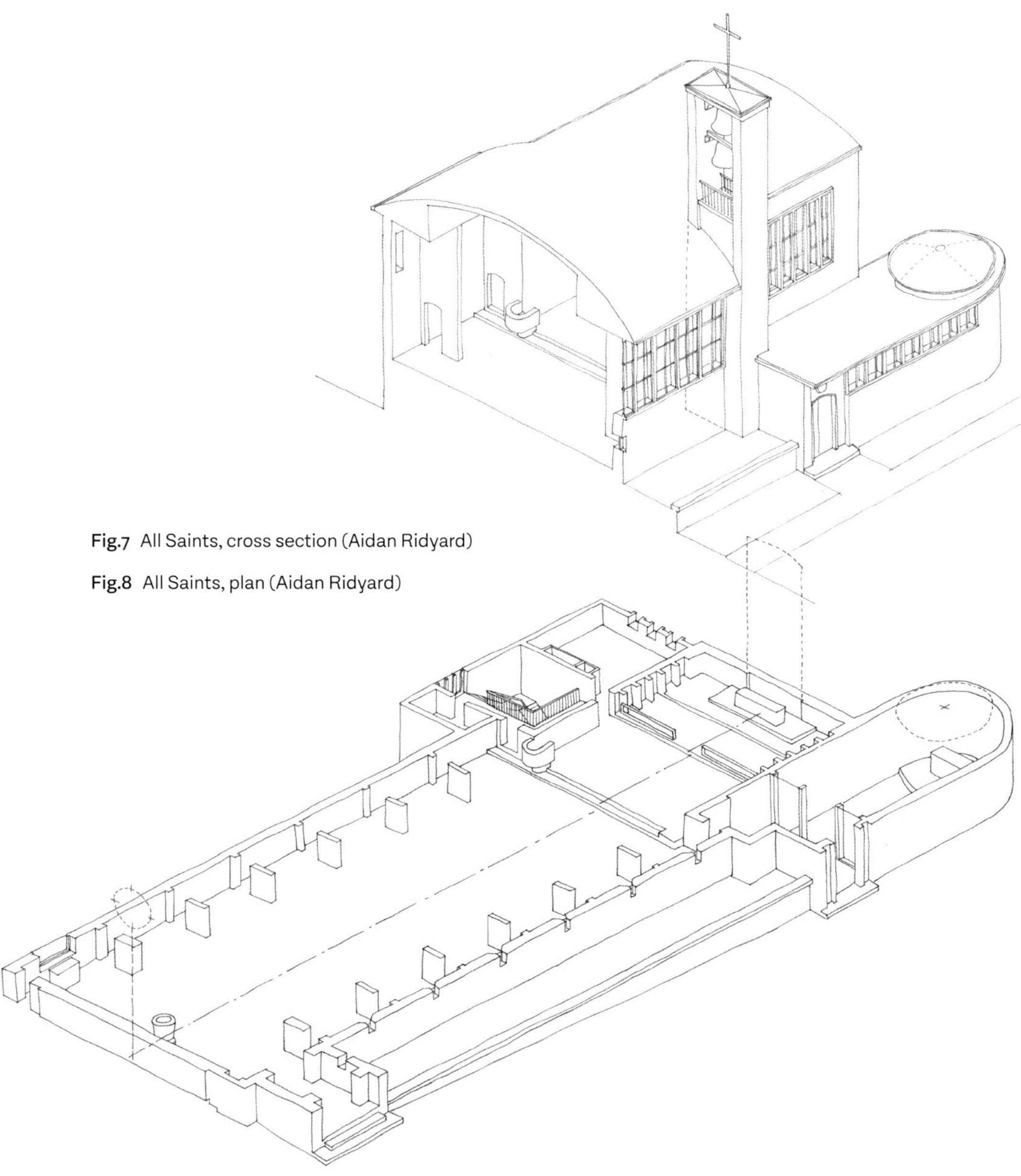

Fig.7 All Saints, cross section (Aidan Ridyard)

Fig.8 All Saints, plan (Aidan Ridyard)

Fig.9 All Saints, lectern by Don Potter (John East)

Fig.10 All Saints, chancel (John East)

There are two south entrances to the church, one main projecting porch on the south-west corner leading into the west end of the nave, the other providing an alternative entry into the Lady Chapel at a reduced level, reflecting the slight slope across the site west to east. The west porch consists of a rectangular double doorway with a segmental curved copper roof recalling the main curved roof. The wooden doors are fluted with round bronze door knobs set in circular plates, a signature Twentyman design. Framing the entrance, carved in situ out of the Portland stone surround, is another sculpture by Donald Potter – after St Martin his next commission from Twentyman. Three angels are sculpted either side of the portal, and the frieze above the door portrays the central figure of Christ with outstretched arms and the four evangelists.[31]

The interior view from the west end to the east at All Saints resembles that at St Martin in that the nave is divided from the choir by steps, and the choir from the

sanctuary by shallow steps and altar rails. The demarcation is less pronounced than at St Martin's with its chancel arch, for the nave is simply narrowed by the organ loft and tower to the north and south respectively; this enhances the effect of openness and space, and makes the high curved sanctuary ceiling visible from the nave. Full-length north and south windows illuminate the chancel with typically deep reveals masking the source of the light.

Unlike the transverse nave arcades at St Martin's, a series of concrete cross-wall partitions from floor to ceiling level act as internal north/south buttresses and define the six nave bays. They are pierced with low, slightly curved and wood-lined archways to form passage aisles that shield the congregation and celebrant from the glare of the large south windows, their softening effect like that of the deep concrete mullions in the north and south sanctuary windows.

The chapel altar with Alpha and Omega symbols on ribbed timber probably resembles the original high altar, which was moved from the east wall in 1974 so that the vicar could face the congregation and allowing the installation of the tapestry.[32] Twentyman developed this fluted style in all his subsequent churches. Running from west to east, the ribbed effect of the concrete nave ceiling emphasises the perspective and contrasts with the oak-faced plywood soffits of the aisle openings. In the choir, the curved coffered plaster ceiling was originally painted blue-grey, with a conscious display of veneered surfaces typical of the Festival era. The east wall is of polished travertine slabs, a tapestry now replacing the original dorsal hanging. Twentyman's church hall, opened in 1956, is accessed through a glazed link that separates it from the west front, creating an impressive street frontage nearly 230 feet (70m) long.

Don Potter created three further works at All Saints, all functional objects necessary for performance of the liturgy. Placed centrally at the west end, the font is made of a black granite incised with gilded lattice work and a sycamore cover with engraved fishes. The simple curved concrete pulpit with an unusual blue-green mosaic base has an Agnus Dei carved in a stone panel, similar to that in St Martin. The carved oak lectern is surmounted by an impressively stern eagle of St John the Evangelist. All four creations reflect Twentyman's view that any decoration should be used sparingly but purposefully and should avoid over-dramatic effects. The stained-glass panels at the west end were added in the 1960s, and the original blue-grey dorsal curtain hanging centrally at the east end was replaced in the 1970s by a tapestry, then the third largest in the country, designed by Stephen Lee and woven by parishioners over a two-year period. Don Potter also worked for Twentyman at Bushbury Crematorium, Wolverhampton (1954) and St Nicholas, Radford, Coventry (1954–5).

CONCLUSION

The two churches described here demonstrate how Twentyman moved from designing massive and defensive looking structures to more modern conceptions, emphasising lightness of structure and spatial openness, in both phases concerned with utilising the power of natural light. His architecture continued to evolve over the fifteen years following All Saints. As society changed and ecclesiastical demands changed with it, Twentyman adapted and developed a variety of churches ranging from the utilitarian simplicity of a small multi-purpose church like the Good Shepherd, Castlecroft (1955), to the imposing Emmanuel, Bentley (1955–7) and the austere St Andrew, Whitmore Reans (1965–7), whose interior reflects the demands of a more modern liturgy.

ACKNOWLEDGEMENTS

We would like to thank John East for his photographs. Line drawings are by Aidan Ridyard. Information supplied by clergy and parishioners was invaluable, as was that of those who knew the Twentyman family, or who are connected with Twentyman's patrons such as David Owen, son of Sir Alfred Owen, whose family funded the building of Emmanuel, Bentley Walsall. This article is intended as a forerunner to a book, *The Church Architecture of Richard Twentyman,* by Chris Kennedy and Aidan Ridyard, published by Forest of Arden Press in 2023.[33]

NOTES

1 Derek Mills, Rough Hills, Wolverhampton (Cirencester: Mereo Books, 2017), p.100.

2 Letter to Rev. Roach, Shrewsbury, 21 October 1938, P253/K/1/11, Shropshire Archives.

3 Peter Larkham, 'Rebuilding the Industrial Town: Wolverhampton', *Urban History*, vol.29, no.3, 2002, p.392.

4 Mills, op. cit., p.197.

5 Nikolaus Pevsner, The Buildings of England, *Staffordshire* (Harmondsworth: Penguin, 1975), p.322.

6 R. J. McNally, *Fifty Modern Churches* (London: Incorporated Church Building Society, 1947), p.30.

7 Böhm's church of Christ König (1928), Leverkusen-Küppersteg, near Cologne, Germany, could be the model.

8 Le Corbusier, translated by Frederick Etchells, Towards a New Architecture (London: John Rodker, 1927), p.29.

9 *Architect and Building News*, vol.162, 18 August 1939, pp.181–4.

10 Vivienne Light, *Don Potter: an Inspiring Century* (Brook, Hampshire: Canterton Books, 2002), p.160.

11 Alan Powers, 'Art and Artefacts', in S. Charlton, E. Harwood and C. Price, eds., *100 Churches, 100 Years* (London: Batsford, 2019), pp.157–61.

12 Peter Anson, *Fashions in Church Furnishings* (London: Faith Press, 1960), p.339.

13 Richard Twentyman, 'The Design and Layout of Crematoria', in *Royal Sanitary Institute Journal*, vol.75, July 1955, pp.504–5.

14 Pevsner, op. cit., p.332.

15 McNally op. cit., pp.46–8, 118–19.

16 Edward Maufe, *Modern Church Architecture* (London: Incorporated Church Building Society, 1948), pp.30–1.

17 Lawrence Israel, letter about Wolverhampton Civic Centre, 1979, http://www.yourwolvescivic.co.uk/history/plans-and-drawings.html, accessed 3 December 2020.

18 James Thomas, *Albi Cathedral and British Church Architecture* (London: Ecclesiological Society, 2002), p.30.

19 Elain Harwood, 'Liturgy and Architecture', Twentieth Century Architecture, no.3, *The Twentieth Century Church*, 1998, pp.49–74.

20 Peter Hammond, *Towards a Church Architecture* (London: Architectural Press, 1962), p.28.

21 Maufe, op. cit., p.6.

22 Hammond, op. cit., p.10.

23 From a conversation with Ernest Lavender's daughter reported by Father Tony Hutchinson of St Martin.

24 John Hares, letter to RIBA Librarian, 25 November 1994, in 'Alfred Richard Twentyman', biography file, RIBA Library and Archives.

25 Twentyman, op. cit., p.504.

26 Hammond, op. cit., p.10.

27 Robert Proctor, *Building the Modern Church* (Farnham: Ashgate, 2014), p.69.

28 Billy Parker, 'A History of Darlaston: The inter-war years', http://www.historywebsite.co.uk/articles/Darlaston/interwar.htm, accessed 20 November 2020.

29 Uttoxeter Advertiser, 18 May 1966, B/A/26/11/2/2, Stafford Record Office.

30 'All Saints Church, Darlaston', *Architect and Building News*, vol.203, 12 February 1953, pp.193–8.

31 Light, op. cit., p.162.

32 Aidan Ridyard, personal communication.

33 Details at www.RichardTwentyman.com.

ELAIN HARWOOD

7 The Churches of Robert Potter and Richard Hare

Fig.1 All Saints, Clifton, Bristol, 1963–7, with Perspex windows by John Piper (all photos Elain Harwood)

Robert Potter (1909–2010) had a long and varied career, centred on Salisbury and later Hampshire. It can be compared with that of George Pace, a near-contemporary and fellow churchman who similarly combined new churches with restoration work; Potter's wide-ranging portfolio included Oxford's Bodleian Library as well as many churches and Salisbury, Chichester and St Paul's cathedrals. He wrote extensively on the monitoring of cracks and movement at St Paul's using pioneering electronic technology, and in the 1970s he became an expert in digging out and underpinning undercrofts to make parish facilities, for example at All Soul's, Langham Place and St Nicholas Sevenoaks.[1] From his restoration work, which he regarded as his most important contribution to architecture, it is possible to identify two key features of his new churches, a real understanding of structure and a passion for fine art. He worked closely with the artists Geoffrey Clarke and John Piper, and with the Southampton-based engineer Edwin W. H. Gifford (1921–2014), who pioneered the use of pre-stressing for concrete structures in Britain and contributed dynamic roof structures to Potter's most interesting churches (while his practice prospered producing bridges and hovercraft). These churches are significant, too, for bringing the celebrant and congregation closer together some years ahead of Peter Hammond's call-to-arms of 1960, *Liturgy and Architecture*.

Robert James Potter was born in Guildford, where his father Jack engraved printing blocks for the Bank of England. After schooling at the local technical college, he enrolled at the Regent Street Polytechnic while also serving articles with the church architect William Henry Randoll Blacking (1889–1958), who in late 1928 or 1929 moved from Guildford to Salisbury.[2] Potter followed in his footsteps, and he too settled in Salisbury (marrying in 1935) before opening a Southampton office in 1960. Blacking had served articles with Ninian Comper before launching an independent career working for the Warham Guild established by Percy Dearmer to produce vestments and church furnishings. He went on to become a successful designer of modest, spare yet quietly elegant churches in the 1930s, many for Anglo-Catholic parishes in the dioceses of Chichester and Salisbury where he was also the cathedral architect. He paid careful attention to fittings and the position of the altar, preferring an English altar complete with riddel posts; where possible he also installed a chancel screen, usually of classical design, and Comper's influence is also evident in his selective use of colour as a highlight. At St Albans Cathedral, he refurnished St Michael's Chapel in 1927 and introduced a ciborium. In a pamphlet issued by the Incorporated Church Building Society in the late 1930s, Blacking wrote that 'A church is the simplest of buildings; it is the House of God, where He is to be worshipped, and where the two sacraments of the Prayer Book rite are to be administered and the ministry of the Word spoken; the essentials are, therefore, a

Fig.2 St Francis, Ashton Gate, Bristol, 1952–3

Fig.3 St Francis, Salisbury, 1939, remodelled in 2017–18, the apse is the least altered part

Holy Table (which should be the focal point of the place), a Font, and accommodation for the ministers and worshippers: all other considerations are of secondary importance.'[3] Here was Potter's starting point.

While he acclaimed Blacking as a great draftsman who had introduced new standards to the repair of churches, Potter was proudest of his lineal descent from Ninian Comper. The single greatest influence on his work was St Philip, Cosham, built rapidly in 1935–7 and Comper's most succinct distillation of Greek and Gothic sources into what he termed 'unity by inclusion'. Detailed research had convinced Comper that the fourth-century church layout, with the altar 'in the midst of the worshippers, and not separated from them by a choir but only by a very open screen, or merely by low *cancelli*', was far more suited to modern secular worship than the accepted plan of nave and chancel.[4] St Philip's modest four-bay interior, with its ciborium, rear choir gallery and carefully focussed use of gilding and bright colour, offered a perfect model for architects working with limited budgets after 1945.

First for Potter, however, came a more modest commission. His first church was St Leonard, Redfield, Bristol, won in competition in 1937 and completed in 1939 to supersede an earlier church built in 1907 by W. V. Gough, which became the church hall. It is a vestigially Gothic building, only a little larger than Gough's, rendered and with a four-bay nave and chancel abutted by a single aisle, and became the Coptic Orthodox Church of St Marina in 2014. His next church, St Francis, Salisbury, in 1939 enabled him to briefly form his own practice. A substantial building on a prominent rising site in the city's northern suburbs, its exterior suggests the influence of Willem Dudok in its brick details and (albeit somewhat stumpy) tower, while the attenuated nave windows follow the style made fashionable by Ragnar Östberg. The interior is reminiscent of N. F. Cachemaille-Day's St Nicholas, Burnage, in the Art Deco treatment of its flat ceiling and the prominent Lady chapel raised high in the apsed east end behind the altar. Potter spent the Second World War serving with the Royal Engineers in India, rising to the rank of lieutenant-colonel, and the church was only fully completed at its end. It survived well until 2017–18, when it was transformed by a large side addition and stripped of most of its internal fittings.

Returning to England in 1946, Potter asked Blacking to make him a partner. Both had the promise of new churches in Bristol: Potter's commission for St Francis of Assisi, Ashton Gate, was the first built in the city after the war, but Blacking's reconstruction of All Saints, Clifton, was thwarted by a legal battle. St Francis, Ashton Gate, had been a large rectangular brick church of 1886–7 by John Bevan with a single (north) aisle before suffering irreparable damage in air raids of December 1940 and April 1941. Potter reused the foundations of the old nave and aisle, but his rebuilding of 1952–3 adopted a more delicate pale-yellow brick with Bath stone dressings on a concrete frame, the main doorway eccentrically splayed, taking its shape from a tapered tower intended to rise above it which was never realised.[5] He also made the west window slightly curved to make a baptistery, a space enlarged by setting the choir gallery slightly forward of the west end, which – so Potter insisted – encouraged more sound from the choir to percolate downwards and became a feature in subsequent churches.[6] The aisle is low but highly glazed, and the east window has glass by Christopher Webb, who had also served articles with Comper and was one of Blacking's closest friends.[7]

Meanwhile, in 1953 Potter formed a partnership with Richard Hare (1924–89), educated at Westminster School and the Bartlett School of Architecture. They designed schools, a car showroom and many office buildings in the Salisbury area, student accommodation at Southampton University including a seventeen-storey tower block connected to South Stoneham House, and large commissions for the Ministry of Defence in addition to church and conservation work. Hare assumed responsibility for Salisbury Cathedral Close and a range of sacred and secular commissions, until retiring in 1975 to devote himself to the study of conservation philosophies and methods across Europe. Their first church collaborations were small. St Matthew, Bridgemary, was built in 1955 to serve a housing estate on the outskirts of Gosport after a town centre church to that dedication was demolished. Its main feature is an angled east window of timber, partly boarded on the interior. It was followed by a slightly more ambitious church for the Diocese of Salisbury,

Fig.4 All Saints, Ulwell, Swanage, 1956–7. The (liturgical) north side has been extended

All Saints, Ulwell, near Swanage, built in 1956–7 to replace a wooden hut that had begun life as a recreation centre for troops stationed in the village. The east end again has a slight prow, but this time only with a small lozenge or vesica-shaped window. Inside, precast parabolic arches with a fine granular finish define narrow aisles (and a large north extension) then die into the high roof.

More important commissions followed Blacking's retirement and death. Potter succeeded him as architect to Chichester Cathedral in 1957 at the request of Dean Walter Hussey, with whom he worked first on the refurbishment of the Chapel of St Mary Magdalen in 1957–61. His new altar provided a setting for Graham Sutherland's radiant painting, *Noli Me Tangere*, while Geoffrey Clarke designed the altar rails and candlesticks. Potter then enacted Blacking's proposals for the reinstatement of the so-called Arundel Screen, actually a medieval pulpitum which had closed the west of the choir until 1860; in the restoration he opened up its three arches to create long views between the nave and choir, where in 1966–7 he installed a new high altar backed with tapestries designed by John Piper, brought in to the project during 1964.[8]

Potter's first major new work was the Church of the Ascension, Crownhill, Plymouth, in 1956, described by Peter Hammond as 'one of the most satisfactory buildings for liturgy completed in this country since the war'.[9] The first housing appeared at Crownhill in the 1930s, though Abercrombie and Paton Watson

Fig.5 Ascension, Crownhill, Plymouth, 1956–8

Fig.6 Ascension, Crownhill, interior with glass at the east end by Geoffrey Clarke

commented in 1943 that the suburb 'does not appear to have formed a community, due, no doubt, to the overwhelming influence of the service population' at nearby Manadon.[10] The church had a complicated gestation out of a tiny chapel of ease from 1842, Holy Trinity, which was replaced by the hall church of St Christopher's in 1939, whence services moved to St Alban's Garrison Church in 1951.[11] It was largely paid for by war damage settlements from the bombed-out St George, Stonehouse, and inherited its white-painted pews from St Catharine's Church in Lockyer Street, an organ from St Mary the Virgin and St Mary Magdalene at Cattedown and a bell from Widley Court. The site was gifted by the St Aubyn Estate, and was still surrounded by fields when the foundation stone was laid in May 1956.

Potter revised his design in August and November, the principal change being to the top of the tower, where the first drawings showed a band of glazing under a shallow coolie-hat top. He was quick to acknowledge the debt to St Philip's Cosham in setting a freestanding altar under a ciborium, from which the priest faced the congregation from the first. There was again a choir gallery with a font in the gap between it and the west end. In the absence of an altar against the east wall, Potter introduced small hexagonal windows of stained glass. Coventry was being built and he was excited to meet Epstein, then working on the top half of his sculpture of St Michael – the whole thing being too big for his studio. He commissioned twelve windows depicting the apostles, with Christ in the middle, but Epstein produced only one design 'and some bits' before his death.[12] Potter then turned to Geoffrey Clarke, with whom he had established a rapport at Chichester.

Work was set to start in January 1957 and again in March, amid rising inflation; after two builders went bankrupt over the foundations Potter took on the second

Fig.7 St George, Oakdale, built in 1959–60

set of men as a direct labour force. The church was dedicated on 6 December 1958, the first by Potter and Hare to be engineered by Gifford & Partners. The plan is a four-bay nave with a raised altar under a ciborium designed by Robert Medley set between narrow transepts, and a small space to the liturgical east end (actually north-east), shown as a Lady chapel on plans but not used as such. Vestries and a boiler room were tucked out of site to the north-west. The concrete structure was faced externally in green-tinted Buckfast Abbey stone and Tyrolean render, with Delabole slate roofs and, internally, slim columns faced in polished grey stone and a shallow-vaulted timber ceiling in the style of Coventry Cathedral, physically light though coloured a dark red. Potter & Hare added the large vicarage to the north-east later in 1958. The St Aubyn estate went on to build houses and flats close to the church in 1963–5, in return paying for a church hall designed by John Taylor of Truro on the site of the original car park.[13]

Potter and Hare were commissioned by the Salisbury diocese in 1955 to design St George, Oakdale, a fast-growing suburb of Poole. They took over a project originally to have been funded by the Mothers' Union, who required that there should be a Lady chapel. Two early sets of proposals survive at the church, the first from

September 1955 straight-sided with a conventional east end and a Lady chapel at the end of the south aisle. The elevation shows offices behind the east end and an angled, rather Scandinavian tower over the porch, both elements as intended at St Francis, Ashton Gate. The second scheme, undated, anticipates the final version of March 1958 in having a central raised altar and a Lady chapel to the east, with extra banks of seats to north and south made possible by angling the side walls of the nave to form what Potter described as a 'boat shape', so that the church is broadest in the middle. A fleche over the altar was never realised. Hammond published a plan showing the Lady chapel in the south transepts, but this revision seems never to have been adopted, and it has always been at the east end, which was remodelled in 2010 by Sophie Hacker, who also designed the frontal for the main altar.

The top of the tower was also a little more conventional as built than the jaunty trilby design shown in the undated scheme. Stairs in the tower lead to the gallery, again set forward to allow light from the staircase window on to the large font just inside the main door. The six bells were added in 1985. Most impressive are the nave columns, again finished in green aggregate above a narrow flash gap, and the shallow angles of Gifford's timber roof, again reminiscent of the vault of Coventry Cathedral. There are close similarities with Ascension, Crownhill, but the emphasis is on space and light rather than artworks, with the practice designing all the furniture (in afrormosia wood); Potter designed the candlesticks and other fittings were by his assistant, later associate partner, Donald Hargreaves. A large church hall, meeting room, kitchen and offices were added to the north-west in 1965 by Morley & Bolton of Parkstone on a footprint determined earlier by Potter & Hare.[14]

A crematorium and chapel at Taunton was one of the first and most picturesque in a wave of crematoria built by local authorities between the mid-1950s and late-1960s. Potter & Hare won second place in a competition but nevertheless secured the commission to work with the landscape architect Peter Youngman. The landscape has been altered but the main chapel and a near-circular gazebo housing the book of remembrance, built in 1961–3 and connected by a porte cochère, survive well. Potter visited crematoria in Britain and Europe before submitting his design. The two buildings are faced in random pieces of lias and sandstone, quarried locally, with copper roofs. The chapel dominates the view from the entrance at the foot of the steeply sloping site to the north. Largely rectangular, it is fully glazed on its long west side, while long, narrow slits in the stone north wall are inset with glass by Geoffrey Clarke, who also designed the altar fittings. A folded plate roof is expressed internally by a slatted timber ceiling. The chapel is full of light, but the glazed wall gives on to a grassy courtyard with only narrow gaps in a north wall which provides privacy for the mourners. The crematory, offices and waiting areas are set low against the hillside to the south.[15]

St Mary Magdalene, Peckham, was a rebuilding in 1961–2 of Robert Palmer Browne's church of 1839–41, destroyed in 1940. Hare led this project, where in the absence of ornament the dominant features were Gifford's tall roof structure, clad in copper, and four entirely glazed ends to the cruciform plan. The organ, choir and clergy stalls were in the eastern arm and the congregation filled the other three sides round the central altar. A similar fleche to that designed at Oakdale was set over this crossing point. The building was simple, yet the geometry of the soaring roof was uplifting; however, the congregation saw only its leaks and campaigned vigorously for its demolition and replacement in 2010–11 by a modest brick structure of no interest. A much smaller cruciform church, of laminated timber,

Fig.8 [following pages] Taunton Deane Crematorium, built in 1961–3, with glass by Geoffrey Clarke

was built as Our Lady Queen of Heaven, Durrington, Wiltshire, in 1960, again with Gifford as the engineer. It was closed by the Roman Catholic Church in 2003 and is now a workshop.[16] Hare also designed a new chapel and study hall for the Roman Catholic St Anthony's School, Leweston, Dorset, built in 1968–70 in the grounds of a late Georgian house close to the seventeenth-century Holy Trinity Church. The study hall is pentagonal, as is the chapel above it, but this is turned through some fifty degrees to form a star-shaped plan with a tall central belfry.[17]

Fig.9 St Aldate, Gloucester, 1962–4

Potter's greatest collaboration with Edwin Gifford was at St Aldate, Gloucester, the rebuilding in the suburbs of an eighteenth-century city church which itself had replaced a Saxon foundation. The old church had been demolished in 1927 and Randoll Blacking had built a vicarage at the new site, but it was only in 1958 that the new parish determined on a permanent building, following a bequest; a temporary timber structure became the church hall. Potter was approached on the advice of the Diocesan Board of Finance, and the parochial church council studied photographs of his earlier churches before confirming his appointment. The earliest plans show a larger and more regular, geometrical design, but then Gifford suggested the use of a timber hyperbolic paraboloid or 'hypar' structure to give it what Potter termed 'thrust', which was then developed in conjunction with the Faculty of Engineering at Southampton University.[18]

The vicar, Donald F. Matthews, was an enthusiast for the new liturgy and welcomed the design. A sharply angled double entrance under a west choir gallery leads to a fan-shaped auditorium with a slightly raked floor. The simple altar is set on a single step forward of a curved white wall, with the congregation occupying two angled banks of seating. There are chapels to either side (now screened off) below large clear-glazed windows and vestries behind the east end. The font, set between the seating, came from the old church but was heavily retooled and given a new base. Potter sought to use a wide palate of materials inside the church, notably slate under the windows, but the congregation requested Iroko hardwood and clear glazing, producing a more austere interior than he had wished. The exterior is, by contrast, uncompromising in its bravado, and a model was a highlight of an exhibition by the Central Council for the Care of Churches in 1963. The impact of the hypar roof is enforced by the needle-like concrete spirelet over the west doors. The final design was completed by Easter 1961, the Bishop of Tewkesbury laid the foundation stone in May 1962 and the Bishop of Gloucester consecrated the completed church in June 1964.[19]

All Saints, Clifton, was one of the pioneering churches of High Anglicanism, built in phases by G. E. Street in 1866–72 and celebrated for its choral music. The church was orientated north-south, to which G. F. Bodley designed a narthex, completed posthumously in 1909, and in 1928 F. C. Eden erected a large vestry at the other end. He also completed Street's stump of a tower over the central entrance by adding an exuberant pepper pot. The body of the church was burned out by incendiaries in December 1940, but the narthex and sacristy survived remarkably little touched. Randoll Blacking was commissioned as early as 1943, and in 1952 erected a ciborium in the nearby parish hall where services were being held. Then in 1953, in a zealous programme of church closures, the Bishop of Bristol, Dr Frederic Cockin, proposed that the benefice be merged with those of Emmanuel, Clifton, and St Mary, Tyndall's Park, so that the substantial sum expected from the War Damage Commission could be used to build new churches in the suburbs. It was particularly insensitive to suggest a merger with Emmanuel, an evangelical church built in

Fig.10 All Saints, Clifton, with Randoll Blacking's ciborium (1952) and organ by J. W. Walker and Sons, Ltd (1967)

rivalry to All Saints. Both parishes resisted, All Saints arguing that it attracted Anglo-Catholics from long distances and had already raised £30,000 towards its rebuilding. The situation came to a head in 1959 when the diocese applied to demolish the church, leading the parish priest, Father Albert H. Luetchford, to submit Randoll Blacking's restoration scheme to the city council's Planning and Public Works Committee as an alternative. The council refused to make a decision while a spirited elderly parishioner, (Ella) Madeline Hodgson, appealed to the Privy Council for All Saints' rebuilding. On a second appeal by Hodgson and the parish in 1961, it ruled that the diocese had not heeded the congregation's wishes nor paid sufficient respect to the different traditions and characteristics of All Saints and Emmanuel.[20]

At last, All Saints could be rebuilt. Blacking's scheme, presented in 1947, had retained as much of the old fabric as possible. He died in 1958, to be succeeded by Potter, who found that the old walls had become unstable. While new liturgical thinking suggested a less regular plan, his first proposals in 1962 nevertheless followed the old footprint, dominated by an angled east end featuring a great mullioned window on the corner of Alma Vale Road and a new lantern for Street's tower. The nave was, however, shortened, with a courtyard between a fully glazed west end and Bodley's narthex.[21] Over the next year, Potter produced a new scheme within the fixed points of the surviving narthex, sacristy and tower. Courtyard and church changed places with the latter set at right angles, so it was at last correctly orientated, with a gallery along the long south side. On the north, the narthex was restored as a chapel to St Richard of Chichester, where Christopher Webb designed a new east window, the last before his death, partly paid for by a legacy from Madeline Hodgson and featuring the figure of Fr Luetchford holding a model of the new church.

The foundation stone was laid in November 1963 but building only began in earnest a year later. The new church, faced in rubblestone but clearly of concrete construction, was consecrated in July 1967.[22] Again a dominant feature was a full-height mullion window, now facing Pembroke Road and cranked to form the baptistery, with next to it an entrance under the tower leading to a clear-glazed cloister that links Eden's sacristy and new offices to the south. To the north, the dominant feature of the church is the high altar of polished Portland stone set forward under Blacking's ciborium, with an aumbry of silver and lapis lazuli by Eden. The south gallery doubles as a Lady chapel, its altar the only survivor of four in the old church. Edwin Gifford's roof of canted slabs determines the shape of four brilliantly coloured windows by John Piper, brought in at Potter's suggestion in September 1962 just as his baptistery window at Coventry Cathedral had been completed and ahead of their collaboration at Chichester. Potter suggested the themes, the baptistry with windows to the River and Tree of Life from the Book of Revelation and the Lady chapel window based on the first lines of Genesis, but it was Piper who determined on fibreglass and resin to achieve a painterly effect without leads.

Potter & Hare's later churches were more modest. In 1950 Potter had remodelled St Mary, Rowner, to serve a new estate built as part of Gosport's ambitious housing programme, restoring the twelfth-century chancel (which had been reduced to a vestry following the building of a new chancel in additions of 1874) as a Lady chapel with glass by Hugh Eaton. He returned in 1965–8 to rebuild the 1874 nave, which was rebuilt again by the Sarum Partnership following a fire in 1992. In 1968, Potter & Hare joined forces with Sutcliffe Brandt & Partners, another Southampton practice, led by Jack Brandt (1908–92), becoming the Brandt Potter Hare Partnership, later Brandt Potter & Partners. Other late works included Guildford Baptist Church, Millmead, built in 1972 and largely remodelled in 2014; and St Andrew's, Goldsworth Park, Woking, an evangelical church centre consecrated in 1988. Potter also made large additions in 1989 to Randoll Blacking's Roman Catholic church of St Edward, Chandler's Ford, built in 1938 and for which he had been the assistant for some of the working drawings. He reoriented the church through ninety degrees and demolished most of the north wall to make a broad church seating 350 people with a new sanctuary, once again with a prominent prow. This features stained glass by David Wasley, while statues by Christopher Webb and the original reredos by Harry Stammers were resited.[23] Potter himself settled in Chandler's Ford with his second wife, continuing to advise on restoration works into his 80s and living to the great age of 101.

NOTES

1 *Monumentum*, vol.25, no.3, September 1992, pp.215–27; *Building*, vol.232, 28 January 1977, pp.55–61; *Arup Journal*, vol.31, March 1996, pp.20–2.

2 Much of this article is based on an interview with Robert Potter at his home in Chandlers Ford in August 1996.

3 W. H. Randoll Blacking, *The Arrangement and Furnishing of a Church*, London, Incorporated Church Building Society, *c.*1938, p.1.

4 J. N. Comper, *Of the Atmosphere of a Church* (London: Sheldon Press, 1947), p.21

5 *The Builder*, vol.187, 23 July 1954, pp.127–33.

6 Robert Potter in conversation, 6 August 1996.

7 *The Builder*, vol.187, 23 July 1954, pp.127–33.

8 Hussey 5/2/6/3/160 and 165, West Sussex Archives.

9 Peter Hammond, *Liturgy and Architecture* (London: Barrie and Rockliff, 1960), p.118.

10 J. Paton Watson and Patrick Abercrombie, *A Plan for Plymouth* (Plymouth: Underhill, 1943), p.84.

11 *Western Morning News*, 7 December 1950, p.5

12 Robert Potter in conversation, 6 August 1996.

13 Plans 20228/1–5; *Plymouth Herald*, 10 January 1957, Press Cuttings Book 15; *Morning News*, 8 June 1966, Press Cuttings Book 33; Plymouth Archives, The Box.

14 Plans and information held at the church, visited January 2022.

15 Robert Potter in conversation, 6 August 1996; *The Builder*, vol.205, 8 November 1963, pp.937–41.

16 *Wood*, vol.26, June 1962, pp.228–9

17 *Architect and Building News*, vol.7, 5 November 1970, pp.36–8.

18 Robert Potter in conversation, 6 August 1996.

19 *Architectural Review*, vol.131, January 1962, pp.30–1; plans and information held at the church, visited January 1999.

20 P.ASC/PM/7, P.ASC/HM/4, Bristol Archives; All Saints' Archives; Peter Cobb, *The Rebuilding of All Saints, Clifton* (Bristol: 1992); John Hudson, *All Saints for All People, 150 years of All Saints, Clifton* (Bristol: Redcliffe, 2018).

21 *Bristol Evening Post*, 4 October 1962, p.27, with many thanks to Wendy Mortimer, All Saints' parish office manager.

22 *Concrete Quarterly*, no.77, April-June 1968, pp.5–6.

23 *Church Building*, no.15, Summer 1990, pp.30–4.

ROBERT DRAKE

9 Thomas Ford and Hans Feibusch: A Unique Collaboration

Fig.1 St Michael and All Angels, Harrow Weald, Thomas Ford, 1958, featuring Hans Feibusch's mural of the Adoration of the Cross (Elain Harwood)

The architect Thomas F. Ford (1891–1971) and the painter Hans Feibusch (1898–1998) collaborated on over a dozen new churches, mostly in the Diocese of Southwark, for which Ford was surveyor. The result is probably the largest body of mural decoration in the Church of England from the 1950s and 1960s. While Feibusch is relatively well known, Ford – like the majority of non-modern architects of his period – is not.

Ford founded his practice in 1926, specialising in church work and influenced by the English Regency and Sir John Soane. He was initially in practice with William Harkess, then was joined post-war in the practice by his sons John and Alan, and son-in-law Harold Cooper. They all became partners in 1964 when the practice known as Thomas Ford & Partners came into being. Ford's grandson Jim Cooper (Harold's son) was also an architect but did not join the practice, which has nonetheless continued up to the present with a specialism in conservation. In addition to a prolific architectural career, Ford collaborated with his brother Ralph on a revision of the King James Bible, published in 1948.

After attending Bedford Modern School and farm working during the First World War, Thomas Ford spent three years at the Royal Academy School of Architecture. He showed early talent as an architect, winning the Ashpitel Prize in 1919 for achieving the highest marks in the final RIBA examinations before working for W. A. Forsyth and setting up his own practice with William Harkess in 1926. He built cinemas – mainly for the Union chain at Maidenhead and in Hampshire – as well as private houses. However, Ford soon began to specialise in churches, beginning with St Michael the Archangel, East Wickham, Kent, built in 1932–3 beside a small medieval church which had become hopelessly small following the huge growth of housing in the area between Woolwich, Plumstead and Bexleyheath. Although built for a fairly modest sum of £10,000, Ford's church is spacious if sparsely decorated. It has a starkness and severity unlike the neo-Regency typical of Ford's post-war churches.

Ford and Harkess were involved before 1939 in various adaptations and repairs to historic churches in the outer London suburbs. His other new churches in the 1930s, several commissioned through Bishop Garbett of Southwark's 'Twenty-Five Churches Fund', consisted of dual churches and halls, built with the hope that a proper church could be constructed later. Owing to the war, a group consisting of St Mary the Virgin, Welling; St Peter Bexleyheath; St James, Merton Park and, in the Diocese of London, St Michael and All Angels, Harrow Weald, were delayed until the late 1950s. A major process began in 1945 of deciding which Anglican churches could or should be restored because of their historic significance. Others needed replacement, while population decline and displacement made some redundant.

New churches were also needed, in areas of population growth or insufficient existing provision.

The Ford-Feibusch collaboration began at St John the Evangelist, Waterloo Road, Lambeth, designated as the 'Festival church' opened by Princess Elizabeth in April 1951. There was pressure for the Festival of Britain to include some religious content, and Francis Bedford's 1824 church, close to the South Bank site and visible from two of its entrance gates, answered the need. During the Festival, St John's hosted several Christian denominations, unusually including the Free churches. This severe Greek Revival 'Waterloo Church' provided upper seating galleries on three sides, while in 1928 Sir Ninian Comper placed a large Corinthian ciborium over the altar, all of which were lost in the bombing. Ford replaced the west gallery, but the side galleries and ciborium were omitted on grounds of cost. The colouring and decoration were a mixture of replacements of the original features with a novel variation on Regency classical themes.[1] An unusual feature of the reconstruction was the provision of a matching pair of pulpit and lectern, on a Georgian 'two-decker' model with testers, forming what was known as an 'Anglican Ambo', intended to frame the view towards the altar in place of the lost side galleries.[2] This appreciation of the Regency was very much part of architectural thought in the 1940s, considered 'perfectly mannered architecture'. In 1948, Paul Reilly contributed a slim volume on Regency architecture to a series of books edited by Hugh Casson, well on cue for the creation of the Festival Church.[3]

For Thomas Ford, the Regency provided an appropriate template for rebuilding churches in South London, and while fashionable among interior decorators, it had not been used for churches before. With modest brick exteriors, his designs are largely traditional in layout although sanctuary and nave are brought closer together. Ford's churches in the two decades following St John's have well-lit

Fig.2 St John the Evangelist, Lambeth (the Festival Church), restored 1951 by Thomas Ford with murals of the Crucifixion and Adoration of the Shepherds (above altar) by Hans Feibusch (John East)

interiors, with shallow curved ceilings, vaults and arches providing a constant theme. If the church was replacing one that had been bombed, the War Damage Commission was willing to commute the cost of replacing glass into a fee for a mural painting, chiming with a feeling at the time that an east window might dazzle the worshippers on a bright morning.

As for the specific influence of Sir John Soane, which can be detected in Ford's spatial compositions as well as in his 'primitive' incised detailing, a clue may lie in a lecture, 'Soane: the case-history of a personal style' given by John Summerson at the Royal Institute of British Architects in December 1950 and published the following month in the *RIBA Journal*. The opening image was of the Bank Stock Office of 1792, to which Summerson drew attention, discussing at length the possible origins of this smooth-surfaced exercise in volume and 'the *lumière mystérieuse* of certain French churches which Soane mentions approvingly in his lectures'.[4] Ford would certainly have received this journal and read it with interest, just as he was working on Bedford's Waterloo church. There the scope for continuing Soane's style was strictly limited, but he would presumably have stored up its suggestive text and images for later use, although as a south Londoner he was probably familiar with the Dulwich Picture Gallery, where Soane's reduction of classical orders to the bare essentials of brick piers is most clearly apparent.
At St John's, Hans Feibusch's two paintings form a crucial part of the ensemble. A panel of the Adoration with angels is framed over the high altar, while the east window space was filled with a crucifixion in a harsher, expressionist style. Hugh Casson, knighted for his role as director of architecture for the Festival, suggested Feibusch for these murals. He had already worked extensively under the patronage of Bishop George Bell in the Chichester diocese, and had become an Anglican. His book on mural painting was published in 1946. Feibusch was an obvious choice on this occasion, probably seen as more modern in spirit than others in the church art field, sitting between the extreme modernism of the South Bank exhibition artists and the conservatism of his chief rival in church commissions, the Rome Scholar Brian D. L. Thomas. Feibusch wrote that painting 'should be an integral part of the architecture, the conclusion and highlight of the architectural space and the logical consequence of the structure'. It was always Thomas Ford who commissioned him rather than an incumbent or parish council, and Alan Ford explains that his father was so impressed with Feibusch's first mural for him that commissions for eleven more churches followed, some the rebuilding of damaged structures but mostly new.

Feibusch wrote in a letter of 1991 that Thomas Ford 'took me on rather suspiciously, a foreign man of Jewish origin, and was critical over my designs. In the end, when he saw what was appearing on the wall, he changed completely and became very pleased. In fact, he made me paint in every church he restored' – only a slight exaggeration. The two preliminary versions of the Crucifixion at St John's in Thomas Ford & Partners' archive may explain some of the initial suspicion. One has a black background which says at the side 'Approved by [Southwark] Diocesan Advisory Committee, Hon. Sec. 18/12/50', although the background was later intensified. Writing up the reopening in April 1951, the *Church Times* said that 'in its final form, [the painting] produced a much harsher effect than the quiet dignity of the artist's preliminary sketch'. 'The striking composition in modernist idiom', the reviewer continued, 'may appeal to some tastes. Others are likely to find its crude realism a hindrance to devotion.'[5]

Fig.3 St Mary the Virgin, Shoulder of Mutton Green, Welling, 1954–5 by Thomas Ford, with sgraffito scenes by Augustus Lunn (John East)

Alan Ford wrote that Feibusch always accepted the designated spaces for his murals, whether an embrasure or framed space, a lunette or a whole apse. Ascension and Crucifixion subjects were the favourites and, having secured the parish's agreement, Feibusch had free rein to design the mural using the colours he wished, with Stic-B paint his favoured medium. Cartoons had always to be approved and sometimes a few modifications were made, but the realisation of the mural was down to Feibusch, with architect, incumbent and congregation generally very pleased with the result. The interior at St John, Waterloo, had not been redecorated since 1951 when Thomas Ford & Partners returned in 1990 to undertake a major eight-year restoration to arrest decay and restore the interior. At the same time, the crypt was remodelled as a homeless centre and ramps for disabled access inserted.[6] Meanwhile, more collaborations between Feibusch and Thomas Ford followed, mainly in the Diocese of Southwark, but with one each in London, Rochester and Portsmouth dioceses.

St Mary the Virgin, Shoulder of Mutton Green, Welling, from 1954–5, recalls Ford's pre-war style with a dark red brick Italian-style exterior, complete with Lombardic campanile. This was the last church supported by Bishop Garbett's Twenty-five Churches Fund, for which Sir Charles Nicholson (1867–1949) had been the favourite architect. Ford had completed the church hall here in 1934, which was used for worship until 1954 when Ford and Harold Cooper were able to return to the job.

A tripartite plan of nave and aisles was precluded on cost grounds and the structure had to be roofed in a single span. Ford wrote of 'a danger lest the interior should be more like an enlarged Hall'; yet the clarity of external volume proved an asset, showing Ford's capacity for simplification, perhaps recalling Inigo Jones's 'handsomest barn in England' at St Paul, Covent Garden.[7] The deep archway sheltering the deeply recessed west door imparted a monumental character, offset by a tympanum decorated with a sgraffito panel depicting five 'joyful' scenes in the life of the Virgin created by Augustus Lunn (1905–86) using three layers of coloured plaster in a technique not much used since its revival by Heywood Sumner in the 1880s. To break up the single span interior, Ford introduced side aisles running under small cross vaults so giving a feeling of greater length and creating an illusion of space 'by the screening of the windows and the play of light and shade on the piers and curved surfaces', a device, as Ford noted, 'frequently adopted in the age of classic architecture to make a building look larger than it really is'. He explained his strategy of using line and colour 'to heighten the optical illusion of space and bring out the very shallow surface modelling'.[8] Four piers mark out a Wren-like central square within the plan.

The matching pulpit and lectern flanking the level-change toward the sanctuary are simpler than at St John's, having less need to fill the empty volume. Feibusch's altarpiece featuring the Ascension is in a neo-classical frame like that at Waterloo but is a calmer and more classical composition, with a quality of weightlessness in the main figure often found in Feibusch's work. Other artists also worked at the church: Clare Dawson (1891–1988) painted eight lunettes in the west-facing cross vaults, in a 'neo-primitive' style reminiscent of children's book illustrations of the era with deep blues predominating. The statue of the Virgin to the right of the altar

Fig.4 St Mary the Virgin, interior with Feibusch's altarpiece featuring the Ascension (John East)

in limewood is by Philip Bentham (1910–81), who also worked at Christ Church, Battersea.[9] On the south side, a chapel of St Thomas of Canterbury (appropriate as the church is close to the pilgrim route) is lit by small, ogee-curved 'Strawberry Hill Gothick' windows and contains a late nineteenth-century reredos and other fittings from All Saints, Streatham, made redundant in 1968.

In his notes on the design, Ford commended classicism as a solution to spatial problem-solving, writing that 'it is desirable that every part should be in harmony with the rest, and therefore the dimensions of piers, arches, moulding and wall surfaces have been related by the classical method of proportion, which has produced some of the world's most lovely buildings and which is still capable, even in these days of limited expenditure, of imparting a feeling of peaceful devotion'.[10] John Newman is more grudging in his praise, considering that 'A building like this epitomises all that mid-20 architecture ought not to be, yet one feels at least that Mr Ford got a kick out of designing it'.[11]

Fig.5 St Michael and All Angels, Paulsgrove, Portsmouth, 1955–7 by Thomas Ford with a reredos by Feibusch depicting the Temptation of Christ (John East)

Fig.6 All Saints, Plumstead, 1956–7 by Thomas Ford (John East)

St Faith, Landport, is one of two churches by Ford in the Portsmouth diocese, and in 1956–7 replaced two bombed churches, St Faith and St Barnabas. It has both a Dutch and a marine character described by Charles O'Brien as 'eclectic and rather demure'.[12] There is stained glass by Clare Dawson, but Feibusch was not employed here. The second church, St Michael, Paulsgrove, was built in 1955–7 in an area of rather bleak social housing, on a dramatic site that rises towards Portsdown Hill with its vast mid-nineteenth-century fortifications. The brown brick exterior is austerely neo-Georgian in a brown brick, reminiscent of the eighteenth-century terraces in Portsmouth Dockyard and showing Ford's attention to detail, with trimmings in orange brick. The south face of the church is parallel to the street, broken up into different volumes anchored by a plain tower with a belfry cupola, austerely ornamented with Greek details.

The unexpectedly spacious and serene interior (cut in two by the insertion of a screen in the 1970s) leaves the eastern portion intact, where transverse vaults carve into the shallow main vault setting up a play of curves, leading through a triumphal arch-style chancel screen that frames the reredos by Feibusch depicting the Temptation of Christ. Most dramatically, openings to either side of the high altar with engraved glass figures of St Gabriel and St Michael, show a glimpse of the Lady Chapel beyond, an extension of the space similar to some of N. F. Cachemaille-Day's pre-war plans. Out of sight from the nave, a brightly coloured painted glass window by Arthur Buss of Goddard & Gibbs (of the Annunciation) enhances the Regency effect that is, nonetheless, quite unlike any actual Regency church.

Feibusch's composition has Jesus pointing a finger to banish the devil from his mountain top in a palette of browns and buffs with cobalt blue hills behind, darker than his usual searing pastels. The narrow spandrels of the chancel arch have the reclining Wise and Foolish Virgins in Flaxman-like classical style grisaille. This axial ensemble is completed with a roundel depicting a flight of four angels in his more familiar Tiepolo mode. The church and murals were paid for by diverting funds from an abandoned bombed church on Portsea Island, sources of some of the furnishings along with pews donated by the Wren church of St Edmund King and Martyr, Lombard Street in the City of London. The combination of an unusual plan and a range of murals and other works of art make this an outstanding example of Ford and Feibusch's collaboration. The church was recently able to clean and stabilise its Feibusch murals through funding from the Hampshire and the Islands Historic Churches Trust.

Fig.7 Mural depicting the Ascension by Hans Feibusch, All Saints, Plumstead (John East)

Returning to the Diocese of Southwark, All Saints, Plumstead, of 1956–7, is another Ford church replacing a bombed-out Victorian church, this of 1873. Thomas Ford decided to build on the site of the church schools, also destroyed by bombing, which provided a suitable setting further down the hill, surrounded by sloping green lawns. Now-familiar Ford elements, such as a tower with an octagonal top and copper cap, and the broken pediment expressed in the eaves of the west end over triple blind arches are recombined, here with the novel effect of a long run of full-height windows, punctuated by mullions to make narrow vertical panes, on both aisle walls. These bring a sense of spaciousness inside and out, making it one of Ford's most successful churches, with a shallow groin vault framing a square between four clustered piers that add a hint of Gothick. The fall of the site allowed for a large crypt under the west end and a higher entrance at the side of the church leading to the priest's and separate men and women's choir vestries. It has star designs on the concrete panels below the windows on the north and south sides, a common Ford feature.

Feibusch's mural of the Ascension fills the whole wall above the high altar, again framed in a recessed space with concealed side light. Christ ascends above two angels with Apostles below, standing in wonderment. Feibusch claimed to have learnt the rules of composition when he attended the academy of André Lhote in Paris in the 1920s. In his book, *Mural Painting* of 1946, however, Feibusch felt that work of this complexity and scale when attempted by English artists could result only in a formulaic application of such rules. As he wrote, 'an art in which great directness and warmth are necessary to assimilate the formal elements imposed from the outside, if a really live work is to be the result, attracts just those artists of lower vision and vitality who cannot express anything'.[13] While tastes differ over the colour schemes of Feibusch's murals, his skill in interpreting architectural space cannot be denied.

In the consecration programme, Thomas Ford said that he sought to avoid boxiness in an almost square church; a feeling of length was given to the nave by grouping the pews in a compact mass and making a broad choir space in front of the altar. He repeated his defence of classicism, writing that 'The architectural style of the building is derived from the Greek Classic of the early nineteenth century, modified and adapted to suit modern materials and requirements. What little detail there is, of mouldings and enrichment, retains that precision of line and care for proportion which earned for this style the title of "The Reign of Elegance".'[14]

St Peter, Pickford Lane, Bexleyheath, was built in 1957 with Alan Ford as the job architect. It stands out from other work with its square plan and a pyramidal roof topped by a cross from which a sanctuary, transepts and portico are projected. The effect of a shallow neo-classical portico *in antis* is produced with thin brick columns – Ford at his most Soanic – allowing for a west window spanning the opening. North and south transepts repeat the columnar effect with closer spacing. Ford wrote that 'the great transept windows and portico are designed in classical proportion and projections and recesses have been designed to break up its mass and scale', making an unusually transparent effect. Other Ford church plans are suggestive of a central square space, a device used by Wren and Hawksmoor to emphasise the 'auditory' character of Stuart Anglican worship, and this chimed with principles of the Liturgical Movement that was rising at the time, but normally linked to modernism.

Fig.8 St Peter, Bexleyheath, 1957 by Thomas Ford and Alan Ford (John East)

The nave ceiling is unusual, consisting of an outer dome rising without any intermediate moulding from an unequal-sided octagonal base formed by the transept soffits, the canted walls to east and west, and the shallow arches between them. Inscribed within this shape is an inner dome of steeper pitch, rising out of it like a bubble and floating above the heads of the congregation. This inner ceiling was richly painted by Feibusch with sky and angel figures receding in perspective and giving the appearance of space and solid plaster. The most arresting feature of the interior today is the purple and mauve paintwork, apparently a source of controversy when recently agreed by Rochester DAC. However, it is close to the original colour scheme and effective for example for the paired doors into the chancel, reflecting the church's tradition of evangelical worship. The other fitting to highlight is the paired pulpit and reading desk in a neo-Georgian style.

On the east wall of the sanctuary, Feibusch created a triptych with the Resurrection in the centre, scenes from the life of St Peter on either side. The left panel shows his attempt to walk on stormy waters with the hand of the Lord to protect and sustain him and the right is a fishing scene on the Sea of Galilee with Christ beckoning St Peter to become his disciple. The colours are quite muted: browns, purples, greens, terracotta and buff. According to Ford, 'the panels are well lit by day and by concealed sources at night. The whole interior therefore comes alive with a variety of modelling, of curved surfaces, colour and movement of figures. In essence it is a centrally planned Renaissance church stripped of its classical trimmings and reduced to its simplest expression as a modelled chunk of solid space.'[15] Briefly illustrated in *The Builder* and omitted from The Buildings of England, this unusual church deserves to be better known.[16]

Feibusch's contribution to St James the Apostle, Merton Park, 1957, was another Ressurection triptych. Built of sand-faced multi-coloured bricks with reconstituted stone dressings to the windows, buttresses and parapets, the church is more conventional in plan than Bexleyheath. A vaulted nave runs into a shallow barrel-vaulted sanctuary, with touches of Ford's now familiar ornament. The mural panels are particularly successful and complemented by stained glass by John Hayward.

The year 1957 was extraordinarily successful for the Ford practice, in which it also completed St Barnabas, Eltham. This was not, however, a completely new church, since it incorporated parts of an iron-columned Gothic church with brick walls and a tower from Woolwich Dockyard, built by George Gilbert Scott in 1857–9. Well Hall, the suburb largely constructed during the First World War with houses for munitions workers, lacked a proper church, so the dockyard structure, iron and brick alike, arose under Ford's supervision on a new site on Rochester Way in 1933, paid for by the Twenty-Five Churches Fund. It lasted barely eleven years in this form, however, being hit by incendiary bombs in 1944.

When Thomas and Alan Ford returned to repair it, they retained the Victorian shell, but transformed the interior with a lower ceiling to reduce heating costs and all the seating confined to the nave. Square piers encased the damaged cast iron, with a continuous entablature that supports a barrel vault marked out with alternating coffered panels and star patterns. At a lower level between the piers is a secondary order of Adamesque columns linked by beams, on which kneeling angels face towards the altar, and other fittings brought from lost churches.[17] The Feibusch mural of 'Christ in Majesty' surrounded by angels was painted high up on the chancel vault with pinks and oranges predominant, which the pink walls complement. In a publication for the rebuilding fund, Feibusch wrote that '[The mural] shows the Saviour enthroned, with arms outstretched, and surrounded by adoring angels and by clouds which are partly lit up by his Glory, but are grey where they face the outer world in which we dwell'.[18]

Moving north of the river, St Michael and All Angels, Harrow Weald, built in 1958, appears an insignificant mission church with a small belfry amidst 1930s' suburban housing. A church hall had been the parish's first place of worship, but with Alan Ford as job architect a surprisingly capacious church was created. A vigorously carved statue of St Michael by another émigré, David Paul Königsburger from Vienna (known as 'David Paul' in the UK) was placed over the entrance, with a commemorative tablet to mid-century refugees. This was also a tribute to Bishop Bell of Chichester, who had furthered Feibusch's career in church decoration during the war.

Thomas Ford's familiar touches include twin columns with palm-leaf capitals, internal transepts marked by shallow lunette windows, and a gently apsed east end with light streaming in from the north and south sides. The Feibusch mural depicts the Adoration of the Cross, one of his best and most dramatic works, extending right

Fig.9 Christ Church and St Stephen, Battersea, 1959 by Thomas Ford with Feibusch's mural of the Last Judgement (John East)

Fig.10 St Crispin, Bermondsey, mural of the saint with St Crispinian handing out sandals, 1959 by Hans Feibusch (John East)

across the low chancel and down to floor level, with ascending figures ranged round a red-orange altar cross; a nimbus behind it is so convincing that light appears to emanate from the cross itself. Intense turquoises of the sky dominate with rocky scenes at either end and framed by double palmette topped columns. In the lunettes of the shallow curved ceiling, there are small murals of the four Evangelists in subdued purple and grey tones created by Feibusch and stained glass on each side possibly by Goddard & Gibbs.

Feibusch, Augustus Lunn, Philip Bentham and Arthur Buss reconvened to work on Christ Church and St Stephen's, Battersea, in 1959, replacing another bomb-damaged Victorian church on the same foundations. A traditional plan of nave, transepts and aisles has a copper covered barrel roof over the nave and transepts (and felt-covered flat roofs over aisles and vestries). The aisles project as porches on the west front, where tapering door frames with small roundels recall Soane's Dulwich Picture Gallery, and linked to a triangular park created in 1952 with wooden seating in memory of those who lost their lives in Battersea during the war.

In the interior, a Festival of Britain lightness complements ecclesiastical decorum – the essence of the Ford and Feibusch style. The nave and short chancel are in one space, ceiled by a coved plaster vault, and lit from three clerestory lunettes on each side, which let in plenty of light. There are chairs rather than pews, as Ford preferred. He is at his most Soanic here, not just in details, but in the complexity of space at the east end, that, from some angles, suggest the 1792 Bank Stock Office.

A large Feibusch mural of the Last Judgement fills the east wall behind the high altar in an unusual keyhole shape, using a typical range of colours, ranging from blue/greens at the sides to intense purples and oranges towards the centre. In front of the font, he depicted the sacrament of Baptism; it is in a more restricted colour palette, using an irregular outline as he had done in several pre-war domestic commissions. Complementing these, but not interfering with them, is a charming grisaille mural by Augustus Lunn of a nativity scene in tones of grey with contrasting flashes of blue for the Virgin's robe in the Chapel of the Adoration of the Virgin (to the right of the chancel) reminiscent of fifteenth-century Bruges.

The original St Crispin's in Southwark Park Road of 1879 was another bomb victim, giving Ford the opportunity to create what may be his best church, St Crispin with Christchurch, in 1959. It is regrettably now out of use, although the majority of fittings remain in place and this, exceptionally, is protected by a listing from 2000, a year after closure. Ford used a four-square plan, liturgically reversed so the east end faces west, with wide multiple-light windows and large halls.

St Crispin is the patron saint of cobblers and, reflecting leather work in the district, the interior has leather seat coverings and doors. The roof treatments are perhaps the most Regency of all the Ford and Feibusch churches with a high trapezoidal roof, given greater height by a 'sky' mural by Phyllis Bray (1911–91), Feibusch's assistant on several other projects. The sanctuary has high-set side windows shedding light onto the altar and its mural beneath a shallow arch. This is complemented by Ford's usual bowed altar rails painted white and gilded in Georgian style. The broad nave is lined with shallow pilasters and delicate anthemion and palmette capitals set in the frieze. The mural itself shows St Crispin and St Crispinian handing out sandals with a shadowy haloed figure of Christ behind, set in an arid Holy Land scene with a wide colour range. Stained glass by Michael Farrar-Bell (1911–93) in the side chapel to the left of the high altar commemorates

Fig.11 Holy Trinity, Rotherhithe, 1960 by Thomas Ford, 1960 (John East)

the union with Christ Church, Bermondsey, now demolished, with a background of Thames scenery.

The smallest and last of the Ford and Feibusch collaborations was Holy Trinity, Rotherhithe, from 1960. It is a low, simple Dutch-style church in pale brick with a copper roof sitting sideways onto Rotherhithe Street and with a green quadrangle in front, somehow fitting for its Docklands location. By the time of the church's consecration, however, the Surrey Docks – which traditionally handled Baltic timber – were on the verge of closure. Its fortunes have revived as the area has regenerated with a more socially mixed population and improved transport links. Apart from the eighteenth-century riverside church of St Mary, Rotherhithe, it is the last functioning Anglican church in the district.

Narrow aisles are divided from the nave by simple columns and two arched openings with a sanctuary in an alcove at the east end. This is filled completely with a Feibusch mural of the Crucifixion depicting Jerusalem behind the cross,

including some elements of Portmeirion in North Wales where Feibusch had painted external murals for Clough Williams-Ellis.

This article is the first record of a remarkable set of collaborative works, unmatched in number by any comparable partnership of architect and artists. Apart from the listing of St John, Waterloo, which reflects the original Bedford shell and the Festival interest, St Crispin's is the only other example with national protection. Of the Thomas Ford churches in the Feibusch murals, five are locally listed: St Peter, Bexleyheath; St Mary the Virgin, Welling; St Barnabas, Eltham; St James the Apostle, Merton Park; and St Michael and All Angels, Harrow. All Saints, Plumstead; Christ Church, Battersea; Holy Trinity, Rotherhithe and St Michael and All Angels, Paulsgrove, have no heritage protection of any sort at present.

While Feibusch's work has acquired status in its context of émigré artists and mural painters, Ford's architecture has hitherto lacked champions, but his series of churches surely stands out as a distinctive contribution to post-war Anglican building and the variety of classical modes of the time. They are no pale hangover from the 1930s, since their planning, construction, scale and materials are of their time, although not in the way that is usually recognised. It seems evident that they continue to serve their congregations well.

NOTES

1 'Restoration of St John's Church, Waterloo Road (the Festival Church)', *The Builder*, vol.180, 8 May 1951, pp.618–22.

2 It seems likely that Ford had read G. W. O. Addleshaw and Frederick Etchells, *The Architectural Setting of Anglican Worship* (London: Faber & Faber, 1948), which commends the Anglican Ambo, citing precedents such as St Philip, Regent Street, by G. S. Repton, 1820.

3 Paul Reilly, *An Introduction to Regency Architecture* (London: Art and Technics, 1948); Hugh Casson, An Introduction to Victorian Architecture (London: Art and Technics, 1948).

4 John Summerson, 'Soane: The case-history of a personal style', *RIBA Journal*, vol.58, January 1951, p.89.

5 *Church Times*, vol.134, 27 April 1951, p.1.

6 Spirit of the Festival', *Architects' Journal*, vol.194, 11 & 18 December 1991, p.14.

7 *Architect and Surveyor*, vol.1, May/June 1956, pp.49–52, also printed as 'From our Architect' in the consecration brochure, 1955.

8 ibid.

9 Bentham was a member of the Art Workers' Guild from 1947, joined by Feibusch and Lunn in 1956; Ford was never a member.

10 Ford, 'From our Architect', op. cit.

11 John Newman, in Bridget Cherry and Nikolaus Pevsner, The Buildings of England, *London 2: South* (Harmondsworth: Penguin, 1983), p.152.

12 Charles O'Brien, Bruce Bailey, Nikolaus Pevsner and David W. Lloyd, The Buildings of England, *Hampshire South* (London: Yale, 2018), p.465.

13 Hans Feibusch, *Mural Painting* (London: A & C Black, 1946), p.64.

14 Thomas Ford, 'Message from the Architect', *Consecration of New Church, Saturday 6 July 1957, All Saints Parish Church Shooters Hill, Ripon Road, Plumstead* (Plumstead: 1957).

15 Thomas Ford, Consecration leaflet, 1958.

16 'Saint Peter's Church, Bexleyheath', *The Builder*, vol.194, 6 June 1958, pp.1030–1.

17 The choir stalls, pews, font and organ came from St Michael's, Lant Street, Southwark.

18 Thomas Ford, 'The Rebirth of St Barnabas', and Hans Feibusch, 'Our Painting', *St Barnabas Church Rededicated*, leaflet produced in aid of the Rebuilding Fund, June 1957.

ROBERT PROCTOR

10 Churches for Towns and Suburbs:

Sir Percy Thomas & Son and the Percy Thomas Partnership

Fig.1 Roman Catholic Cathedral of Saints Peter and Paul, Clifton, Bristol (author).

With the exception of the Roman Catholic Cathedral of Saints Peter and Paul in Clifton, Bristol, the Cardiff architect Sir Percy Thomas (1883–1969) and his subsequent practice the Percy Thomas Partnership are known for secular civic buildings rather than churches. Under his son Norman Percy Thomas (1915–89), the practice had modernised, expanded and diversified, and when the Clifton commission arrived in 1965, most of its work was for the welfare state and industry, from the new steelworks and power stations of south Wales to hospitals and universities.[1] By comparison its religious commissions were modest, overlooked by the architectural media (and historians). This essay considers how and why this practice attracted these commissions and how its secular background contributed to its ecclesiastical projects.

Despite a diversity of clients, and, indeed, of architects working in the practice, one thread connecting the firm's religious and secular buildings is a civic ethos, articulated by Percy Thomas himself as RIBA president and as a founder of the Cardiff Civic Society in 1933, and applied in his earliest buildings.[2] Some religious clients evidently chose the practice because of that civic background. Religious organisations considered the church building's relationship to its urban context an expression of the congregation's place in the civic body, a concern articulated in the choice of site as well as architectural form.[3] The firm's architects gave expression to the congregation's thinking about the civic realm in their chosen place, designing churches for towns and suburbs, not merely within them.

ANGLICAN RECONSTRUCTION

Such concerns surrounded Percy Thomas's first religious commission, for reconstructing Arthur Blomfield's bombed Gothic Revival Anglican church of St Mary in Swansea town centre.[4] Despite a diminishing parish population as post-war planning dispersed housing into suburban estates, the bishop Edward Williamson shared the parishioners' preference to rebuild on the existing foundations. At a vestry meeting, the vicar Jack Thomas affirmed the civic purpose of this historic church: 'St Mary's is the town church & it is unthinkable that we sh[ou]ld rebuild the town w[ith]out rebuilding the Church wh[ich] was its heart & soul for something like 1,000 y[ear]s'. 'We are building not simply for the parish but for the town', he argued.[5] The borough engineer J. Richard Heath also wanted to keep the church as a singular focal monument in the newly planned centre, along with the medieval castle and Percy Thomas's interwar neoclassical Guildhall, surrounding them with modern shopping streets.[6] Thus it suited the aims of both planner and clergy to rebuild the church in broad conformity with its predecessor. Ostensibly, reusing the foundations would save money, but sentiment surely outweighed rational concerns.

Williamson wanted 'the best possible architect' to account for both 'the ancient side' and 'the shopping-centre side of our problem', to evoke the long-lost medieval church while addressing its modern context. Favouring Edward Maufe, he initially rejected Percy Thomas alongside N. F. Cachemaille-Day and H. S. Goodhart-Rendel as 'thorough-paced moderns'.[7] Though Williamson considered him too strictly Gothic, in 1943 the diocese appointed Leslie T. Moore, who sketched rough plans before resigning in 1949 citing age and distance. It then approached Norman Thomas in the Swansea office, who with his colleagues did much of the work of design, though Percy Thomas commandeered parts for himself, relishing the Gothic exercise.[8]

Designed from 1953 and built in 1955–9 in rubble masonry with Bath stone details, the church gained improvements in height and layout, including larger windows in the aisles and an additional chapel for smaller services, while war damage compensation limits encouraged a simpler and more contempory architecture than Blomfield's.[9] Windows were groups of lancets, only one transept window employing tracery; the oak hammerbeam nave ceiling disguised a steel structure, and the aisles were roofed in reinforced concrete.[10] After a fundraising effort in the parish and town, Percy Thomas commissioned stained glass for the chancel from E. Liddell Armitage of Whitefriars Studios, encouraging him to take a distinctively twentieth-century approach combining arts and crafts principles with an expressionist style, thick lead lines emphasising the gem-like nature of the glass to give

Fig.2 St Mary's Church, Swansea (author).

'a tapestry effect' to complement Margaret Kaye's altar frontal.[11] Percy Thomas designed the Gothic revival furnishings himself, including richly carved choir stalls, transept screen and pulpit.[12] After the church's opening, the parish commissioned further significant artworks, notably a painting by Ceri Richards, and, for the Trinity chapel, windows and a reredos by John Piper.[13]

The clergy considered St Mary's close to a cathedral in status, 'the greatest parish church in Wales', and endowed it with the responsibility of representing for its town a continuity with the past, as surrounding traces were effaced.[14] Modernist planning often showcased isolated monuments in modern settings: Swansea echoes Coventry, for example, whose modern shopping centre was aligned with the medieval spire preserved alongside Basil Spence's new cathedral. Though Sir Percy Thomas & Son was known by then for modernism, therefore, it could also embrace the civic symbolism of a historicist restoration as a modern project.

Similarly, on a smaller scale, the practice reinstated the late Victorian Anglican church of All Saints, Penarth, also bombed in the war. Budget constraints demanded a simpler design than the original, but there was good Gothic detailing and a vividly painted timber ceiling likened to those of Stephen Dykes Bower.[15]

CIVIC MISSION: NONCONFORMIST CHURCHES IN ENGLAND AND WALES

Around the same time the practice received independent clusters of commissions for various Methodist chapels, reflecting the continuing vitality of this element of Welsh culture. Their first Methodist commissions, however, were English. The Didsbury Theological College in Westbury-on-Trym in Bristol was a residential seminary, named after its precursor, a Methodist college in Manchester, closed in 1945 and moved to meet the needs of congregations in south Wales and south-west England.[16] Percy Thomas's former colleague and occasional collaborator Ernest Prestwich of Leigh was advising E. Benson Perkins and Albert Hearn of the Methodist Church's General Chapel Committee on its post-war building programme, so probably recommended the architect, though Thomas was also consultant architect to Bristol University, to which Didsbury College became attached as an 'associate college'.[17]

Didsbury College was a notable landmark on a hillside overlooking the growing suburb when completed in 1953. Thomas employed an austere brick neo-Georgian style closely resembling student halls he had recently built for the University College of North Wales at Bangor.[18] The chapel was a simple tall barrel-vaulted and aisleless volume projecting from the rear.[19] Large, plain round-arched windows flooded its interior with light and overlooked the garden: in college principal Frederic Greeves's interpretation demonstrating that 'the world is God's creation as well as our parish and we want the outside world to come in to our worship'.[20] Plainness coincided with contemporary Methodist thinking, the period's enforced austerity becoming a 'salutary factor' that encouraged 'simple design with reliance upon form and line for genuine beauty of structure', as Perkins and Hearn argued. They urged a return to the spirit of Wesley and the eighteenth-century preaching house, when 'there was a feeling for churches which were light, and open to the whole congregation'.[21]

In 1969–70 Sir Percy Thomas & Son returned to add a separate building for an experimental chapel and additional teaching spaces, probably designed by Ronald Weeks from the Bristol office. Three teaching rooms surrounded a central, top-lit chapel, separated by folding partitions that could be opened into one large, cruciform worship space. Brick walls wrapped each space, the chapel rising up behind them over a clerestory, in a logical modernist expression of internal volumes. This liturgically innovative building followed two Roman Catholic churches where the practice engaged with liturgical design.[22]

The firm's earliest Methodist church was a replacement for the bombed Victorian King Street Methodist Church in Plymouth. Perkins, as secretary of the General Chapel Committee, recommended Thomas in 1948, and he made initial designs the following year.[23] The old building, seating 1,500 and described as 'the Cathedral of Western Methodism', had been close to the city centre in a dense area of Victorian terraces.[24] In Patrick Abercrombie and James Paton Watson's *A Plan for Plymouth* in 1943, the church and surrounding housing were subsumed into the shopping centre: the Pannier Market was eventually built on the site; and the plan suggested no location for a replacement. An early revision gave the surviving interwar Methodist Central Hall a prominent position on an approach road, clearing surrounding buildings, thereby threatening to make a new King Street church superfluous.[25] The Plymouth and Devonport Mission Circuit (which did not include King Street) proposed using King Street's war damage compensation for missions in new suburban estates at Devonport, Ernesettle and elsewhere.[26] The King Street trustees demurred, however, and pursued a central church, though clearly anticipated smaller congregations, providing seats for only 500.[27] Perkins encouraged them, contradicting his advice elsewhere, awarding a grant from funds sent by American Methodists for rebuilding war-damaged churches in Britain.[28]

The city council eventually offered a site behind the future Royal Parade, where bombs had destroyed several houses on the end of the Crescent, a Regency terrace, on condition that the church 'conform in style to that of the existing buildings'.[29] Thomas's neo-Georgian design, similar to Didsbury College in style, nevertheless contrasted with the stucco-fronted terrace, its silver-grey brick indicating the church's public function: more than half the site was dedicated to a complex for secular activities, especially for the young. Thomas positioned the domestically-scaled Church House for social activities beside the terrace; a hall followed with similar sash windows, suggestive of a secular civic function by comparison with the church. A vestibule turning the corner linked to the church, defined by a projecting gable, with pedimented doorcase and circular window.[30]

On receiving Thomas's sketch design the trustees had asked for the church 'to be re-designed in a more beautiful & more typically "Methodist" manner'.[31] Perkins and Hearn preferred simple forms without ornament, stating that a church 'should rely upon its line and the suitability of its material for its dignity and attraction'. Though more Romanesque than neo-Georgian in feel, their suggested model church showed a building close to King Street's final design.[32] As finalised by practice partner William Marsden around 1955, and completed in 1957 (demolished *c.*2002), the elevations were broadly similar and almost as plain; a proposed flèche was omitted for even greater simplicity; and the plan also adopted Perkins and Hearn's recommended passage aisles.[33]

Perkins and Hearn considered the relationship between choir and congregation a defining Methodist feature, rejecting the Anglican convention of a choir in front of the altar.[34] After Marsden experimented with different layouts, the trustees accepted a design positioning the fifty choristers in a block forward of the communion table and to one side, balanced by the deacons' seats and pulpit opposite.[35] This arrangement did, however, resemble many new Anglican churches, while the choir emulated Anglican practice in wearing gowns, becoming the first robed Methodist choir in the

Fig.3 King Street Methodist Church, Plymouth, photograph of c. 1960 (The Box, Plymouth).

region. Modest design touches, including a recess and steps up to the communion table and a decorative cloth behind it, balanced the desire to recapture the grandeur and sacredness of the lost church with adaptation to the modern city and a revitalised idea of Methodism.[36]

Meanwhile in Swansea, the site of the elegant but bomb-damaged Calvinistic Methodist Trinity Chapel of 1829 was also lost to the town's new shopping centre.[37] With other churches, members of its congregation initially pressed the council for a central site, but by the time they consulted Percy Thomas in 1950, few lived centrally and they had been worshipping in their pre-war schoolroom in the suburb of Sketty for almost a decade.[38] Thomas convinced them to rebuild there, reassuring them that there was adequate room on their land.[39]

Didsbury College was not yet built, and the Calvinistic Methodists (or Presbyterian Church of Wales) were a separate denomination unconnected with the English Methodist Church, so Thomas was not an obvious choice. He spoke no Welsh, the chapel's principal language; but its members approached him personally in Cardiff rather than the Swansea office, likely motivated by his national prestige. Some chapel members had links to the University College of Swansea which his practice was planning, and others to the council, working in Thomas's Guildhall.[40]

Fig.4 Trinity Welsh Calvinistic Methodist Chapel, Sketty, Swansea (author).

The chapel committee was evidently disappointed when, at a meeting in the schoolroom, Thomas handed over to his son.[41] Norman Thomas negotiated war damage compensation and produced a sketch plan, in 1951, that he thoroughly revised after listening to the committee's discussion.[42]

Externally, Trinity Chapel was similar to the King Street Church: a narrow pitched-roof box gable-on to the street with projecting passage aisles. The basilican plan departed from the Welsh Nonconformist tradition of wide, almost square plans, partly because of the restricted site. Members however prohibited a central aisle, and even a centre line in the pews, as over-emphasising the communion table. Communion was taken in the pews, which had holes in the book rest for cups. Some members wanted a traditional gallery on three sides; this was impractical on the narrow site, but a rear gallery was included. This made the chapel larger than necessary for the congregation, but suited to the Welsh custom of singing festivals involving neighbouring chapels. Others requested a *sêt fawr*, a seat for the elders under the pulpit, though the minister H. Wynne Griffiths negotiated a more discrete screened bench between the organ console and communion table.[43] A visually dominant, central high pulpit behind the low communion table strongly maintained Welsh traditions. Norman Thomas designed these elements in modern forms, with grey brick walls, warm oak furnishings, conical light fittings and a decorative timber panel behind the pulpit in a Festival of Britain style.

In Cardiff, too, the Wesleyan Methodists of the Roath Circuit decided against rebuilding their bombed Gothic Revival church in the city centre, apportioning

Fig.5 St Andrew's Methodist Church, Birchgrove, Cardiff (author).

the compensation to three suburban churches in the circuit.[44] Two of them, at Birchgrove and Rumney, had older buildings, outgrown as Cardiff's population expanded outwards; the third arose on a post-war council estate at Llanrumney. Marsden seems to have designed all three when the practice was appointed in 1950, in a more distinctly modern version of the Plymouth church.[45] Plans had to be checked by the Methodist office in Manchester, where Hearn was advising the trustees, so he may have recommended the architects.[46]

Birchgrove was the largest of the three, dedicated by the minister T. Dixon Jones to St Andrew, against objections from some in the congregation who thought the use of a saint's name too close to Anglican practice.[47] The English-speaking Wesleyan Methodists followed a relatively more high church style of worship than at Sketty, with a central aisle, pulpit to one side and altar-like communion table.[48] Nevertheless, the design's basis in Perkins and Hearn's model made it quite distinctive as a Methodist church. The old church was converted into a hall, linked to the new building with a block for use as a Sunday school and weekday activities for young people, as at Plymouth a characteristic Methodist activity. The old chapel was on a side street, while the new church confronted the main artery of Caerphilly Road, presenting an overt public statement to the suburb.[49] The gable roughly duplicated the end houses on its Victorian terrace, suggesting integration with secular and domestic surroundings, though its distinctive orange brickwork and simple modern forms denoted a public character. The architecture reflects the congregation's missionary approach to the suburb: at its opening in 1956, the superintendent

Fig.6 Dowlais Wesley Methodist Church, Merthyr Tydfil (author).

minister A. W. Abbotts wrote that 'With the new church should go a new vision. We must be a missionary church, looking outwards beyond our fellowship towards the churchless multitude for whom Christ died ... dedicated to the task of claiming this neighbourhood of Birchgrove for Christ.'[50]

The church in Rumney, opened earlier that year (demolished *c*.2010), was almost identical, with a shorter nave and recycled furnishings from the bombed Roath church reworked to Marsden's design.[51] The bricks were grey rather than orange, 'toned pleasantly with the predominantly grey colour of the other buildings in the neighbourhood', as the opening booklet noted.[52] It too brought the church to the street frontage, the old church behind linked to it and converted into classrooms. Its congregation was also charged with establishing the new church in nearby Llanrumney, and war damage funding from Roath made it possible to do so speedily, on a landscaped junction at the heart of the estate.[53] The church, smaller and simpler than the others, opened in 1959 (but has since also been demolished).[54]

Nearly two decades later, the Percy Thomas Partnership built another Wesleyan Methodist church at Dowlais, a suburb of Merthyr Tydfil that was also an industrial town overlooking an ironworks in the valley below it. In the 1960s the borough council replaced many of its Victorian terraces with social housing and created

a new road layout through the valley as smaller factories replaced the ironworks. After demolishing the old church in 1967 it eventually allocated a new site in 1971 on the hillside overlooking the valley in an area of new housing.[55] The congregation seems to have chosen Sir Percy Thomas & Son simply because of its prestige, rather than because it knew its earlier churches. The building was designed by Dale Owen and Edward Kluge, and subsequently reduced in size and detailed by Roy Page, none of whom had significant involvement with the practice's other churches.[56] They rejected the traditional typology of the 1950s churches, taking a more radical approach, as with their contemporary Roman Catholic work. As with other Wesleyan Methodist churches, secular missionary activity was especially important: the architects positioned a hall at the top of the sloping site, separated from the church space lower down by a foyer containing a social room, kitchen and connecting stair, and a classroom was tucked underneath the hall. The church, opened in 1972, is low and almost domestic in nature, but its inverted asymmetrical pitched roofs, echoing the valley's topography, express a higher purpose as a public building. Its overt modernity suggests the congregation's desire to participate in the contemporary development of the town with a church that would be 'of value and use to the community around'.[57]

This was a coherent body of work for Nonconformist congregations, largely adapting a simple template. Yet the commissions were separate and sometimes unrelated, and differences of expression developed from context and from congregations' articulations of civic purpose, besides the different tendencies of the several architects involved. Decisions about whether to build in the centre or the suburb could be both pragmatic and symbolic, concerning the church's mission to the wider population.

Fig.7 Gwent Crematorium, Croesyceiliog, Cwmbran (author).

A RURAL CHAPEL

The Gwent Crematorium at Croesyceiliog, near the new town of Cwmbran, opened in 1960, was a civic project more typical of Thomas's background, though the prominent cross on its façade made the crematorium chapel explicitly Christian in character, and it was dedicated by the Anglican Archbishop of Wales.[58] Its location, rural when built, was loosely related to Cwmbran but primarily convenient for road access for the several local authorities that built it, coordinated by Newport Borough Council in 1943.[59] When the site was decided and Thomas commissioned in 1954, Monmouthshire, one of the participants, was planning a new county hall in Croesyceiliog, built later in the 1960s; the crematorium was close to this complex, though still in a marginal position outside the new town.[60] The crematorium committee requested 'an unobtrusive and tastefully and simply designed building ... that will fit naturally into its rural surroundings'.[61]

As built with assistance from Marsden and Frank Buckley, the crematorium chapel was a simple, pitched-roofed hall fronted with a cloister walkway of cut-out arches and enclosed in stark, white-rendered elevations. A rubble stone tower with an arched opening disguised the flue, and the incinerator was attached to the rear as a flat-roofed modern box. There was a distinct Arts and Crafts feel, in the stone window surrounds, for example, though Thomas's characteristic simplicity of forms also evoked modernity, and rubble stonework gave a contemporary style. The plain interior balanced the suggestion of a church atmosphere with enough abstraction to put Nonconformist mourners at ease.

LITURGY AND COMMUNITY: THREE ROMAN CATHOLIC CHURCHES

Given the practice's relatively modest body of work in church architecture, it seems remarkable that Roman Catholics also commissioned Sir Percy Thomas & Son in the 1960s. Most Catholic dioceses favoured trusted architects: in Wales, F. R. Bates, Price & Son around Cardiff, and Weightman & Bullen in Menevia, which until 1987 served Swansea and rural mid-Wales. The practice's three Roman Catholic churches had different strands of patronage, and each was designed by a different architect. Bishop John Petit of Menevia, who often resided at Wrexham near the architects' Shrewsbury office, might feasibly have commissioned the practice himself and recommended them for Clifton. An important unifying factor, however, was the donor, the Van Neste Foundation, created by the Bristol philanthropist Francis van Neste, the principal funder of two Welsh Roman Catholic churches, Our Lady Star of the Sea in Burry Port and Our Lady Help of Christians in Machynlleth, which also awarded half of the cost of Clifton Cathedral. Burry Port's parish priest James Howard claimed that the Foundation wanted him to build 'a Replica of [a church] in Avonmouth, Bristol.[62] This was the Catholic church of St Brendan by Sydney Gerald Howitt, a plain Romanesque building of 1956.[63] Howard's first contact with Percy Thomas's Swansea office in 1963 was with a Howitt, presumably also the 'S. G. H.' who signed the drawings.[64] Perhaps van Neste knew Howitt before and after his move to Sir Percy Thomas & Son and recommended the practice. Each project went to a different office, however; and after Howard and Howitt's initial meeting, Wallace Sweet led the Burry Port project as partner, and their modern approach was radically different to that at Avonmouth.[65]

Despite a restricted budget and modest brief for a church seating fewer than 200, Sweet and Howitt proved enthusiastic, submitting a design within a month with a report emphasising its liturgical basis. An elongated hexagon in plan would,

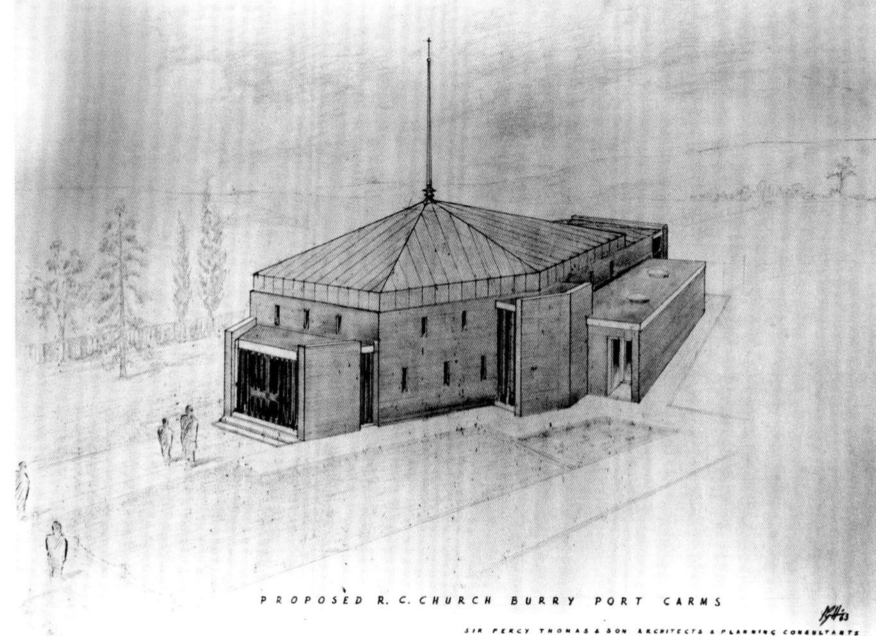

Fig.8 Our Lady Star of the Sea, Burry Port, presentation drawing by SGH of Sir Percy Thomas & Son, 1963 (Menevia Roman Catholic Diocesan Archives; courtesy of Percy Thomas Architects (Capita Real Estate and Infrastructure Ltd.)).

they thought, bring the congregation closer to the altar. A Lady chapel projected from one side for smaller congregations, a baptistery opposite. Their report made liturgical suggestions beyond conventional practice in the Church, closely following the Second Vatican Council, then in progress: they proposed a forward altar for the priest to face the congregation across it (a year before this was authorised in Britain), and chairs instead of pews so the congregation could turn towards the font to make baptism a parish ceremony. The bishop insisted on pews, the font was positioned near the entrance and the baptistery redesigned as a sacristy, but a forward altar was built as suggested.[66] The liturgical movement had by now entered mainstream architectural discourse, and Dale Owen in the Cardiff office was advising colleagues to read Peter Hammond's edited book *Towards a Church Architecture*, so its ideas were current in the practice.[67]

The architects were enthusiastic also for the economical use of basic materials, suggesting awareness of the liturgical movement's emphasis on simplicity and poverty, following Maguire and Murray's church at Bow Common and its interpretation by Hammond. At Burry Port they proposed a brick structure with a steel roof, and inside, a 'simple rugged vernacular' of white-painted brick, hexagonal concrete floor tiles and 'robust and simple' joinery, the steelwork exposed and heavy concrete lintels over side chapels. Colourful vestments and a cloth hanging would add richness to liturgical ceremonies.[68] The immediate surroundings, a residential street of terraced houses and more recent post-war housing, they felt to be 'grey' and lacking 'character', but they intended the church's brown brickwork and chunky timber windows and doors as sympathetic to the context.[69] They also wanted to demonstrate 'the progressive nature of the Catholic faith ... by designing in a frankly contemporary manner', with a pyramidal roof and flèche rising over the nave, visible from surrounding streets.[70]

Our Lady Help of Christians in Machynlleth, opened a year later in 1965 (now called St Mair, interior altered), was designed from the Shrewsbury office, probably

Fig.9 Our Lady Help of Christians (now St Mair), Machynlleth (James Crowley).

by Marsden. It was even smaller, seating only 120. The building took an equally contemporary, though different, form, a flat-roofed rectangular structure set back from the main road running through the market town, in brutalist yellow brick with slot windows and chunky projecting concrete beams. The same materials continued inside, with exposed brick walls and a reinforced concrete roof. This church also followed the new liturgical thinking: the sanctuary was a raised platform projecting into an open nave; seating was on three sides, one block facing a side chapel.[71] It had a simple, plain interior similar to some of Rudolf Schwarz's churches.

The client was a group of Redemptorist priests, appointed by the diocese before the war to administer the parish. In 1949 they accepted the role of 'Welsh Travelling Mission' to the few, sparsely distributed Catholics of central Wales. At Machynlleth they had acquired a house, built a temporary chapel and attracted a complementary convent of nuns.[72] The church, opened in 1965, resembles the modest civic structures of the contemporary welfare state such as libraries and community centres, perhaps partly to deflect hostility in this area where Catholics were unusual, though also for economy: the congregation was too small and poor to afford a church, and the Van Neste Foundation donated most of its cost.[73]

Such modest work was hardly adequate preparation for one of the most important British church buildings of the twentieth century, but these two tiny churches were the practice's only previous Roman Catholic work before the Cathedral Church of Saints Peter and Paul in Bristol for the Diocese of Clifton. In promising funds towards a new Clifton Cathedral, van Neste encouraged the diocese to abandon the nineteenth-century pro-cathedral, and motivated Bishop Joseph Rudderham to appoint architects for a new building. While van Neste urged Rudderham to build a lasting monument, he also claimed it would be mainly a parish church for Clifton with, incidentally, cathedral status.[74] Nevertheless, it was designed on a generous scale, seating almost a thousand. Van Neste sat on the Cathedral Working Party throughout the process of design, though whether he recommended the architects is unrecorded. The bishop decided against a competition, and instead asked the RIBA for a list of suitable architects, whom he interviewed in 1965.[75] Sir Percy Thomas & Son's reputation for civic buildings must have weighed in their favour, as the cathedral's purpose exceeded the purely religious, with a wider duty to represent Catholic identity in the city, including events welcoming local dignitaries. The firm's experience of complex work such as university campuses and the proximity of its Bristol office in Clifton offered further reassurance.

The architects helped choose the site a short walk north from the pro-cathedral, set deeper into a more suburban area of Clifton surrounded by Victorian and late-Georgian terraces. Kenneth Nugent (a priest and former architect) criticised its location as diminishing the cathedral's presence in the city's everyday life; but its position distinguished it from the city centre church of St Mary on the Quay, and brought it closer to the parish population, particularly associated with the university, then building a new students' union nearby.[76]

The partner appointed was Frederick Jennett, who attended many working party meetings before giving up design for a managerial role in 1971.[77] Dale Owen seems to have had initial involvement, as he travelled in Italy with Clifton in mind, studying the urban settings of cathedrals.[78] A specialist in planning, he may have outlined the scheme's parameters, which followed modernist principles he used elsewhere: the cathedral was set in the centre of the site, and a sunken car park was bridged by broad, stepped walkways creating processional and gathering spaces related to the surrounding streets. Owen had no direct contact with the diocese, however, and the architect who did most of the design work was Ronald Weeks.

Weeks gave several accounts of the design process which are supported by the evidence of preparatory drawings.[79] He and Jennett understood the liturgical movement: even Jennett's letter accepting their appointment hoped that 'a close working relationship between Architect and Client can achieve the level of "Architectural Seriousness" advanced by the New Liturgical Movement', referring to an essay by Lance Wright in *Towards a Church Architecture*.[80] By avoiding a competition, the diocese ensured a collaborative approach to design (impossible, for example, at Liverpool Metropolitan Cathedral).[81] Their architects coaxed the clergy to articulate their interpretation of the liturgy. This the cathedral's working party was unusually competent to do: members included Dom Gregory Murray, a Benedictine expert on Gregorian chant involved in the pre-war liturgical revival, and Lancelot Sheppard, lay liturgical writer.[82] Weeks and Jennett sketched out the movements of liturgies as they were explained by a committee member. Then they created diagrammatic plans for every spatial and physical aspect of the cathedral and its furnishings in relation to liturgical requirements, with alternative configurations for discussion with the committee.[83]

The hexagonal geometry was different to that used at Burry Port: at Clifton a beehive grid enabled a free placing of liturgical elements forming axial relationships in different directions. Font, ambo and altar form a linear sequence at an angle to the axis of the nave, for example; the Blessed Sacrament chapel is contained by walls between sanctuary and baptistery, opening in different directions for visual and processional access; the geometry integrated all elements around a fan-shaped nave. The principal doors to the east brought occupants in a spiral motion around the baptistery. The elevations resulted logically from the spatial volumes and expressive use of daylight. Despite such a functionalist approach to design, a precedent noted at the time was Maguire and Murray's St Matthew, Perry Beeches, with a

Fig.10 [following pages] Clifton Cathedral (author).

similar rotating spiral geometry organising its liturgical plan.[84] Nevertheless, there were only a handful of churches in Britain where architects took such a rigorous modern approach to design, as advocated by liturgical movement writers.

Completed in 1973 (recently restored by Purcell), the cathedral benefited from Weeks's obsessive attention to detail, including a modular proportioning system determining the concrete shuttering. *Concrete Quarterly* found the building 'supremely well made' by John Laing and engineer Felix J. Samuely, with concrete 'of an exceptionally high standard', cast in situ with board-marked surfaces, and precast cladding of Aberdeen granite aggregate recalling the purple stone in surrounding buildings.[85] The cathedral's few artworks complemented its material treatment. William Mitchell made Stations of the Cross panels of fast-setting cement, as well as ambo and doors. The latter had rugged, metallic surfaces on fibreglass panels incorporating the arms of Bristol, celebrating their donation to the cathedral by the city council. Henry Haig's windows formed two friezes of abstract *dalle de verre*, inspired, he said, by the Pembrokeshire coast, where he made preparatory drawings for the commission.[86]

Besides this Welsh element, the cathedral was a building for its English diocese and its city. It allowed the new liturgy to be celebrated generously, with room for congregations from across the diocese, made intimate by their arrangement around the altar. It presented a contemporary image to the city: despite its suburban location the concrete spire is visible from many distant viewpoints; and its open external platforms encouraged events in sight of surrounding streets. The diocese expressed this civic purpose in the opening ceremonies, which juxtaposed liturgical rites with a musical festival, including an ecumenical concert with church choirs from around the city and a 'religious opera' performed by children from local schools.[87]

CLIFTON'S OFFSPRING

Despite praise from the architectural press, the Percy Thomas Partnership received no further church commissions for twenty years. This was partly because few new churches were built in Britain after 1970, as church attendance for all denominations sharply dropped. Clifton Cathedral did have two late offspring, where Weeks, architect for both, applied its lessons and forms to similar purposes. The first was a competition win of 1989 for the Roman Catholic church of St John Vianney at Kirkland near Seattle, which Weeks designed in collaboration with his brother-in-law Wojtek Koczarski, an accomplished Polish architect who had designed many Catholic churches for the Archdiocese of Seattle.[88] The building, completed a few years later, was a flattened, neo-vernacular version of Clifton Cathedral, with a timber roof structure and low projecting eaves. It reworked Clifton's fan-shaped hexagonal nave in simplified form. A substantial attached parish centre followed the same geometry for community use in its sprawling suburb.

Weeks also designed the Anglican church of St Luke in his home town of Buckfastleigh, Devon, for the Percy Thomas Partnership as a miniature, economical version of Clifton Cathedral from 1999 to 2002 (recently closed; future uncertain). Workshops with the parochial church council elicited a detailed brief, and concern for provision of community spaces. With similar liturgical priorities, Weeks felt justified in adapting Clifton's design to the new setting, with a similar hexagonal geometry, fan-shaped nave and baptistery.[89] As at Clifton there was a basement

Fig.11 St Luke, Buckfastleigh (author).

hall and social rooms, but also a 'lounge' on the street frontage for use by townsfolk which could be opened inside to augment the nave. The church's stark modernism contrasts with its village setting, but stepping it back from the building line softened its impact on the townscape. The building resulted from a fire that ruined the old parish church of Holy Trinity, and as that was outside the town, the parish replaced the small Victorian chapel of St Luke in the town centre with the new building. Weeks incorporated fragments of the old churches, including stained glass windows and font, into the new, symbolising a continuous identity for its community – a feature also at Clifton, where the pro-cathedral's bells hang from the spire.[90]

CONCLUSION

The practice's work in religious architecture was modest compared to others that specialised in churches. Clifton Cathedral stands out because their lack of consistent church patronage led them to a unique design process and an unprecedented result. There was no consistent pattern of patronage from religious bodies; there was no single architect within the practice with religious connections or specialist interest, but many different architects involved; and between the 1940s and the end of the century, the practice took diverse approaches, from historicist neo-Gothic and neo-Georgian to radical modernism, via modern interpretations of conventional patterns. Superficially similar buildings represent different architects and even different denominations. Nevertheless, all demonstrate a civic ethos, an important aspect of the practice originating in Percy Thomas's pre-war work, with a distinctive public presence and a generous relationship to surrounding settlements, often achieved in partnership with civic authorities. Architects and clients saw religious buildings as contributions to the civic culture and community of the place, as well as forming congregations into communities with shared identities. Such concerns encompassed the changing nature of town centres and the dispersal of populations to the suburbs. Percy Thomas and his practice did not offer a single answer to that question, but rather articulated their clients' visions and resolved their needs empirically for each community in turn.

ACKNOWLEDGEMENTS

This article was written as part of a project that received funding support in the form of a British Academy/Leverhulme Small Research Grant and a Paul Mellon Centre Mid-Career Fellowship, for both of which I am most grateful. I would also like to thank Susan Fielding, Rev. Jill Hailey-Harris, Howard Williams, Rhidian Griffiths, Alan Randall and Canon J. A. Harding for assistance with the research.

NOTES

1 The author is in the process of writing a book on the practice; currently the best overviews are Elaine Davey, 'A National Architect? The Percy Thomas Practice and Welsh national identity', PhD thesis, Cardiff University (2013); Elaine Davey and Huw Thomas, '"Chief Creator of Modern Wales": The neglected legacy of Percy Thomas', *North American Journal of Welsh Studies*, no.9, 2014, pp.54–70.

2 See e.g. John B. Hilling, *The History and Architecture of Cardiff Civic Centre: Black Gold, White City* (Cardiff: University of Wales Press, 2016).

3 See for example Sven Sterken and Eva Weyns, eds., *Territories of Faith: Religion, Urban Planning and Demographic Change in Post-War Europe* (Leuven: Leuven University Press, 2022); C. Dwyer, D. Gilbert and B. Shah, 'Faith and Suburbia: Secularisation, modernity and the changing geographies of religion in London's suburbs', *Transactions of the Institute of British Geographers*, vol.38, no.3, July 2013, pp.403–19; Gretchen Buggein, *The Suburban Church: Modernism and Community in Postwar America* (Minneapolis: University of Minnesota Press, 2015).

4 Leslie T. Moore, 'Report: St Mary's Church, Swansea', 12 October 1944, in 'St Mary's, War Damage 1941–54: with Minutes of the Diocesan War Damage Consultative Committee', P/123/cw/547, West Glamorgan Archive Service.

5 Notes on vicar's speech, Annual Easter Vestry meeting, 30 April 1957, in PCC Minute Book, 1956–58, P/123/cw/442, West Glamorgan Archive Service.

6 Edward Williamson (Bishop of Swansea and Brecon) to D. Edwards-Davies (Diocesan Chancellor), 29 January 1942, P/123/cw/547, West Glamorgan Archive Service; see also Dinah Evans, *A New, Even Better, Abertawe: Rebuilding Swansea 1941–1961* (Llandysul: West Glamorgan Archive Service, 2019), p.60.

7 Williamson to Edwards-Davies, 5 November 1943 and (for first quotation) Edward-Davies to Williamson, 24 October 1943, P/123/cw/547, West Glamorgan Archive Service.

8 Swansea and Brecon Diocesan War Damage Consultative Committee, 22 March 1949, P/123/cw/547, West Glamorgan Archive Service; much of the correspondence over design in 1956–9 is with Percy Thomas in person, at P/123/cw/500, West Glamorgan Archive Service; Percy Edward Thomas, *Pupil to President: Memoirs of an architect* (Leigh-on-Sea: F. Lewis, 1963), p.49.

9 The main drawings date from December 1953, at P/123/cw/663, West Glamorgan Archive Service.

10 Drawing, Sir Percy Thomas & Son, 'The Church of Saint Mary Swansea: Part Cross Section Thro Nave & Aisle', 15 December 1953, P/123/cw/663/k, West Glamorgan Archive Service.

11 E. Liddell Armitage (Whitefriars Stained Glass Studios) to J. J. A. Thomas (Archdeacon of Gower and Vicar of St Mary's Swansea), 26 March 1957, and further correspondence between Armitage and Percy Thomas, P/123/cw/550, West Glamorgan Archive Service.

12 Correspondence of 1959 on furnishings between Percy Thomas, T. G. Middleton (Sir

Percy Thomas & Son) and H. C. Williams (St Mary's, Swansea), P/123/cw/554, West Glamorgan Archive Service.

13 Correspondence with John Piper of 1963–5 on the Holy Trinity Chapel is from Jack Thomas, though Howell Mendus of Percy Thomas & Son's Swansea office was invited to view the works once installed, suggesting some involvement; P/123/cw/554, West Glamorgan Archive Service.

14 [D. Edwards-Davies] to Leslie T. Moore, 11 December 1943, P/123/cw/547; Annual Easter Vestry, 26 April 1943, PCC Minute Book, 1940–55, P/123/cw/441, West Glamorgan Archive Service.

15 John Newman, The Buildings of Wales: *Glamorgan* (London: Yale University Press, 2004), p.491.

16 'Didsbury College, New Buildings: Didsbury College, Westbury-on-Trym, Bristol', leaflet, n.d. [*c.*1950], in A4/9, Wesley College Archives, University of Manchester Library Special Collections; 'Didsbury, Past and Future', *Methodist Recorder*, 3 May 1945, p.1, in newspaper cuttings collection, E3/34/1, Wesley College Archives, University of Manchester Library Special Collections.

17 E. Benson Perkins and Albert Hearn, *The Methodist Church Builds Again: A Consideration of the Purpose, Principles, and Plans for Methodist Church Building* (London: Epworth Press, 1946), pp.13, 17,21; Didsbury College meetings of 19 September 1947 and 13 September 1951, in Didsbury College Meeting Minutes, A1/9/3, Wesley College Archives, University of Manchester Library Special Collections.

18 'New Men's Hall of Residence, University College of North Wales, Bangor', *The Builder*, vol.163, 20 November 1942, pp.435–40.

19 'Didsbury Theological College, Bristol. Architects' Sir Percy Thomas & Son', *Architect and Building News*, vol.203, 4 June 1953, pp.651–4.

20 Frederic Greeves, 'Didsbury College, Bristol', pamphlet, n.d. [*c.*1953], A4/12, Wesley College Archives, University of Manchester Library Special Collections.

21 Perkins and Hearn, op. cit., pp.13, 17, 21.

22 'Percy Thomas Partnership: Architects & Planning Consultants', n.d. [*c.*1977, containing sketches signed by Weeks], unpaginated, 05/05; 'Percy Thomas Partnership: Architects & Planning Consultants', n.d. [*c.*1975], unpaginated, 05/04, Percy Thomas Archive, Archives of the Royal Commission on the Ancient and Historic Monuments of Wales.

23 King Street Methodist Church trustees' meetings of 5 April 1948 and 16 December 1949, 'King Street Methodist Church, Plymouth: Minute Book, 1940', 2597/3, Plymouth Archives and Local Studies.

24 Pauline Raine, *Blitzed Church is Rebuilt: The Storey of King Street Methodist Church, Plymouth*, n. pub., n.d. [*c.*1986], 3878/13, Plymouth Archives and Local Studies.

25 Patrick Abercrombie and James Paton Watson, *A Plan for Plymouth* (Plymouth: Underhill, 1943); Jeremy Gould, *Plymouth: Vision of a Modern City* (Swindon: English Heritage, 2010) pp.5–7, 13–14.

26 John E. Trevithick, 'Methodism in the New Plymouth: The observations of the Plymouth and Devonport Mission Circuit to the Conference Commission', 30 January 1947, for Quarterly Meeting of the Plymouth and Devonport Mission Circuit, Joint Leaders' and Trustees' Meeting, 26 March 1947, 2957/3, Plymouth Archives and Local Studies.

27 Trustees' meeting, 10 October 1946, 2957/3, Plymouth Archives and Local Studies.

28 Trustees' meeting, 5 April 1948, 2957/3, Plymouth Archives and Local Studies; on the relationship between centre and suburbs, which would imply support for Trevithick's view, see Perkins and Hearn, op. cit., pp.26–8.

29 Trustees' meetings of 23 February and 16 December 1948, 2957/3, Plymouth Archives and Local Studies.

30 Various plans dated 1954–7 at PCC/60/1/17169, Plymouth Archives and Local Studies.

31 Trustees' meeting, 6 January 1950, 2957/3, Plymouth Archives and Local Studies.

32 Perkins and Hearn, op. cit., p.54 and plates, e.g. Plate II; the plates are not attributed and other architects besides Prestwich are also named as advisers.

33 Percy Thomas attended early committee meetings in person, and Marsden first appeared on 20 April 1955, where he was described as 'the Architect for the new Building', suggesting significant design input; 2957/3, Plymouth Archives and Local Studies.

34 Perkins and Hearn, op. cit., p.34.

35 Choir seating discussed at trustees' meetings of 15 October 1956 and 28 November 1956, and robes discussed on 2 August 1957, 2957/3; photograph of interior and further discussion in Raine, op. cit., pp.18 and 20 respectively, 3878/13, Plymouth Archives and Local Studies.

36 These ideas are hinted at in the 'Order of Service for the Opening and Dedication of the New King Street Methodist Church, Plymouth', booklet of 4 December 1957, 3543/2, Plymouth Archives and Local Studies.

37 E. Llewellyn John to regional licensing officer, Ministry of Works, Cardiff, 3 May 1952, in 'Capel y Trinity: Adeiladau Newydd. Gohebiaethau Cofnodion', EZ1/85/33, Calvinistic Methodist Archives, National Library of Wales Archives.

38 'County Borough of Swansea: Re-Planning of the Central Town Area; Places of Worship', report of meeting of 10 January 1944 between corporation officials and the Swansea Churches' War Damage and Town Planning Committee, BE 52/95, West Glamorgan Archive Service.

39 Report of 25 October 1950, EZ1/85/33, Calvinistic Methodist Archives, National Library of Wales Archives; additional information from Rhidian Griffiths (son of minister H. Wynne Griffiths), correspondence with the author, 9 July 2018.

40 Rhidian Griffiths, interview with the author, 11 July 2018.

41 Report of 25 October 1950, EZ1/85/33, Calvinistic Methodist Archives, National Library of Wales Archives.

42 E.g. meeting of 7 November 1951, Trinity Chapel Swansea, New Chapel Building Committee Minute Book, 1951–8, EZ1/85/29, Calvinistic Methodist Archives, National Library of Wales Archives.

43 Correspondence at EZ1/85/33, Calvinist Methodist Archives, National Library of Wales Archives; for further information, especially on Welsh Methodist custom, I am grateful to Rhidian Griffiths and the minister at the time of my visit, Jill-Hailey Harries.

44 G. P. Williams, 'Acorn-Oak, 1742–1956', in 'Saint Andrew's Methodist Church, Birchgrove: Opening Ceremony, Saturday, September 1st, 1742–1956', pp.5–7, DWESCR/20/2, Glamorgan Archives.

45 ibid., p.6; Marsden is named in most of the written documentation at Glamorgan Archives and is pictured attending the opening ceremony at Rumney (D761/7/1, Glamorgan Archives).

46 Trustees' meeting, 14 October 1953, in Rumney Methodist Church Trust Minutes, 1953–76, D761/1/4, Glamorgan Archives.

47 T. Dixon Jones (minister), 'Why St Andrew?', in 'Saint Andrew's Methodist Church, Birchgrove: Opening Ceremony', op. cit., pp.3–4, DWESCR/20/2; leaders' meetings of 8 March and 29 August 1956, Birchgrove Methodist Church: Minutes of Leaders' Meetings and Annual Society Meetings, 1937–60, DWESCR/20/1/1, Glamorgan Archives.

48 E.g. explained in 'The New Church', in 'Souvenir: Opening and Consecration of the New Methodist Church at Rumney, Cardiff, 17th March 1956', pp.8 and 11, D761/7/1, Glamorgan Archives.

49 Drawings submitted for planning permission dated 1954, BC/S/1/44594, Glamorgan Archives.

50 A. W. Abbotts, untitled text, in 'Saint Andrew's Methodist Church, Birchgrove: Opening Ceremony', op. cit., p.4, DWESCR/20/2, Glamorgan Archives.

51 Drawings dated 1954, BC/S/1/44149; trustees' meeting, 1 April 1954, in Rumney Methodist Church Trust Minutes, 1953–76, D761/1/4, Glamorgan Archives.

52 'Souvenir: Opening and Consecration of the New Methodist Church at Rumney, Cardiff, 17th March 1956', pp.8 and 11, D761/7/1, Glamorgan Archives.

53 Leaders' meeting, 1 September 1952, in Rumney Methodist Church Leaders' Meetings and Society Meetings, 1944–53, D761/1/2; leaders' meetings of 29 November 1954 and 7 March 1955, in Rumney Methodist Church Leaders' Meetings, 1953–64, D761/1/3; trustees meeting, 11 June 1953, in Rumney Methodist Church Trust Minutes, 1953–76, D761/1/4, Glamorgan Archives.

54 'The Methodist Church. Cardiff (Roath) Circuit. Opening and Dedication of the New Church at Llanrumney. Saturday, 13th June 1959', D761/7/2, Glamorgan Archives.

55 https://www.merthyr-history.com/?p=3804, accessed 10 November 2021.

56 E.g. Sir Percy Thomas & Son, 'Notes of Meeting held in the Architect's Offices on Friday 3rd May, 1968', DWES/MT/144/1/4, Glamorgan Archives; summary of position in George Graham (minister at Dowlais) to Herbert Simpson (Department for Chapel Affairs, Methodist Church), 15 January 1971, DWES/MT/144/1/1, Glamorgan Archives.

57 'History of Dowlais "Wesley" Methodist Church, 1932–1972: 40 Years', DWES/MT/144/1/2, Glamorgan Archives.

58 Invitation to opening ceremony, Gwent Crematorium archive.

59 'Local Authorities Confer at Newport', *South Wales Gazette*, no.2931, 16 July 1943, p.7.

60 'County's 20-Year Development Plan', *Western Mail & South Wales News*, no.26893, 20 October 1955, p.8; dates of crematorium commission from meetings of Monmouthshire and Newport Joint Cremation Committee, 15 November 1954 and 13 May 1955, Gwent Crematorium archive.

61 Monmouthshire and Newport Joint Cremation Committee, 24 June 1955, Gwent Crematorium archive.

62 James Howard (parish priest, Our Lady Star of the Sea, Burry Port) to John Edward Petit (Bishop of Menevia), 2 April 1963, parish file, Menevia Diocesan Archives.

63 *Catholic Building Review*, southern edition, 1957, pp.137–8 and *Catholic Building Review*, southern edition, 1958, p.176.

64 Various drawings of May 1963, parish file, Menevia Diocesan Archives.

65 Howard to Petit, 2 April 1963; Wallace Sweet (Sir Percy Thomas & Son) to Petit, 2 April 1963, parish file, Menevia Diocesan Archives.

66 Sweet to Petit, 16 May 1963, with accompanying report and drawings, parish file, Menevia Diocesan Archives; alterations shown in drawings by S. G. H. of 24 June 1963, parish file, Menevia Diocesan Archives.

67 IDO [Dale Owen] and FSJ [Frederick Jennett], 'Design Note 1', n.d. [1964]; 'Design Method & Procedure, 1962–64', D900/U/6, Dale Owen Papers, Glamorgan Archives.

68 Sweet to Petit, 16 May 1963 and accompanying report; Sweet to Petit, 21 May 1963; parish file, Menevia Diocesan Archives.

69 On the historical background to the church's site, see https://taking-stock.org.uk/building/burry-port-our-lady-star-of-the-sea/, accessed 15 November 2021.

70 All quotations from Sweet to Petit, 16 May and accompanying report, parish file, Menevia Diocesan Archives.

71 *Catholic Building Review*, northern edition, 1965, pp.159–61.

72 Christopher Magner, *Saint Mair, Machynlleth: A parish history, 1927 to 1997* (n.pl: n.pub, 1997); 'Redemptorists Take Over Travelling Mission', *Catholic Standard*, vol.23, no.13, 30 March 1951, p.3; H. W. J. Edwards, 'The Toman Church in Wales To-Day', *Western Mail & South Wales News*, no.25729, 19 January 1952, p.4; https://taking-stock.org.uk/building/machynlleth-st-mair-our-lady-help-of-christians/, accessed 12 November 2021.

73 *Catholic Building Review*, northern edition, 1965, p.159.

74 Francis van Neste to Bishop Rudderham of Clifton, 18 February 1970, and '£250,000 Promise for New R. C. Cathedral', *Bristol Evening Post*, 17 January 1966, unpaginated cutting, in 'Miscellaneous Correspondence', cathedral box, Clifton Roman Catholic Diocesan Archives.

75 Peter Ansdell Evans, 'Clifton's Catholic Cathedral', *Architects' Journal*, vol.158, no.28, 11 July 1973, pp.70–2 (71).

76 Kenneth Nugent, 'Clifton Cathedral Church of ss Peter and Paul', *Clergy Review*, vol.58, September 1973, pp.737–44 (739–40)

77 Tony Aldous, 'Portrait of a Practice: Percy Thomas Partnership', *Building Design*, no.374, 2 December 1977, pp.13–16 (15).

78 Maureen Kelly Owen, interview with the author, 23 June 2017.

79 Ronald Weeks, 'The Design and Construction of the Cathedral Church of ss. Peter and Paul, Clifton', *Pax: The Review of the Benedictine Monks of Prinknash*, vol.63, autumn/winter 1973, pp.60–9; Kate Wharton, 'Genesis of a Cathedral', *Architect and Building News*, vol.2, no.1, 1 January 1969, pp.22–9; Kate Wharton and Ronald Weeks, 'Architectural Heritage Year 2075…?', *The Architect*, vol.121, no.3, May 1975, pp.24–5.

80 Lance Wright, 'Architectural Seriousness', in Peter Hammond, ed., *Towards a Church Architecture* (London: Architectural Press, 1962) pp.220–44.

81 Robert Proctor, 'Uncertainty and the Modern Church: Two Roman Catholic cathedrals in Britain', in Vladimir Kuliç, Monica Penick and Timothy Parker, eds., *Sanctioning Modernism: Architecture and the making of post-war identities* (Austin: University of Texas Press, 2015), pp.113–38.

82 Robert Proctor, *Building the Modern Church: Roman Catholic church architecture in Britain, 1955 to 1975* (Farnham: Ashgate, 2014), p.160.

83 For detailed analysis of this design process, see Robert Proctor, 'Modern Church Architect as Ritual Anthropologist: Architecture and Liturgy at Clifton Cathedral', *ARQ*, vol.15, no.4, 2011, pp.359–72; evidence for this process includes booklets of drawings of High Mass and Pontifical High Mass of 29 November 1965 and 2 December 1965, 'Plans & Construction Details of Clifton Cathedral', cathedral box; 'R. C. Cathedral Bristol Liturgical Brief (rev. Dec' 65)' and another similar, undated, cathedral box, Clifton Roman Catholic Diocesan Archives (viewed there by author *c.*2010); Ronald Weeks, telephone interviews with the author, 9 November 2007 and 24 September 2008.

84 Evans, op. cit., p.71.

85 George Perkin, 'Cathedral Craft: Cathedral Church of ss. Peter and Paul, Clifton, Bristol', *Concrete Quarterly*, no.100, January to March 1974, pp.22–32 (24, 29–30).

86 Henry Haig, 'Clifton Cathedral: Designing and Making the Windows', *Clergy Review*, vol.59, January 1974, pp.81–8.

87 'Clifton Cathedral Souvenir Brochure', 29 June 1973, p.12, cathedral box, Clifton Roman Catholic Diocesan Archives.

88 Untitled elevation image and caption, *Architects' Journal*, vol.190, no.15, 11 October 1989, p.12; https://www/nwsmiles.com/blog?p=wojteck-jan-koczarski-a-biography, accessed 18 November 2021; https://www.seattlepolishnews.org/2021/04/roy-wojtek-koczarski-has-died/, accessed 18 November 2021.

89 Ronald Weeks, telephone interview with the author, 4 May 2011.

90 Ronald Weeks, 'Church of St Luke, Buckfastleigh, Devon', *Church Building*, no.78, November-December 2002, pp.27–32.

KAROLINA SZYNALSKA McALEAVEY AND HARRY PATRICK FOLEY

11 Yesterday's Church of Tomorrow:

St John the Baptist, Ermine Estate, Lincoln

Fig.1 Church interior; the concrete font and altar (St John Ermine archive)

Consecrated in 1963, the church of St John the Baptist remains a central feature of the Ermine Estate on the north side of Lincoln. It was commissioned by Rev. John Hodgkinson over a cup of tea shared one afternoon with Eric Scorer, a clerk to Lindsey County Council. Scorer showed the vicar an image of a projected modern church in Welwyn Garden City designed by his son, Hugh Segar 'Sam' Scorer (1923–2003), a talented and recent alumnus of the Architectural Association, in collaboration with Peter Bridges, a priest architect engaged in innovative church planning, and Kalman Hajnal-Kónyi, a London-based Hungarian engineer and refugee.

The proposed church at Welwyn had a square plan with the altar positioned on the diagonal axis, beneath a dramatic hyperbolic paraboloid roof. The radical design was enthusiastically previewed in the *Architectural Review* and in the book *Liturgy and Architecture* by Peter Hammond (1960), a priest and architectural theorist, who sought 'a church which reflects a new theological outlook, a deeper understanding of the liturgy'.[1] In what is now thought to be 'one of the most important books for church design of the twentieth century', Hammond suggested that the Welwyn design promised 'to be one of the more interesting churches built in this country since the war'.[2] Sadly the scheme failed to find funding and remained unbuilt.

The dominant feature of the design for Welwyn Garden City was a gracefully sweeping, tent-like, concrete roof structure.[3] Precariously supported at only two points, it encloses a large area, free from columns; an uninterrupted, flexible, *functional* space. Though not new, the single-saddle form, or hyperbolic paraboloid (hypar, for short), was unfamiliar in the context of modern church design. However, it had been afforded a greater audience during the 1950s and 1960s owing to continued post-war steel rationing, the excitement surrounding the possibilities of engineering and a desire from the ecclesiastical community to better engage their congregations in more open plans.

HYPERBOLIC PARABOLOIDS

The hypar is a double-curved surface, generated by a more primitive linear geometry, allowing it to be easily constructed with a formwork of straight planks. The shape is a continuous plane that develops from a parabolic arch in one direction, and a similar but inverted parabola in the other – a principle of two arch systems, one in compression and one in tension. A high-tech solution executed via low-tech methods, the architectural application of the hypar was largely developed in Mexico in the 1950s by Félix Candela and notably featured in Le Corbusier's Philips Pavilion for the Expo'58 in Brussels. After seeing Candela lecture in London, Scorer and Hajnal-Kónyi had already employed the hypar on three previous occasions.

The first was incorporated into the tank tower that sat awkwardly on the corner of the five-storey Charnos lingerie factory in Ilkeston, Derbyshire, in 1956 (demolished). The second, much larger, hypar formed a roof over a petrol station along the A1 at Markham Moor, Nottinghamshire, in 1960 (since 2020 a Starbucks coffee shop). Their most ambitious application, consisting of four concrete hyperbolic paraboloid shells separated by a roof-light running along the entire depth of the building, was a feature of the Lincolnshire Motor Company's garage, offices and showrooms in Lincoln, opened in 1959. This was briefly the largest hyperbolic paraboloid to have been built in the United Kingdom, until exceeded in 1962 by the Commonwealth Institute in Kensington designed by Robert Matthew, Johnson-Marshall & Partners. By comparison with these commercial facilities, St John the Baptist was a more exciting, but also more challenging, prospect; its architectural language was expected to have liturgical justification.

Fig.2 St John the Baptist (Karolina Szynalska McAleavey, 2010)

THE LITURGICAL MOVEMENT

In 1957, the year that Scorer and Hajnal-Kónyi were commissioned to begin work at Ermine, the subject of the Liturgical Movement reached the British architectural press. Peter Hammond first criticised modern church architecture in Britain in *The Listener*, and followed it the next year with an equally biting article for the *Architectural Review*.[4] Like Scorer and Hajnal-Kónyi, Hammond prioritised function over aesthetics, seeking 'a church which reflects a new theological outlook, a deepened understanding of the liturgy which gives the building its *raison d'être*'.[5] Inspired by two seminal texts, Fr A. G. Hebert's *Liturgy and Society* (1936) and Dom Gregory Dix's *The Shape of the Liturgy* (1945), Hammond's concerns aligned with those of the Liturgical Movement, which originated in France and Belgium during the 1830s and 1840s, then developed across northern Europe and the United States. He admired the work of Gottfried Böhm and Rudolf Schwarz, and became interested in the potential of square, round, or elliptical plans that featured in their work. On the subject, Rudolf Wittkower had argued in 1948–9, 'how could the relation of man to God be better expressed, we feel now justified in asking, than by building the house of God in accordance with the fundamental geometry of square and circle'.[6]

Wittkower provided a historical justification for a strong geometry in church design, along with a prioritisation of function over aesthetic. His book grew out of a series of lectures at the Warburg Institute attended by, significantly, Peter Smithson, and in 1951 he and his wife Alison – self-appointed heroes of British modernism – entered a competition for Coventry Cathedral. Their proposed scheme was a vast, functional, diamond-shaped space featuring a forward altar and a remarkable hyperbolic paraboloid, according to the Smithsons a form 'quite unsuitable for a church unless handled in a very special way'.[7] The scheme was later published in *Churchbuilding*, the magazine of the New Churches Research Group, by another Wittkower follower, Robert Maguire. His editorial emphasised how function determined the choice of the structure (engineered by the Smithsons' friend Ronald Jenkins), though the Smithsons also stressed the importance of a modern image.

> *It is hoped by the competitors that the building of this cathedral will finally explode the fallacy that Modern Architecture is incapable of expressing abstract ideas and will prove that only Modern Architecture is capable of creating a symbol of the dogmatic truths of the Christian faith and 'thrusting them at the man who comes in from the street' with the dynamism that so great a Faith demands.*[8]

Scorer was the same age as Peter Smithson, belonging to a generation that stretched the term 'functional' beyond its earlier meanings to include the expression of abstract or symbolic values.[9] St John the Baptist is the product of an alliance to this school of thought; the single uninterrupted space was a functional solution to the question of the new liturgy, where process, form and detail are employed to express narratives relating to a sense of place, truth and individuality.

DESIGN PROCESS

For Scorer and Hajnal-Kónyi, the timing of Hammond's intervention was impeccable, allowing the duo to pursue a reimagined model of the modern church whilst understanding that they could rely on the 'Church of England's leading architectural theorist' for support. St John the Baptist's unique arrangement originally took shape in response to a simple sketch representing a focal point of some activity (a speaker in Hyde Park, for example). During early discussions, Scorer had invited Fr

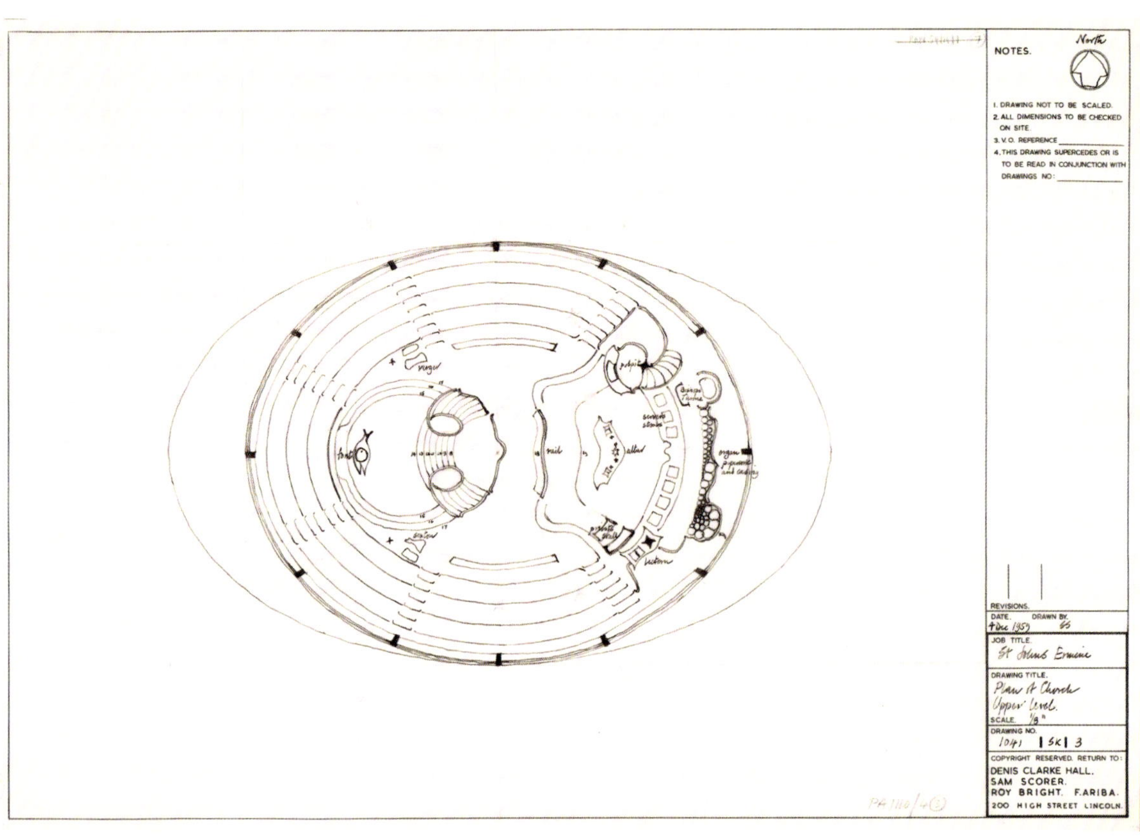
NOTES.
North
1. DRAWING NOT TO BE SCALED.
2. ALL DIMENSIONS TO BE CHECKED ON SITE.
3. V.O. REFERENCE
4. THIS DRAWING SUPERCEDES OR IS TO BE READ IN CONJUNCTION WITH DRAWINGS NO:
REVISIONS.
DATE. 4 Dec 1959
DRAWN BY. SS
JOB TITLE. St Johns Ermine
DRAWING TITLE. Plan of Church Upper Level.
SCALE. 1/8"
DRAWING NO. 1041 | SK | 3
COPYRIGHT RESERVED. RETURN TO:
DENIS CLARKE HALL.
SAM SCORER.
ROY BRIGHT. F.ARIBA.
200 HIGH STREET LINCOLN.

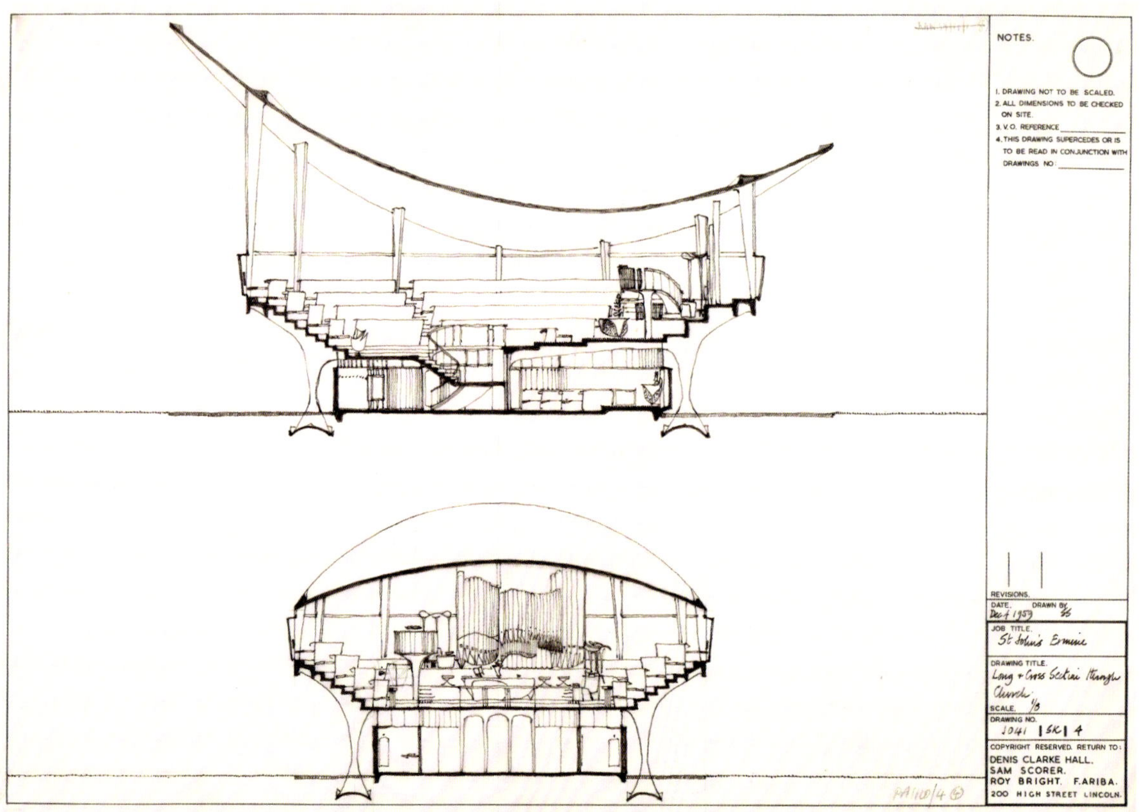
NOTES.
1. DRAWING NOT TO BE SCALED.
2. ALL DIMENSIONS TO BE CHECKED ON SITE.
3. V.O. REFERENCE
4. THIS DRAWING SUPERCEDES OR IS TO BE READ IN CONJUNCTION WITH DRAWINGS NO:
REVISIONS.
DATE. Dec 4 1959
DRAWN BY. SS
JOB TITLE. St John's Ermine
DRAWING TITLE. Long + Cross Section through Church
SCALE. 1/8
DRAWING NO. 1041 | SK | 4
COPYRIGHT RESERVED. RETURN TO:
DENIS CLARKE HALL.
SAM SCORER.
ROY BRIGHT. F.ARIBA.
200 HIGH STREET LINCOLN.

Fig.3 1959 version of the church; plan (RIBA collections)

Fig.4 1959 version of the church; sections (RIBA collections)

Hodgkinson to draw how he imagined the congregation would gather in the church; his sketch conveyed a series of circles of people to the front of the eucharistic space, with a row of people to the rear. Scorer's realised design adheres to this concept. Curved pews are positioned theatrically on a gentle downward slope, encircling the central font at the lowest point of the church, constituting a symbolic descent into the water of baptism.

With this arrangement, St John the Baptist became one of the first Anglican churches to be developed on a fan-shaped plan. But Scorer was confident that by employing this layout with the uninhibited sightlines afforded by the unique application of a tent-like hypar roof, the eucharistic space would greatly improve the quality of worship for the congregation. Scorer's intuition was later vindicated by an application to list the church that recognised the significance of the architect's decision to remove the altar from a central location, where the celebrant must have his back to part of the congregation. The building's importance lies in its combination of innovative minimalist architectural thinking with advanced liturgical planning.

The first designs, in 1959, however, aroused consternation with the parish committee. It was a minimalistic concrete form on an elliptical plan with a flamboyant interior, balanced on a plinth. The architect from the beginning wanted to discuss with the parish committee such fundamental questions as its belief in God, and the purpose and function of a church.[10] In order to design the building, the concepts of the church as the 'People of God', the 'Body of Christ', and a community, had to be redefined. The new structure was to represent a 'Tent of Meeting, rather than a static temple'. This image was evoked from the Old and New Testaments; it was the place where pilgrims would pass through this world 'travelling lightly (free of excess baggage) to the promised land'.[11] Hodgkinson recalled that 'the emphasis was very much on church as people rather than a building'; the function of the church building was to protect the community from the elements.

The eventual, 'value-engineered', built version is a comparatively modest, single floor form following the principles of functional design. Hodgkinson reminisced that 'the old church was very cluttered up with various objects and they [the designers] arrived at a principle that nothing would be included unless it was used'.[12] He explained, 'None of you would include any item in a factory or a warehouse unless it functioned and that was the line we took. We wanted the church to be functional. Instead of having a separate lectern and pulpit, it was decided to combine the two and not to 'clutter it with a cross and candles'. Hodgkinson thought that people often ignored crosses if they saw them when they were out. He stated, 'they did not do much for them'. 'It was felt that the cross on the altar was unnecessary so the only one in the church was the processional cross, which was purely functional. ... it was not intended to be there for decoration.'[13]

FUNDING AND PROCUREMENT

The parish had precious little money available, so an intensive fundraising campaign ensued to help realise Scorer's proposal. It began in 1958 when an issue of the *Ermine News*, a monthly church newsletter edited by Fr Hodgkinson, featured an article entitled '8,000 Shares for Sale'. An early attempt to raise finances for the construction of Scorer's design, the article explained how certificates provided in exchange for donations would make for 'unusual souvenirs ... signed by the Lord Bishop of Lincoln and they state that the owner has had a share in the building of the Parish Church'.[14]

Fig.5 The revised design included a bell tower, which remains unbuilt (St John Ermine archive)

To build the church, Hodgkinson was utterly reliant on appeals of this type and on the generosity of others, despite remarking as late as January 1959 that, owing to uncertainties concerning the budget, the appearance of the church remained uncertain. One year later, he identified a shortfall of £15,000, despite the receipt of £5,250 from the diocese. So he extended his plea to the local and national press, of which this early declaration to the *Lincolnshire Echo* was typical in describing the project as a 'Do-It-Yourself' operation:

> *The people of the Ermine housing estate, in the Stewardship Campaign held some time ago, proved that not only do they want their church but that they are prepared to support it financially and otherwise. So far, they have had to be content with the two dual-purpose buildings – a church when services are held, then down with the screens and on with the dance.*[15]

This was in 1961, when Hodgkinson claimed to have gathered only £17,000, still well below Scorer's original estimate. He was fortunate, then, that in the absence of more substantial contributions, the Ermine congregation was so willing to aid the scheme. The young vicar acknowledged that 'it is obvious that we must be prepared to do a considerable amount of the construction ourselves. We should of course, use only skilled men for skilled work, but there are many of us prepared to work as labourers.'[16]

Having received a promise of payment upon completion of the design, Scorer agreed to provide further drawings and a physical model, to be used to promote the funding campaign and eventually appearing in parish magazines, local and national newspapers, architectural journals and on television. The model was also exhibited at Coventry Cathedral, until it was sat on and destroyed by a member of the congregation.

Finally, in July 1962, having now raised a total of £20,000 after much press coverage, an article in the *Ermine News* witnessed the signing of the contract for the first stage of building. This included the concrete shell of the church.[17] The piece confessed that, unless large sums were received by the end of the year, the rest of the work would have to be carried out by the congregation, including laying the floor; making the pews, furniture and fittings; decorating the walls and landscaping the outside area.

To mark the occasion, at a 'very vigorous eighty', Canon Dalby operated a bulldozer himself to begin clearance of the site before laying the foundation stone to represent 'the building up of a community on the estate'.[18] It did not take long before a maze of scaffolding and planks quickly erupted on site for the construction of the hyperbolic paraboloid roof, drawing some inquisitive residents to question, 'is it going to be a funfair ride?'.[19] Despite setbacks by frost, with the aid of floodlights and oil burners the contractors 'continued work right into the night and, within a week ... they completed the operation'.[20] This day marked a further setback, however, when negotiations for a £2,000 loan for the walls of the church fell through 'because the charity concerned ... found that it must secure a mortgage,

Fig.6 Model of the church (St John Ermine archive)

Fig.7 Church interior with the original formwork left in place (St John Ermine archive)

Fig.8 The parishioners taking part in the construction process (St John Ermine archive)

and it is not possible to mortgage a church'.[21] Unfortunately for Hodgkinson, this marked the beginning of a series of setbacks, and it was not long before the church was forced to abandon the final phase for the scheme, including the erection of a bell tower, estimated at an additional cost of £1,000 according to a list of works in 1963.[22]

Abandoning the second phase of the scheme, however, allowed the main structure of the church to be considered finished. The ceiling formwork was left in place as the finishing layer. At the request of the vicar, in August 1963, 25 male members of the congregation appeared at the entrance of the building to decorate, make cupboards, complete the site works and many other jobs to be ready for the Consecration Day of 6 October. On Tuesdays and Thursdays, the main work nights, women and children were also requested on site to provide cups of tea and carry out needlework. Over three of these evenings, along with the help of Rev. Frank Baker, volunteers from the congregation removed 'thirty tons of earth with shovel and wheelbarrow', a mark of their dedication.[23] The parishioners were responsible for building the pews, decoration and landscaping the site.

The main body of the church was built for £24,000, but over eight per cent of this sum was dedicated to a special artwork. Scorer wanted it to be incorporated to 'illuminate the whole building', while Hodgkinson mysteriously stated, '[t]his was the act of faith which resulted in the magnificent East window by Keith New, filling the church with colour, light and mystery'.[24] New had become famous for some of the windows at Coventry Cathedral. His abstract composition at St John the Baptist, fitted into an industrial patent glazing system, presented the theme of the revelation of God's plan for man's redemption. Both the altar and the font are in a minimalist and primitive style, and both were cast in concrete. The altar is free standing.

In 1963, one month after the consecration, Hodgkinson recalled some of the initial reactions of the congregation and residents of the Ermine Estate. Hundreds of men and women made such remarks as '"I must confess that I didn't think much to it when it was going up, but the result is terrific"; the elderly retracted their earlier qualms that there could be no "atmosphere" in a modern church; a local police sergeant "stopped in amazement" when he looked inside, declaring "I've watched it being built, and I wondered what all the fuss was about, but I can see now. It's beautiful"; teenagers beckoned their friends, "It's a smashing church, come and have a look"; a builder observed out of professional curiosity, "I don't go to church, but if I did, I'd come to this one".'[25]

St John the Baptist was named as the 'Church of Tomorrow' in parish publications.[26] According to Pevsner, it was the first church in Lincolnshire to break the tradition of the Gothic revival.[27] It was revolutionary. The church represented a direct victory over historic architecture.[28] It also continues the modernist tradition of honesty of the materials and rationality derived – paradoxically – from nineteenth-century Viollet-le-Duc's interpretation of Gothic. It is a major contribution to ecclesiastical architecture of the second half of the twentieth century. In spite of how inappropriate a hyperbolic paraboloid may have been for church building, according to the Smithsons, it has been handled in a very special way indeed.

Fig.9 Church interior; the pews (St John Ermine archive)

Fig.10 Church interior; east window by Keith New (Karolina Szynalska McAleavey)

It provided the open space the congregation wanted, as well as the narrative of a modest tent on a pilgrim's path. The community gathered around St John seems successful. It works as a community hub and the event calendar is busy. And a tourism industry among local (and increasingly national) architectural enthusiasts is maintained by volunteers who open the church in the mornings during the summer months.

NOTES

1 Peter Hammond, 'A Liturgical Brief', *Architectural Review*, vol.123, April 1958, pp.240–55.

2 Robert Proctor, *Building the Modern Church: Roman Catholic Church Architecture in Britain, 1955 to 1975* (Farnham: Ashgate, 2014), p.133; Peter Hammond, *Liturgy and Architecture* (London: Barrie and Rockliff, 1960), p.111.

3 *Architectural Review*, vol.125, January 1959, pp.44–5.

4 Peter Hammond, 'Contemporary Architecture and the Church', *The Listener*, vol.57, 23 May 1957, pp.824–6.

5 Hammond, 'A Liturgical Brief', op. cit., p.242.

6 Rudolf Wittkower, *Architectural Principles in the Age of Humanism* (London: Warburg Institute, 1949 / Academy Editions, 1988), p. 25.

7 Alison and Peter Smithson, 'Design for Coventry Cathedral 1951', *Churchbuilding*, no.8, January 1963, pp.3–12 (p.12)

8 ibid.

9 Alison Smithson, *The Emergence of Team 10 out of CIAM* (London: Architectural Association, 1982), p.82.

10 John Hodgkinson, *The Creation of a Parish and the Buildings of its Church: 1956–1964* (Lincoln: St John the Baptist, 2010.

11 ibid, p.8.

12 John Hodgkinson, *The Parish Church of St John the Baptist, Ermine Estate*, undated, R BOX L.LINC.726.5 CLA 00/128, Lincoln City Archives.

13 ibid.

14 '8,000 Shares for Sale', *Ermine News*, February 1958.

15 'Church Design Ultra-Modern', *Lincolnshire Echo*, 14 June 1961, p.1.

16 ibid.

17 'The Church is Growing', *Ermine News*, November 1962.

18 'Bishop Lays Foundation of a Family Church', *Lincolnshire Echo*, 24 July 1962, p.3.

19 Fr Stephen Hoy, interviewed by Harry Patrick Foley, 2018.

20 'New Lincoln Church must be Worthy', *Lincolnshire Echo*, 18 January 1962, p.8.

21 'Churchman's Diary', *Lincolnshire Echo*, 27 December 1962, p.4.

22 *Ermine News*, September 1963.

23 ibid.

24 Hodgkinson, *The Parish Church of St John the Baptist*, op. cit.

25 *Ermine News*, November 1963.

26 Hodgkinson, *The Parish Church of St John the Baptist*, op. cit.

27 Nikolaus Pevsner and John Harris, revised Nicholas Antram, The Buildings of England: *Lincolnshire* (London: Pevsner, 1989) p.71.

28 ibid.

TIMOTHY BRITTAIN-CATLIN

12 An Element of Apprehension: Holy Trinity, Twydall Green, Kent

Fig.1 Holy Trinity, Twydall, from the west (Elain Harwood)

The church of Holy Trinity, Twydall Green, in Gillingham in Kent, was designed by Arthur Bailey of Ansell & Bailey between 1952 and 1964, and is one of the most remarkable buildings of its date. Approaching from the south, one suddenly finds it looming over neighbouring buildings as if it were the great maw of a shark. It sits on an open patch of grassland facing the neighbourhood shopping centre; from the front, that is the north, it looks like a tent pitched over a cascade of wild brickwork. It was a scene that puzzled and troubled John Newman when he wrote his Pevsner entry: 'but what is one to make of it?' he asked. 'Malformed stock bricks are rudely laid in chunks and bastions and buttresses, but never in a straight bit of wall'.[1] Scarcely two miles to the north is another remarkable church, Peter Bosanquet's contemporary and Aaltoesque St Matthew, Wigmore, described by Newman as 'Undoubtedly the finest late C20 church in the county.', Bailey's church should be on the itinerary of every student architect.[2] And yet it is almost unknown.

The story of the building of Holy Trinity was painful for its architect Arthur Bailey (1904–79) and parochial church council (PCC) alike. No phase of its commission and design passed without agony on the part of one side or the other, in contrast to St Matthew's, where a vicar with a clear idea of what he wanted appears to have had his ambitions fulfilled. Both were churches designed for expanded housing estates east of the centre of Gillingham. The corporation's town guide for 1948 explained that 'the high land to the south away from the river, from which extensive views across the Medway can be enjoyed' had been chosen for these new 'neighbourhood units' just within the adjoining parish of Rainham. The 1951 guide recorded that contracts had been placed for most of the proposed housing in Twydall, pronounced 'twiddle', which lay between the hamlet of Wigmore and the river.[3] The new estate was designed by the town surveyor's department in the Anglo-Scandinavian fashion of the 1940s for an eventual population of around 10,000.[4] Its centrepiece was the Green: an L-shaped block of shops and maisonettes, still in its original form although now enclosing a car park instead of a lawn, which might almost be an illustration from Bertil Hultén's *Building Modern Sweden*, a Penguin book of 1951. The site for the church stood to the south of this block, aligned with an avenue of further shops and flats on its eastern side; it was conveyed to the diocese from the town council in September 1954. When that year the foundation stone of the church hall was laid by Dame Sybil Thorndike, whose father had been a minor canon of Rochester Cathedral and a vicar nearby, the local newspaper described Twydall Green as 'Gillingham's pride and joy'.[5]

At this time the Diocese of Rochester was led by the evangelical Bishop Christopher Chavasse, who likewise was planning expansion and development in the new areas of housing. His right-hand man was the archdeacon, Lawrence

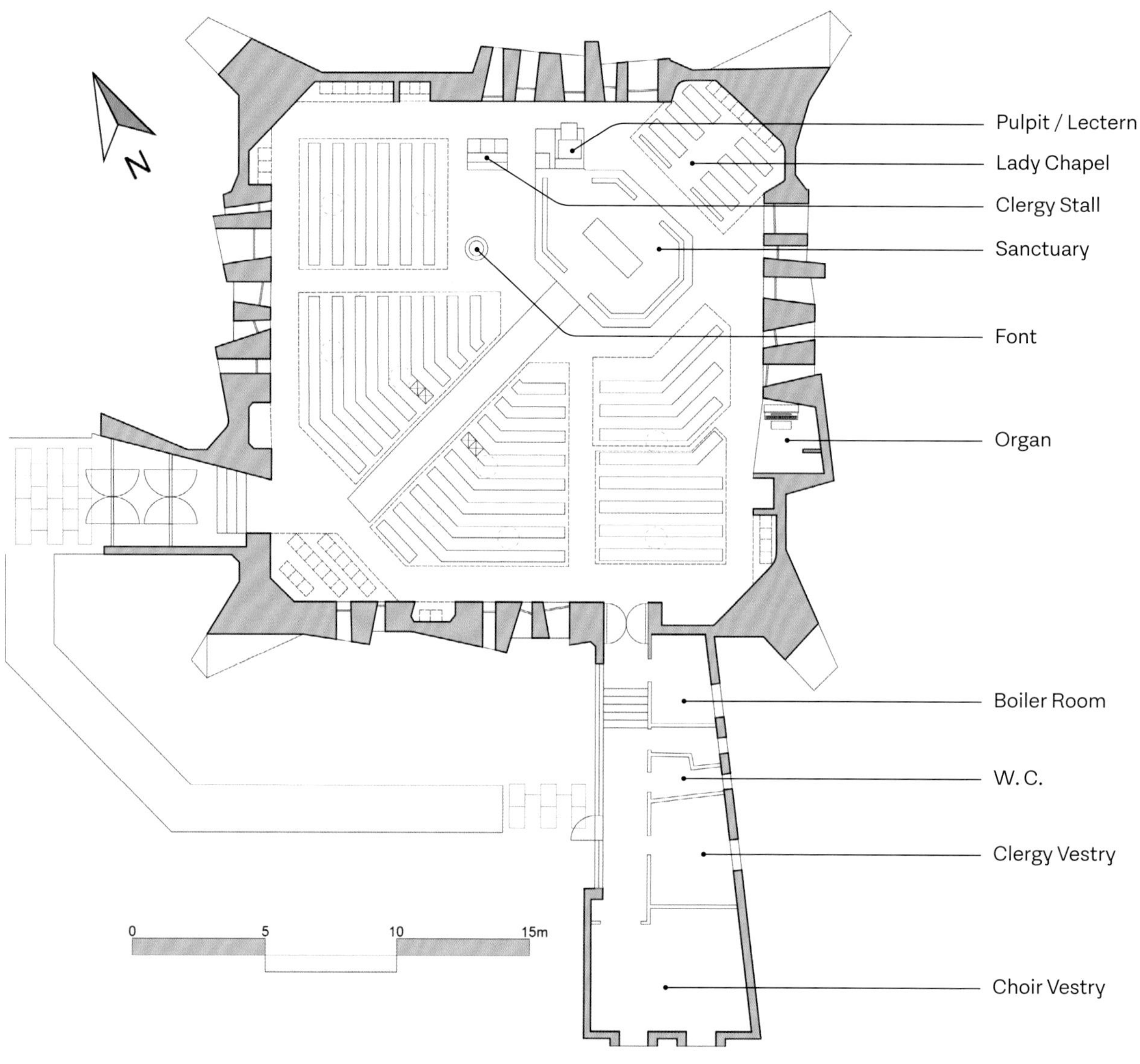

Fig.2 Plan of Holy Trinity, Twydall (Daniel Sables)

Harland, who appears repeatedly in Twydall PCC's minutes and correspondence as their antagonist and as the architect's champion. Canon E. E. Maples Earle, secretary of the Rochester Diocesan Reorganisation Committee, and his successor Major G. D. Gould emerge from the records as level-headed supporters of the scheme. The parish of Twydall Green was to be formed from a sub-division of both Rainham and Gillingham.[6] The new church was to be paid for in part by the sale of land following the demolition of the early Victorian Gothic revival Holy Trinity, Brompton, in the centre of Gillingham – in fact, Gould suggested, perhaps not seriously, that this building should be transported to the new site.[7]

Medway Archives Centre hold all the surviving parish records for the period; sufficient exist to trace how the church building emerged in the face of relentless local ill-feeling. Ansells, the successor to Ansell & Bailey, has not retained its Twydall files, and it has not been possible to ascertain whether Martin Bailey, Arthur's architect son who accompanied him to one particularly hostile public meeting, made any record of what happened or how the design evolved. His father first appears as architect in minutes of a meeting held on 5 April 1951.[8] A roughly

Fig.3 Arthur Bailey's 1951 proposal for the church and hall (P153K/DE0697, Medway Archives Centre)

contemporary but undated outline of events by Earle notes that Ansell & Bailey were appointed by the diocese as the estate layout was being finalised on the town surveyor's advice so that the church plans could be coordinated with him.[9] Bailey was then building the new Dutch Church in Austin Friars in the City of London; he already had a reputation as a designer of mass concrete bridges, but his runner-up scheme for Liverpool's Metropolitan cathedral and remodelling of Nicholas Hawksmoor's war-damaged St George-in-the-East in London lay still some ten years in the future.

Bailey's plan originated in an orthodox – and orthogonal – design for a combined church hall, church and parsonage, linked in that order from west to east across the site.[10] A perspective of this scheme was exhibited at the Royal Academy Summer exhibition in May 1954, a small part of a display overshadowed by Basil Spence's drawings for Coventry cathedral and described overall by *The Builder*'s correspondent as 'a surfeit of mediocrity'.[11] In a surviving print of the scheme, pasted into a Twydall minute book, this was a plain brick building with a tall, pierced cuboid lantern.[12] The plan in the meantime was to build the church hall and parsonage house on the same building contract, and to fit out the hall as a temporary church until funds were raised for the main building.[13]

Tenders were sought in early 1953, and Ward's Construction of Medway submitted the lowest and successful bid for the hall at £10,622. The intention was to negotiate rates and costs with them for the parsonage, on the basis of a similar specification, without further tender.[14] That April, Bailey sent drawings of the proposed house to Rev. F. W. Jordan, the vicar of Rainham and priest-in-charge. This elegant design, with a pantiled catslide roof and neat proportions, was similar, as Bailey pointed out, to his recent one at St Barnabas, St Paul Cray, in the north-west of the county.[15]

It was at this point that the problems began. Jordan did not like the catslide roof; he wanted a gable. The rooms were too big; he wanted them reduced.[16] Bailey reluctantly replaced the catslide with a gable – with the result that the house now looked, in his opinion, 'very ordinary' given the amount of thought invested in the composition of the three buildings.[17] He agreed to reduce the size of the house overall and of some of its rooms, warning that the Church Commissioners would not approve; he was right, and he subsequently had to increase them, resulting in a mishmash.[18] Jordan then interfered with the building specification: he wanted, for example, to install a smaller boiler than either the architect or the Commissioners would allow and he seems to have been particularly affronted that the architect was not making more of an effort to source materials locally for both house and hall.[19] Bailey's letter to Jordan on 30 June 1954 raised 'the strongest objection' to the parish's various interferences in the contract and especially the subcontracting, which at this point included Jordan's opposition to his architects choosing a fireplace. The PCC's copy of a letter from Jordan on this subject is already marked 'Dispute with Bailey', a sign of how the parish was ready to escalate even a minor disagreement.[20] They also turned down Bailey's invitation to join him 'and a small company of friends' on a private visit to his Dutch Church, a prestigious commission.[21] Securing the

Fig.4 Holy Trinity from the east (Elain Harwood)

building licence for the project also required considerable effort: the local MP, F. F. W. Burden, had to lobby David Eccles, the parliamentary secretary to the Ministry of Works; he was rewarded by the autumn of 1953.[22]

The hall is a plain building in good quality brickwork, the choice of which was forced on the architect by the parish, to his annoyance.[23] Its porch, under its own gable at the southern end of the street front to Twydall Lane, is decorated simply with tiles: Bailey's suggestion that the sculptor John Skeaping, who had contributed to the Dutch Church, should create a piece for it was evidently unheeded.[24] Bailey designed plain fittings and presented a silver trowel for the foundation stone ceremony.[25] Given the fuss made about some of the smaller details of the house, it appears that this part of the project at least went relatively smoothly. Leslie Hoskins, a curate with a young family, was appointed to the Rainham parish as priest-in-charge and moved into the new house.[26] And then the PCC turned its attention to the new church for what became, in 1956, a parish in its own right.

The PCC wanted a new architect. Then in late 1957 Hoskins resigned – suddenly it appears. The following January a letter from the PCC secretary to the archdeacon reported that they had at the latter's request put the question of the appointment of an architect for the church itself to his committee and it had been agreed 'that we dispense with the services of Mr Bailey'.[27] Hoskins's successor, Stephen Crookshank, a much more experienced man, was appointed in May (and rapidly found the vicarage under-sized: Bailey was again asked to make the rooms larger).[28] In January 1959, under Crookshank's direction, a group of PCC members took a bus trip to London and visited three economical post-war churches: David Nye's St Andrew, Lambeth; and Ralph Covell's St George, Patmore Street in Battersea and St Agnes, Kennington (which they thought 'beautiful'); they also visited Covell's St Edward, Mottingham, where Crookshank, who had been rector, told them that he had worked 'very harmoniously' with his architect.[29] The PCC interviewed Nye, who told them that 'he liked to produce a building to delight people, not shock them', and at the same meeting, proposed his appointment.[30]

However, a confidential note of 31 August 1959, written by Crookshank, recorded that:

> *The* PCC *did put forward the name of Mr David Nye to be our architect. The diocese did not take kindly to this suggestion and said that they would just as soon have Mr Bailey (who designed the present building) – especially as they were to a certain extent committed to him. The alternative might well be an architect of their choosing who would work with the Kentish* [Church] *Builders.*[31]

Whatever happened behind the scenes during this period is not clear, but on 10 April 1961 the PCC urged the diocesan building committee to appoint Bailey.[32] He and his son Martin came before the PCC meeting that November with plans and a model of the church which at this stage consisted of an almost plain square of plain brickwork, topped with a 90' steel pyramid.[33] This was the only occasion when any explanation of its general form was recorded. The idea, said Bailey, was to create a focal point at the junction at the lower end of the avenue alongside Twydall Green. Many of those present felt 'that the design could best be described as startling'.[34] The notes from the meeting continued:

> *Most members felt inspired by the focal point theme – it was undoubtedly exciting – it had something – and yet there was an element of apprehension as to how the design would be accepted by other people.*
>
> *The chairman* [Crookshank] *... regretted he did not like the design – he could not*

Fig.5 Holy Trinity, the westernmost corner (Elain Harwood)

see people, in general, liking it either, and did not feel that the design had the right idea at all, as initially imagined by most people.[35]

In time however the church guide, probably written by Crookshank, repeated an early comment of Bailey's in noting that the interior layout 'incorporates the latest thoughts in liturgical planning'; and in addition compared the roof to 'a tent [which] also formed the cover of the ark of the covenant'.[36]

The archdeacon reminded the PCC that the money was available, and building could start as soon as the following March.[37] Thirteen members voted in favour of proceeding with the scheme; five voted against, and one person abstained; that implies that W. G. Clements, the PCC secretary, tended to record in detail only the views of those who objected.[38] The Diocesan Building and Advisory Committee approved the plans by December 1961 and forwarded them to the borough council.[39] In March 1962 these went in front of parishioners at the parish's Annual General Meeting and were approved by a large margin.[40] Crookshank told the meeting that he had approached Bailey and

given him our views on specific points. Nevertheless, we are obliged to give him a relatively free hand – we cannot limit him completely. It was not possible to design a conventional type Church, to seat 350 people, for £25,000, hence the Pyramid design which had the Bishop's approval.[41]

The week beforehand the *Gillingham Observer* had reproduced photographs of Bailey's model under the headline 'New "Space-Age" church for Twydall. But will it go up?'.[42] The article recorded that Gillingham council wanted to test public reaction to the 'revolutionary plans' before granting permission. *The Observer* sounded out reactions a week later; these ranged from 'a sacrilegious eyesore' to 'a really beautiful piece of architecture' – it was 'the biggest controversy in the estate's history':

Said 33-years-old Walter Cropper, of Lynstead Road, on the estate: 'I don't like the thing. It isn't vaguely like a church. It has a bleak and desolate look about it, and, judging from the pictures, the inside will certainly not convey a very religious and sacred atmosphere to the congregation'.

A young housewife, Mrs Rosalind Potter, who lives in a flat facing Twydall Green, where the church will stand, was of the same opinion. 'I know that we need a church on the estate', she said, 'but I don't think it should be that shape'.

'Apart from not looking like a church, it reminds me of the Roman amphitheatres where they tortured early Christians – hardly the sort of place one would want to go to pray'.

Bailey attended the PCC's meeting on 14 August in which a revised plan was approved, and again a week later to meet Jordan and more parishioners.[43] The new design had emerged because 'in order to avoid the industrial look and character of the original shape of the church, he had remodelled the wall treatment, and broken it up to prevent a "slab look". Great strength would be required to hold up the roof, so the windows and niches are set in irregular planes'. Bailey had, in other words, taken the opportunity to address comments like those of Walter Cropper:

He had taken away the glass from behind the altar leaving a solid screed [screen?] *with a recess. The recesses around the walls could also accommodate other items, including the organist and console, hymn and prayer books etc. The organist would*

Fig.6 Holy Trinity, north elevation to Twydall Green (Elain Harwood)

> *have a commanding view of both congregation and service. All this had meant a complete recast of the general configuration of the building.*
> *The 'eye-brow'* [window] *of the original had also been re-shaped, to give more protection to the roof lights. The roof light angle had been tilted to ease glazing cleaning and maintenance.*[44]

This seems to have been the only explanation that Bailey ever gave for the final appearance of his unusual design. It was evidently with some fury that Clements then wrote in the minutes that 'A summary of the ensuing discussion could be put as "that we were more or less coerced into this scheme. Only one design was submitted. We were told that if we want a church, it was this or nothing"'; originally he wrote 'blackmailed' in place of 'coerced', and it looks as if Crookshank himself changed the wording before signing it off the following month.[45] The budget was to be £36,000, which seven months later had already risen to £41,217.[46] While PCC members quibbled about details, the contract went ahead with the diocesan's in-house contractors, Kentish Church Builders; parishioners were encouraged to make donations.[47] The parish filmed the laying of the foundation stone on 19 June 1963, and the consecration by the bishop took place on 12 September 1964.[48] Even the diocese described the design as 'challenging'.[49]

If one word could describe Arthur Bailey, his character as much as his building, it would be 'dignified'. That is clearly true of his Dutch Church, consecrated in 1954, designed with austere volumes, outer limestone walls built over a rusticated base, modest ornamental sculpture (by Esmond Burton as well as Skeaping), and what Nikolaus Pevsner called its 'thin, elegant spirelet'.[50] Adjoining the church to the east is a contemporary office block also by Bailey, one of the most elegant of its type. Dignified too is his economical rebuilding of St George-in-the-East, where a plain modern church was inserted within part of the surviving outer walls during the period in which the Twydall church was designed and built. It is true also of his elegant, plastic motorway or by-pass bridges, with their confident, gently mannerist curves, and in 1961 Twydall parishioners might have seen newspaper photographs of his Medway Bridge on the new Maidstone bypass.[51] It is true even of Bailey's parsonages – it had been the lack of dignity in the cheap version forced on him by the rector of Rainham that had distressed him. So where did the astonishing design for the Twydall church come from? The few comments at the August 1962 meeting – the only clues in the parish records – go nowhere near explaining how this expressionist building arose at the centre of a Swedish-inspired housing estate on a flat site in Gillingham.

Bailey had been a pupil of Vincent Harris. As his obituary in *Building* magazine pointed out, grouping him with Donald McMorran and E. Berry Webber, he shared the 'same genius of the logical disposition of the enclosed space as their illustrious mentor'.[52] The only clue as to where the ideas behind the Twydall church might have come from lie in the third-placed scheme he submitted for Liverpool metropolitan cathedral in 1959. Keith Scott, whose description of the competition entries in the *Architect and Building News* was, mostly, harshly critical of the runners up, thought that Bailey's proposals were 'imaginative and fresh' – its drawback was that 'it would not be sufficiently imposing' for its purpose. The building drew direct metaphors from organic forms: a plan shaped like a broad, flat fish supported a folded, ribbed copper-clad concrete roof that rose and fell like the arched spine of some ichthyosaurus: according to Scott, 'even the assessors boggled at its agonised structure and quite how the author intended the mass to be celebrated (or the financial limit to be contained), will fortunately remain a mystery'.[53] This sat over a low perimeter wall that does presage something of that at Twydall: although it is not as thick, it is full of angled openings in plan and elevation.

Bailey's office had had time to think back over this proposal by the time that the Twydall scheme was being finalised. Maybe it had come as a surprise that so wild a design had attracted a prize; possibly, he had entrusted the cathedral design to a junior member of the office, such as his son, and rewarded the author of it with a real commission. Rev. Ann Richardson, until late 2019 the vicar of Twydall, has suggested that the period that Bailey spent working with bombed-out churches and other buildings, including on the War Building programme in 1940–1945, had left its mark on his imagination. It seems as likely a theory as any other. She also points out that not building Bailey's cathedral scheme had deprived the youth of Liverpool of a climbing wall as excellent as the one that allows Twydall boys to peer down into the vicarage garden from the lower part of the church roof, whence they also tear off the timber shingles inspired, according to Bailey, by those of Kentish oast houses.[54]

The planning of the Twydall church is as rational as Bailey's obituarist suggested. It has a single volume, square in plan but for the irregularities in the brick wall, about 60 feet internally (just over eighteen metres) in each dimension. The central axis of this space leads diagonally from the entrance at the

Fig.7 Holy Trinity, Ansell and Bailey's benches, font and lamp standards (Elain Harwood)

Fig.8 [following pages] Holy Trinity, altar with combined pulpit and lectern (Elain Harwood)

westernmost point of a square to an altar on a platform not quite in the eastern corner: beyond this are three rows of stalls which provide a kind of Lady chapel. Thus the plan suited the requirements of the new liturgical movement, as Crookshank and the diocese had intended. Bailey incorporated a single unit to act as a pulpit and lectern on the edge of the platform, and his office also designed all the seating and light fittings, which survive (parishioners' anxiety about the difficulty of replacing light bulbs high up on the underside of the roof turned out to be justified). There is also a fine white concrete egg-shaped font, made up with an aggregate of granite chippings, with a copper lid. Then the steel-framed tented roof, cedar-shingle clad on the outside, rises to a height of about seventy feet above it, so in spite of the irregularity of the external walls the building is contained within a cube. This roof takes the form of a pyramid that has been sliced into two down the centre, with one half slipped down by a few feet to create an eyebrow-window, glazed with amber-coloured Belgian glass, high up at the apex, which is in fact well over the western corner of the nave. Thus, evening sunlight reaches the altar. A bell operated by hand from below was fixed to the underside of the apex of the upper roof where it projects over the skylight.[55]

Fig.9 Holy Trinity, from the southern end of the vestry wing (Elain Harwood)

This type of roof had appeared on Aarno Ruusuvuori's recent church at Hyvinkää in Finland, which had been published in England in December 1963.[56] This is a much larger church and more sophisticated in plan and finish, and its setting is very different from this one. There is no other church as raw as Twydall's: Sigurd Lewerentz's churches at Klippan and Björkhagen in Sweden are refined by comparison. A proposal for a cloister – a simple roofed walkway typical of buildings of the period – connecting the building with Bailey's earlier hall was dropped to save money, so this violent creature, the only progeny of the Liverpool ichthyosaurus, seems to rear up out of nowhere, its violent mouth skywards, its trailing vestry wing providing a kind of tail. The wildness of the brickwork around the base of the building further enhances the sense that this is a feral, slippery creature; if the shingles are like reptilian scales, one is almost looking here at the gnarled lower parts of an alligator or some other dangerous creature. Newman seemed to blame the bricklayers – in his first edition, he asked if they had been blindfolded – but the sureness of touch of the swooping parapets and buttresses, especially at the western corner, is that of a confident designer, possibly one already irritated and provoked by the responses of the conservative churchwardens. Older members of the congregation who were children in the later Victorian era might have remembered the 'New Mother' from Lucy Clifford's *Anyhow Tales* of 1882: a monster with radiating glass eyes (amber, perhaps) and a thumping wooden tail who replaces the kind and loving mother of naughty, inquisitive children; this is what now reared up at the centre of their estate. One of the extraordinary things about the Twydall church for some is that it is both alluring – and yet also shocking.

ACKNOWLEDGEMENTS

I would like to thank the Rev. Ann Richardson for her generous assistance to the church and restricted papers when researching this article; to Jon Salter, church warden; and the new vicar Rev. Mike Nelson, who kindly permitted and arranged access for photography. I am grateful too to Elspeth Millar and the archivists of the Medway Archives Centre; the Revd Canon Brian Senior of Wigmore; Daniel Sables, who drew the plan of the church; Kayleigh Shaw of the parish office of St Barnabas,

St Paul Cray; and to Benjamin Wood. My thanks too to my friend Desmond Day for checking (and correcting) my use of parish and diocesan terminology – although any remaining errors are my responsibility alone.

NOTES

1 John Newman, The Buildings of England: *Kent, West and the Weald* (London: Yale University Press, 2012), p.253.

2 ibid., p.254.

3 *Town Guide*, 1948, p.27; *Town Guide*, 1951, p.15; Medway Archives Centre (MAC), Strood.

4 Canon E. E. Maples Earle, undated note for publication, probably May 1952 ('Earle note'), P153K/DE0697, MAC.

5 *Gillingham Observer*, undated cutting in P/153K/28/1–2, MAC. The foundation ceremony was on 20 April 1954.

6 Earle, note, in P153K/DE0697, MAC.

7 'Provisional Proposals', undated typescript, item (5); moving the old church: Gould to Jordan, 22 April 1954, both in P153K/DE0697, MAC.

8 Untitled minute book from a series of three, no committee name, P153K/DE0697, MAC. William Henry Ansell (1873–1959), past president of the RIBA, entered into partnership with Bailey in 1934 and retired in 1949.

9 Bailey's first appearance: 'Twydall Green – Proposed New Church'; Earle note, both P153K/DE0697, MAC.

10 A block plan survives as part of the revised proposal for the parsonage, 24 July 1953, P153K/DE0697, MAC.

11 G. Maxwell Aylwin, 'The Royal Academy of Arts Summer Exhibition, 1954', *The Builder*, vol.186, 7 May 1954, p.797.

12 Attached to meeting of 6 June 1951, untitled minute book, P153K/DE0697, MAC.

13 Contract; letter from Bailey to Rev. F. W. Jordan, 1 March 1954; Earle note, item 7, P153K/DE0697, MAC.

14 Bailey to Jordan, 1 March 1954, P153K/DE0697, MAC.

15 Drawing dated April 1953; Bailey to Jordan, 22 April 1953; Bailey to Jordan, 24 November 1952, both in P153K/DE0697, MAC. No surviving records could be found for Bailey's vicarage at St Paul Cray.

16 Bailey to Jordan, 18 April 1953; 30 June 1953, P153K/DE0697, MAC.

17 Bailey to Jordan, 14 May 1953, P153K/DE0697, MAC.

18 Diocesan Dilapidations Board to Jordan, 28 April 1953; 20 May 1954, P153K/DE0697, MAC.

19 Bailey to Jordan, 18 June 1954; 28 June 1954, P153K/DE0697, MAC.

20 Jordan to Bailey, 28 June 1954; 13 July 1954, P153K/DE0697, MAC.

21 Bailey to Jordan, 21 June 1954, P153K/DE0697, MAC.

22 Burden to Jordan and Burden to Eccles, 30 June 1953; Ministry of Works to Jordan, 5 September 1953, P153K/DE0697, MAC.

23 Bailey to Jordan, 29 December 1953, P153K/DE0697, MAC.

24 'Main Committee', 29 June 1954, untitled minute book, P153K/DE0697, MAC. The church hall is illustrated with a model of the Skeaping sculpture, perhaps photomontaged, in R. J. McNally, ed., *Sixty Post-War Churches* (London: Incorporated Church Building Society, 1957) pp.56–7.

25 Bailey to Jordan, 1 March 1954, P153K/DE0697, MAC.

26 Jordan to Bailey, 5 January 1953, P153K/DE0697, MAC.

27 W. G. Clements (PCC secretary) to Archdeacon, 17 January 1958, P153K/8/1, MAC.

28 PCC minutes, 24 February 1958, P153K/8/1, MAC.

29 'Strictly Confidential', undated, P153K/8/2, MAC.

30 'Strictly Confidential', 30 January 1959, P153K/8/2, MAC.

31 Untitled memorandum, 31 August 1959, P153K/8/2, MAC.

32 PCC minutes, 10 April 1961, P153K/8/3, MAC.

33 PCC session 61, 14 November 1961, P153K/8/3 MAC; drawings dated 12 October 1961, P153K/6/1, MAC.

34 PCC session 61, ibid., p.4.

35 ibid., p.6.

36 Bailey, undated typescript, probably 1962, in P/153K/28/1–2, MAC; Crookshank, *Holy Trinity Church Twydall Green, Gillingham* [church guide], undated but not before 1968, in P153K/DE0697, MAC.

37 PCC minutes, 10 April 1961, in P153K/8/3, MAC.

38 ibid., p.7.

39 PCC session 62, minutes 14 December 1961, p.1, P153K/DE0697, MAC.

40 Parish AGM 6, minutes 9 March 1962, p.4, P153K/8/3, MAC. The file contains a separate record of parishioners' comments.

41 ibid., p.3.

42 *Gillingham Observer*, 2 March 1962, no page number, in P153K/8/3, MAC. Yuri Gagarin had orbited the earth almost exactly a year beforehand.

43 Ansell & Bailey's drawings are dated 16 July 1962. Incorporated Church Building Society, ICBS14076a/ a1/ a2; available online at http://images.lambethpalacelibrary.org.uk.

44 PCC minutes, 21 August 1962, p.2, P153K/8/3, MAC.

45 ibid., p.5.

46 PCC minutes, 8 April 1963, p.2, P153K/8/4, MAC. The final cost was 'over £47,000' according to the church guide.

47 'To all our parishioners', May 1963, P153K/8/5, MAC.

48 The film is in the care of the parish.

49 Diocesan press release, 19 June 1963, P153K/8/5, MAC.

50 Extant, and published in detail in *The Builder*, vol.187, 10 September 1954, pp.411–17; Nikolaus Pevsner, rev. Bridget Cherry, The Buildings of England: *London, vol.1, The Cities of London and Westminster* (Harmondsworth: Penguin, 1973), p.181.

51 Between what are now junctions 5 and 6 of the M20. It is very hard to see from any position on the ground.

52 I. M. Leslie, 'Last of a Triumvirate', *Building*, vol.236, 29 June 1979, p.15.

53 Keith Scott, 'Cathedral', *Architect and Building News*, vol.218, 31 August 1960, p.266. The proposal is illustrated in pp.273-4.

54 Ann Richardson to author, 18 July 2019. Oast houses: Bailey, in undated typescript, probably 1962, in P/153K/28/1-2, MAC.

55 Church guide.

56 *Architectural Review*, vol.134, December 1963, pp.394-6.

TIMOTHY BRITTAIN-CATLIN was for many years a trustee and deputy chairman of the C20 Society and contributed *Leonard Manasseh & Partners* to its monograph series. He leads the University of Cambridge's Architecture Apprenticeship course and writes mostly on early twentieth-century domestic architecture. His most recent book *The Edwardians and their Houses: The New Life of Old England* was published in 2020.

ROBERT DRAKE has had a long involvement with the C20 Society as its honorary events secretary (1988–99), secretary (2012–16) and on the casework committee to 2022, advising in particular on churches. He contributed an article on public libraries to Journal 13 and to *100 Churches, 100 Years* (2019) and has led many national and foreign events, with an emphasis on places of worship.

HARRY PATRICK FOLEY is course leader for the BA (Hons) Interior Architecture and Design programme at Nottingham Trent University. After an enjoyable period as an architectural designer for Stanton Williams, Harry completed the MA architectural history programme at the Bartlett, University College London, where he is now pursuing a PhD in architectural and urban history and theory.

DUNCAN GREGORY works as the church buildings officer at the Anglican Diocese of Southwark. Prior to completing a master's degree in building history at the University of Cambridge he worked as a data architect in the financial services sector. He is enjoying the transition from conceptual to physical architecture.

ELAIN HARWOOD is an architectural historian with Historic England, honorary fellow of the RIBA and co-editor of *Twentieth Century Architecture* and the monograph series Twentieth Century Architects. She is currently writing on new towns and the architects Ernö Goldfinger and Ralph Erskine.

CHRIS KENNEDY: After a career in applied linguistics at the University of Birmingham, Professor Kennedy gained a master's degree in design history and a certificate in architectural history from Oxford University. Chris has a particular interest in twentieth-century architecture and design, including Richard Twentyman's architecture and the sculpture of his brother Anthony.

KAROLINA SZYNALSKA McALEAVEY is an architect and senior lecturer at the Lincoln School of Architecture and the Built Environment, University of Lincoln. She completed her doctorate at the University of Cambridge. Her doctoral research was shortlisted for the RIBA President's Award for Research 2021. Previously, she graduated with an MA in architectural history from the UCL.

ALAN POWERS, a former chairman of the C20 Society, has written widely on twentieth-century art, architecture and design in Britain. His most recent book is *Bauhaus Goes West* (2019). He teaches at the University of Kent, NYU London and is history leader for the London School of Architecture.

CLARE PRICE is the head of casework for the Twentieth Century Society, responsible for all church casework. She is currently researching interwar churches for a DPhil in architectural history at the University of Oxford. A qualified chartered surveyor and holding an MSc in the conservation of the historic environment, Clare has worked in buildings and conservation for over thirty years.

ROBERT PROCTOR is senior lecturer in architectural history and theory at the University of Bath. He is the author of *Building the Modern Church: Roman Catholic Church Architecture in Britain, 1955 to 1975*, and is currently completing a book on the buildings of Sir Percy Thomas and his subsequent practice.

AIDAN RIDYARD is a partner at Burrell Foley Fischer Architects and a member of the RIBA with conservation accreditation. He has built several notable public buildings in the UK and overseas. He grew up in the Black Country where his father was vicar of All Saints Darlaston, making Twentyman a formative influence on his architectural education.

JOHANNA ROETHE is an architectural historian with Historic England. She is the co-author of *Weston-super-Mare: the town and its seaside heritage* (2019) and has written articles on various aspects of architecture and material culture. Her articles on Quaker meeting houses have been published in the *SPAB Magazine* (spring 2020) and *Studies in Victorian Architecture & Design* (volume 7, 2019).

STEVEN SPENCER is director of the Salvation Army International Heritage Centre and an honorary research fellow in the Centre for Nineteenth-Century Studies at Birkbeck, University of London. He has an MA in history from Canterbury Christ Church University and qualified as an archivist at UCL in 2008. He has published on various aspects of Salvation Army history, including the architecture of its halls.

TWENTIETH CENTURY ARCHITECTURE

Titles in print available from the Society:

2. *The Modern House Revisited*, 1996
5. *Festival of Britain*, 2001
6. *The Sixties*, 2002
7. *The Heroic Period of Conservation*, 2004
9. *Housing the Twentieth Century Nation*, 2008
10. *The Seventies*, 2012
11. *Oxford and Cambridge*, 2013
12. *Houses, Regional Practice and Local Character*, 2015
13. *The Architecture of Public Service*, 2017

ALSO AVAILABLE

Robin Hood Gardens Re-Visions, 2010
100 Buildings, 100 Years (with Batsford, 2016)
100 Houses, 100 Years (with Batsford, 2017, revised 2022)
100 Churches, 100 Years (with Batsford, 2018)
100 Gardens and Landscapes (with Batsford, 2020)

TWENTIETH CENTURY ARCHITECTS

Rutter Carroll, *Ryder and Yates*, 2009
Edward Denison, *McMorran & Whitby*, 2009
Timothy Brittain-Catlin, *Leonard Manasseh & Partners*, 2011
Alan Clawley, *John Madin*, 2011
Elain Harwood, *Chamberlin, Powell & Bon*, 2011
Kenneth Powell, *Ahrends, Burton & Koralek*, 2012
Gerald Adler, *Robert Maguire & Keith Murray*, 2012
Elizabeth Darling, *Wells Coates*, 2012
Geraint Franklin, *Howell, Killick, Partridge & Amis*, 2017
Christine Hui Lan Manley, *Frederick Gibberd*, 2017
Kenneth Powell, *Arup Associates*, 2018
Mark Crinson, *The Smithsons*, 2018
Iain Jackson, Simon Pepper and Peter Richmond, *Herbert Rowse*, 2019
Dominic Wilkinson and Andrew Compton, *F.X. Verlarde*, 2020
Alistair Fair, *Peter Moro & Partners*, 2021
Geraint Franklin, *John Outram*, 2022
Kenneth Powell, *Edward Cullinan Architects*, 2023

The Twentieth Century Society was founded in 1979
to protect and promote twentieth-century architecture and design.
For more information and to join the Society please visit:
www.c20society.org.uk

Twentieth Century Society
70 Cowcross Street · London EC1M 6EJ